Understanding Local G[illegible]

Jeffrey Stanyer obtained first cla[illegible] [illegible]itics and Economics in 1958 and the B.Phi[illegible] [illegible]alliol College, Oxford. He became Research Fello[illegible] [illegible]nment at Exeter University in 1960 and Lecturer in [illegible] in 1962. He has always been interested in local government – [illegible]ther worked for Cheshire County Council for over 40 years, he himself had vacation jobs as a local government officer and had a grant to visit local authorities in many different parts of the United States in 1959. Since coming to Exeter he has been sporadically active in local politics and was for four years a co-opted member of the City Library Committee. His special research interest has been into local government in the geographical county of Devon, but he has also published a number of studies of official reports – The Local Government Commissions, 1958-65; The Maud Committee, 1967; the Redcliffe-Maud Commission, 1969; and the Kilbrandon Commission, 1973. He is author of *County Government in England and Wales* (Routledge and Kegan Paul, 1967) and joint author with Brian C. Smith of *Administering Britain* (Fontana, 1976). He has contributed the *Local Government* Section of the RIPA's *Survey of Adminstrative Developments* since its inception in 1968.

Studies in Public Administration

This is a new series designed to introduce the reader to the study of the different aspects of public administration. Unlike most literature in this field the series will not be directly linked with the study of business administration. The readership foreseen for the series includes administrators, whether or not they are studying for professional exams, students of political science and related subjects, as well as the general reader seeking a more informed appreciation of the key role of the administrative process in political decision making.

This series is edited by F. F. Ridley, who has been Professor of Political Theory and Institutions in the University of Liverpool since 1964. He is Chairman of the Joint University Council for Social and Public Administration, has been Chairman of its Public Administration Committee, and is a founder member of the European Group of the International Institute of Administrative Sciences. He is also Chairman of Examiners in British Government and Politics with the Joint Matriculation Board. He is Editor of *Political Studies*, and his publications include *Public Administration in France* (with J. Blondel), *Specialists and Generalists: A Comparative Survey of Professional Civil Servants* (Editor), and *The Study of Government: Political Science and Public Administration* (in preparation).

Forthcoming volumes in the series are provisionally entitled: *The Policy Perspective:* Dr W. I. Jenkins & Dr G. K. Roberts; *Comparative Administration:* Professor F. F. Ridley; *Governmental Planning:* Professor P. Self; and *The Study of Public Administration* by David Murray.

Jeffrey Stanyer

Understanding Local Government

Fontana/Collins

First published in Fontana 1976

Made and printed in Great Britain by
William Collins Sons and Co. Ltd, Glasgow

Contents

Part Four   Applications

Preface

This book is an essay on the analysis of local government systems, illustrated by reference to England and Wales, but not bound closely to the details of present law and institutions. In the British Isles there are several different patterns of local government, some with common origins and all strongly influenced by the same factors during their development. The two Irish systems started as an extension of the English pattern to a different social and political structure; that of Scotland, though of different origins, has been subjected to the forces that have modified those of England and Wales. Even the Isle of Man and the Channel Islands have within their boundaries their own local government systems. Though all of these are legally distinct and factually different, they can and ought to be analysed in the same terms and with the same framework of concepts.

This is also true of the different local government systems that have succeeded one another in the same country over a long period of time. Though they may be separated by decades and different in principle and detail, yet they can only properly be understood in the light of the same general ideas and the same intellectual orientation. In the last century England and Wales have experienced three different patterns of local government. The first, which originated in the 1830s with the *Poor Law Amendment Act, 1834*, and the *Municipal Corporations Act, 1835*, could scarcely be called a system, as it contained appointed and elected bodies, and both single and multi-purpose authorities – a chaos of authorities, rates and areas, according to Goschen in 1871.[1] This complicated and extravagant pattern was simplified and rationalized according to the lights of the times in the last fifteen years of the nineteenth century, and the second pattern, which was based on three distinct types of local government (the county borough, the administrative county and the London system), survived in recognizably the same form until the 1960s. The third, which only came into full existence in 1974, was created by the *London Government Act, 1963*, and the *Local Government Act, 1972*.

In principle, therefore, it is no more difficult to extend the analysis to local government systems remote in time than to those geographically distant. The problem of *topicality*, which causes so much trouble for books based on legalistic and institutional approaches, has scarcely any relevance here because the aim is to provide a means of understanding all local government systems. The details of systems of government are always changing, particularly in the present century when each new central Government has a massive legislative programme which affects political institutions both directly and indirectly. At the time of writing local government has just completed its biggest basic reorganization since the end of the nineteenth century, and many of the individual services for which local authorities are responsible are under investigation or threat of change. The transfers of the local authority personal health services, water supply, sewerage and sewage disposal, and related activities to newly-created, special-purpose bodies are only striking illustrations of the continuous processes of systems of government.[2] In order to make sense of the apparent confusion and complexity in modern systems of local government what is needed is a proper framework of general ideas, not a knowledge of the latest Act or Royal Commission report.

What the citizen calls *understanding* the academic social scientist calls *explanation;* these are fundamentally the same thing when allowance is made for the greater degree of self-consciousness and commitment to rigour in the latter. Whatever the superficial differences between the point of view of the man in the street and the professional student of public affairs, at heart they are engaged on the same activity – making sense of the world in which they live – and any disparity between their respective 'products' must involve a mistake on one or both sides. There can be only one defensible way of studying local government, and this is true for local councillors, local government officers, interested citizens, members of local political parties and other social scientists.

This book attempts to expound, in ways suitable for both professional students and interested laymen, the framework of ideas that are needed to make sense of local government.

Because the framework is not indissolubly linked to a particular system, specified in time and space, any system would serve to illustrate it. For practical reasons local government in post-war England and Wales has been chosen. This includes the traditional system which finally disappeared on 1 April 1974, and the new system which is still evolving rapidly. The former is included because nearly all current understanding is derived from it; the latter because many readers will want to apply the concepts to the pattern under which they live. The changes of 1972-74 were in any event an extension of the old, rather than the creation of something radically new.

Though it is not possible to define *local government* in exact verbal terms it can be characterized in such a way that it can be recognized as such in different times and places.

Local government is one form of local administration of public services. For much of the time, therefore, it is being contrasted implicitly with other forms of decentralized organization of state activities – such as field administration, where services are provided by the subordinate officials of central departments, and lay-appointed bodies, where a board or committee controls the activity.[3]

A local government *system* is composed of at least one of two basic *types* of local government. *Primary* local government exists when the local authority is directly elected by the people living in its area, and *secondary* local government when the authority is indirectly elected, that is, appointed by one or more primary authorities. Primary local government consists of local authorities who have stable and clearly marked boundaries, are responsible for a range of public services and have an independent power of local taxation, in addition to having their members directly elected. These authorities are the foundation of most modern systems of local government.

Primary local government is of two types: *simple* and *complex.* The latter is found where several local authorities are independently elected and have co-ordinate jurisdiction, though not necessarily in respect of the same services. Simple primary local government therefore occurs where there is only one authority with jurisdiction over a particular territory.

In the traditional pre-1974 system in England the simple type of local government was represented by the *county-borough,* and there were two kinds of complex local government – the *administrative county* and the *Greater London* system. The post-1974 system is based entirely on types of complex local government. The London system remains unchanged, but the rest of England is divided into two types of county. The traditional conurbations of the West Midlands, Greater Manchester, Merseyside, South Yorkshire, West Yorkshire and Tyne-Wear are designated as *metropolitan counties,* having district councils within their boundaries responsible for some of the major local government services and a county council responsible for the whole area. The rest of England outside London is divided into *non-metropolitan counties*, with a county council responsible for major services throughout the whole area and district councils responsible for the rest of the services in their part of the territory. Some parts of non-metropolitan counties have a third tier of local authorities – *parish government*. The Welsh system of local government, though described in separate sections of statutes and statutory instruments, is in practice very close to the English non-metropolitan system, except that the third tier is almost universal and called *community government*.[4]

Built *onto* the system of primary local government there is, and has been, a disparate set of secondary authorities – port health authorities, police authorities, water boards etc. – and built *into* them a variety of area arrangements and local institutions for the provision of particular services – schools, libraries, area social service offices, divisional executives etc. One consequence of the reorganization of primary local government has been a reconsideration of secondary authorities and of the services for which primary ones were responsible. The outcome of this has been the creation of two new types of public body, half local and half central, one for the whole of the personal health services in an area and the other for the whole of the water-cycle group of activities. Other special purpose bodies remain but the most important ones are no longer derived directly and solely from primary local government.

In any given area, therefore, there will be a variety of recognizable and distinct local government units, not all of which are legally *authorities* with their own taxing power and independent existence, but which together form an intricate system of government. Local government is this set of bodies and the relationship between them; the purpose of the book is to provide a way of understanding their behaviour, of making sense of the actions and activities in which individuals and groups are engaged.

The reader must therefore not expect a legal and institutional textbook on local government, nor an academic thesis with every point 'proved' in the accepted manner. Its purpose is to present a generalized picture of the main features of local government, drawn with the aid of a set of concepts intended to promote an understanding of the behaviour of local authorities.

The author has aimed at a very direct method presentation so that the ideas should be intelligible as they stand, without reference to other works. This means that the sources are indicated in only a sketchy manner and no attempt is made to evaluate each one separately. The material relating to the substance of local government behaviour in England and Wales is to be found in the growing list of case-studies of individual authorities, in the weekly and monthly local government journals and in newspapers, particularly local ones. None of these constitute a random sample of local government and thus the picture may be drawn under the influence of many sorts of undetectable bias. The concepts and methods that make up the approach adopted are only sketchily attributed to their sources. They are, in any case, derived quite generally from modern social science, particularly political science of the behavioural type. Human geography, organizational sociology and psychology, studies of electoral and legislative behaviour have all been extensively used in constructing the approach of this book, but it is hoped that the end-product is self-explanatory.

It is impossible to develop, expound and deploy a special approach to a subject without creating a vocabulary to denote the concepts used. I have tried to moderate the pernicious effects of jargon by defining technical terms on their first appearance and in later usage by making the meaning clear from the context.

The essay is divided into four parts. The first two are guides to the rationale of the new approach to understanding local government: first, by contrasting it with a traditional approach with which readers will be implicitly familiar, but which has been discredited for several reasons; and second, by describing the basic concept – that of a *miniature political system.* The third part interprets local authorities as individual political systems in their own right, each with its own distinctive character. Finally, the approach and the ideas it generates are applied to four major topics of traditional local government studies, each corresponding to one of the four main distinguishing characteristics of primary local authorities, to try to show how the new interpretation creates a different understanding from the old.

There are therefore two ways of evaluating the framework presented here. One is in terms of its intrinsic characteristics – the acceptability of the rationale offered for it – and the other in terms of the degree to which it advances understanding of the traditional questions of local government.

Part One

Introduction

Introduction

Part One introduces the reader to the study of local government through a description of traditional approaches, and sets out the reasons for rejecting them in favour of methods that are more rigorous and behavioural. It also provides brief descriptions of two local government systems in England and Wales, the one created in the last two decades of the nineteenth century, which endured until 1974, and the other created by a series of statutes between 1963 and 1974, which is now searching for a stable shape in which to operate in the future.

The reason for combining these two introductions is that understanding local government is largely a matter of grasping the difference between three distinct languages, and mastering the use of two of them. The first is the vernacular language of practitioners, used when engaged in local government activities or when considering them as citizens. But there is also the language of a given legal system, with its precisely defined concepts whose meanings derive from statute, regulations, administrative practice and common law. Those who wish to understand social phenomena are, however, driven to construct and use a third language – a language of analysis.

Everyday language contains elements of both the legal technical language and the language of analysis. But it is confused, inconsistent and incomplete; it can only lead to misunderstanding and misrepresentation. Traditional approaches are a source of error because they rely so much on ordinary language, and this systematically produces mistakes in understanding.

To understand local government it is necessary to create bridges which link the language of the constitutional and administrative system to that of analysis; this is done through rules which translate the terms of one into the terms of the other. It is necessary, therefore, to describe a system of local government in strict institutional terms in order that it may be interpreted in terms of the analytical concepts.

Chapter One

The Study of Local Government

For the last ten years at least local government in England and Wales has been in the forefront of the discussion of constitutional and administrative change. The ferment associated with local government reorganization, the accompanying financial crisis, political demands for devolution and greater decentralization of power, and serious criticisms (whether justified or not) of the performance of central government have all contributed to its growing prominence as the subject of public attention.

Even without the factors making for its current fashionableness, local government is such an important part of the system of government, and therefore of society in general, that it cannot be ignored by anyone concerned with, and interested in, the world in which he lives. Over 10 per cent of the workforce are employed by local authorities and related bodies; over 12 per cent of the national income is spent through local government and a large part of social investment in public land and buildings is owned by it. And, despite all recent efforts to the contrary, it has proved impossible to stop the role of local authorities growing in quantitative terms. Local government is almost twice as important now as it was at the end of the Second World War.[1]

Another way of underlining the importance of local government is simply to mention some of the services for which local authorities are responsible – housing, education, police, fire services, public health, consumer protection, leisure and recreation, town and country planning, the personal social services – all of which are the conventional names for complicated sets of public activities, often of vital importance to the individuals who 'consume' them.[2]

A significant feature of the traditional literature on this large sector of modern society is that much of it was contributed by those who were part of the system – either as council members or, more likely, chief officers – and arose from their reflections about their working lives. It is thus written in the language of practitioners and differs little from journalistic reporting and comment in the newspapers and on radio and television.

Approaches that are rooted in a vernacular language are inadequate to the task of understanding any complex sector of society. No attempt will be made here to defend this assertion, either in general terms or in relation to local government only, but it will be treated as an assumption whose force will become increasingly apparent as the argument of the book unfolds. The reader who is familiar with conventional discussions of *apathy, central-local relations, the quality of councillors, size and performance* and like subjects will soon recognize that the way these are treated in the traditional textbooks and in journalistic comment leads positively to misunderstanding.

Local government has become fashionable in another sense. In recent years much more time and money has been put into empirical investigation of the political and administrative behaviour of local authorities and a new atmosphere has been diffused throughout research and thinking about all the problems in this field. Though the 'behavioural persuasion' has taken a long time seriously to affect the study of local government in Britain, new approaches are as much a protest against traditional methods as was the demand articulated in America in the interwar years for a new 'science of politics'.

The myth of uniformity

The first step, and the only vital one, is to challenge the myth of uniformity. The study of state and local government has always thrived in the United States as a part of orthodox political science and recent developments there have probably contributed to its growth in British universities. The great variety of American state and local political systems has been a feature favouring its early progress, whereas until recently in Britain the study of local government has been restricted by a legalistic bias which obscured the empirical differences between local authorities.

Once each local authority is seen as an individual political unit in its own right, the way is open for the use of the approaches that have become common in the study of central government and in the social sciences generally. When the study of local government is conceived as a combination of modern approaches and the idea of a miniature political system, the student or analyst quickly becomes aware that it has a number of intellectual advantages which were only vaguely appreciated when the new atmosphere was beginning to develop. In the early 1960s, for instance, when these matters were first becoming widely discussed, the stress was almost entirely on the advantages to local government studies of the use of the methods developed in central government research. Today almost the reverse should be argued; that what is important is the contribution that local government studies can make to the study of government, that they should be seen as 'the queen of the (political) sciences'.

Local government is a fruitful field of study for the modern social scientist simply because of the large number of comparable subjects that are found in any local government system. Most modern methods depend on the existence of a large number of 'cases' for their proper use, and these must belong to a sufficiently homogeneous universe to permit them to be treated as members of the same set. By abstracting each local authority from the national system of government of which it is a part, a class of cases – political systems – which is both numerous and homogeneous is created. In particular, those differences of culture and environment which bedevil orthodox comparative government disappear, leaving a universe of study which is sufficiently coherent for the development of an explanatory political science. Though this aim may be remote from the concerns of the general reader, it can readily be appreciated as an important part of the work of the professional student of government. In the long run, also, it is important for the layman; unless political scientists improve their understanding of local government, the interested citizen has no hope of developing his or hers.

To put this point in concrete terms, a comparison of federal systems is very difficult because even if the study is restricted to the classical federations (America, Canada, Australia and Switzerland) there are vast differences of law, society and economy. These differences are accentuated if West Germany, India, Nigeria before the civil war and the other more marginal cases are included in order to raise the number of cases sufficiently to permit justifiable generalizations to be made. But in the pre-1972 local government system there were 61 administrative counties, all sharing the general British political environment and culture, governed by the same general laws and for whom the same statistical information, collected on a uniform basis, was available. Within just one of these – the administrative county of Devon – there were 30 town councils which could be used as the subject of comparative analysis.

The present situation

These newer approaches and the research they have stimulated now coexist uneasily with the traditional literature on local government and the two combined produce a very disparate academic field. A student may find himself at one moment engaged in the baldest moralizing about institutional reform and at the next studying problems involving complex statistics. For instance, since 1931 or before, Professor W. A. Robson has waged a war in unchanging terms on what he regards as over-centralization and the decline of local democracy, which he thought was caused by too many small authorities. As the attitudes underlying this have not been affected by the great mass of relevant evidence that has appeared since the end of the Second World War, it is difficult to treat these demands for radical reform of local government as other than the expression of basic moral attitudes – in fact, a form of utopianism. But, in contrast, the economists employed by the Redcliffe-Maud Commission to study the relationship between size of local authority and the provision of services regarded this as an open question; the elaborate statistical models that they developed showed, as far as this is possible with these techniques, that there was no general relationship between *scale of operations* and *performance in service provision*.[3]

This diversity has been increased by the variety of viewpoints from which the study of local government has been undertaken. The products of the different studies often seem to bear very little relation to each other. For instance, the present discussion of possible new sources of local revenue makes no reference to the existence of statistical research predicated on the view that each local authority is an individual decision maker, which claims to have shown that there are various factors which do, and others which do not, affect local authority financial behaviour.[4]

The traditional approach

Although there is considerable agreement that local government was studied in an unsatisfactory way, not everyone is completely clear about the exact nature of these faults; as a consciousness of them is the basis of the new approach, it is well worthwhile setting them out precisely and in some detail. There are three major faults which are mainly those of the academic and three which are mainly associated with the layman. But, because of the interaction between the two, it is often difficult to ascribe something unambiguously to either category. Many academics in the early years were recruited from the public service, and few public officials have been entirely uninfluenced by what others have written about their roles and the institutions in which they work.

The two related mistakes which laymen commonly make about local government are those of *generalizing* and *particularizing*. In both cases they are the consequences of the problems of interpretation of personal experience.

Generalizing consists of projecting to all local authorities the attributes of the authority with which one is directly acquainted. This is one result of the 'myth of uniformity' mentioned above. The chief effect of this is a failure to appreciate that local government is extremely varied. For instance, those who worked for a county-borough rarely showed any understanding of the nature of county government; those who were familiar with a party-dominated authority had no conception of non-partisanship. The alternative to generalizing is to seek out the dimensions of variation between local authorities in a systematic way; this is one feature of the new approach.

Particularizing is the opposite mistake of believing that one's own authority or area is unique and that no experience of others can ever be useful or relevant in understanding it. This is sometimes a matter of civic pride, but often it is also basically an anti-academic attitude in that it denies the possibility of intellectual analysis of local government behaviour. The alternative to particularizing is to seek out systematically the common elements in the behaviour of local authorities; this is also a feature of the new approach.

The difficulty with both generalizing and particularizing is that they depend on laymen giving accurate and reliable accounts of their own experiences. Those who have undertaken research into an individual local authority have frequently found that participants' memories are markedly at variance with published documents over factual matters; many participants only offer sweeping statements which are more informative about their author than about current events. Laymen also rely on the sort of explanation – for instance, in terms of all-pervasive sinister interests – that social scientists have rightly learned to mistrust on logical grounds.

Pious moralizing is a fault common to both laymen and academics. Many discussions of local government are 'pious' because they embody a touching faith that desired ends will be achieved, even though no suggestion is made as to how this will be realized in practice. Reports of Royal Commissions and committees of enquiry are particularly prone to the simple repetition of 'what ought to be done' and 'what is wrong'.[5] One way this piety spills over into academic writing is through the traditional reliance on official documents as sources of material for textbooks. Moralizing is dangerous because it too has its logical problems.

A precondition of successful reform (that is, reform that will achieve prior stated values) is that its aims be precisely formulated and capable of implementation. Much moralizing depends on values so vague or ambiguous that it is hard to know what would count as success. Another precondition is that the 'world' be properly understood – that is, the causal relationships in what is to be changed must be known – otherwise there is no reason to think that the changes will have the effects imputed to them. Critics of the present system often claim that larger authorities will lead to less central control, that adding services to local government will raise turnout in local elections or attract a better calibre of council member, but even if the values implicit here can be agreed there is still the problem of showing how the world works.

These mistakes are not peculiar to the study of local government but they have had a particular force in the past because of the reliance on the contributions of those who are involved in or with the institutions themselves. Each tends to produce its own characteristic errors of understanding. In discussion it leads to unjustifiable inferences as well as false assertions. The mistakes are also insidious and contagious; those who are not aware of them are unable to avoid them.

The academic study of government was for long dominated by law and history and this dominance was maintained far longer for local government than for many other fields. Reliance on law produced the mistakes usually referred to as *excessive legalism* and *institutionalism*.

The former arises when statements of what the law is are taken as statements of fact and descriptions of behaviour. Laws are of course prescriptive; but they are often cast in a grammatical form so close to that of descriptions that it is easy to slide from one to another. The legalistic approach invariably meets the problem of 'deviant' behaviour – parishes are supposed to hold a parish meeting each year, but as a matter of fact many do not. Laws are often consistent with a range of possible behaviours and a combination of legal provisions may create a situation where a local authority has a choice of what to do. For instance, in the traditional system the law forbade the same person to be both treasurer and clerk of the same authority, but it also specified the duties of a treasurer very narrowly. Thus though treasurers were usually also chief financial officers (a functional term), this was not legally necessary and a number of small authorities appointed the same person as clerk and chief financial officer, disposing of the treasurer's duties through a local bank.

Many laws only become operative if certain prior conditions are fulfilled. If these are rarely or never met then the law is unimportant. For instance, default powers are often presented as fearsome weapons of the centre against the locality,[6] but they do in fact play a negligible part in central-local relations. Again, the relations between law and fact are not straightforward.

Related to excessive legalism is *institutionalism*. This arises from a confusion between what an institution or organization is supposed to achieve and how people are expected to behave on one hand, and what actually happens on the other. Political institutions, like many formal organizations, are described by their creators and those who are members of them partly in terms of their goals, purposes or functions. When public bodies are created or reformed those responsible will make statements about the sort of behaviour they expect to occur. Though a confusion similar to that encountered in respect of the law itself, these conventional descriptions are taken as accounts of what happens. 'What should be' is treated as if it were 'what is'. In a wide range of social science fields those who have done empirical work on organizations have found that the paper account of the working of the body has low predictive value. For instance, close observation of the behaviour of workers on the shop floor revealed that the beliefs, and therefore the accounts, of the leaders of the company were grievously mistaken.[7]

Institutionalism, like legalism, has insidious effects. The aldermanic system, even at the end of its existence, was often described in terms of the values it was originally intended to promote – bringing in outsiders who could not fight elections and providing continuity of membership – yet there is much evidence that the former was largely a dead letter and there were occasions when it promoted instability. Co-option is also supposed to bring experts into the council's deliberations through the committee system, but the use made of these powers shows that this is not a helpful description of the process. In fact both these institutions need a style of analysis of a quite different order.[8]

Many of the conventional textbooks chose to approach local government through its history. This is not in itself bad, but it has encouraged a stress on matters that have a traditional and ceremonial importance rather than those that make a contribution to the understanding of contemporary behaviour. In addition, the history that appears in conventional local government studies is not always the history of professional historians. The latter have also been influenced by the increasing prestige of orthodox science and the more advanced social sciences, and this has been reflected in their methods of study.

The study of local government has been pervaded by sweeping historical generalizations which are at best misleading if not literally mistaken. The Labour Party is often 'blamed' for introducing party politics in local government in the post-war period, yet in many authorities – for instance, Cheshire, Exeter, London, Glossop – a long established Conservative-Liberal conflict preceded the rise of the Labour Party. The Maud Committee repeated the claim that the number of committees in individual local authorities had increased over time, but did not offer any evidence for this. In both these cases the facts to support the generalizations can only be amassed by the traditional crafts of the historian – through chasing thousands of documentary sources – but in other cases more sophisticated techniques are required. Has local government been in decline continuously for many years, due to the loss of services to central government and *ad hoc* bodies? To answer this properly requires the use of the techniques for studying the changing patterns of social activity and for estimating their relative importance as resource-users – in other words, an exercise in modern economic history.

So far attention has been focused rather negatively on the mistakes that have hindered the development of local government studies in this country. The rest of the book is devoted to expounding and illustrating an approach which is based on a different set of considerations.

Alternative perspectives on local government

There are at least three perspectives from which local government has been studied by political scientists. Each one has given rise to its own set of topics and problems, which often bear little relation to those of the others. The first of these has traditionally dominated the field and the two latter are relative latecomers.

The first perspective is one that sees local government as part of a national system of public administration and from its own point of view rightly treats it as only one part of a complex system of government. For instance, S. E. Finer's *A Primer of Public Administration*[9] has a substantial section devoted to decentralization. Under this heading students look at the distribution of functions between different types of public body, at relationships between different types of decentralized organization, and at the degree of autonomy achieved by local administration. Very often a strong normative element enters into discussions of this type. The questions posed have a large evaluative element, for instance, what is the best form of local administration?; how much autonomy should elected councils enjoy?; should the police service be administered nationally, regionally or locally? The discussion of the 'theory' or 'foundations' of local government belongs to this tradition, as do discussions of the reform of local government structure and new sources of local revenue. This is the aspect in which economists have taken an interest when they have looked at local government as part of the national economy. Social administrators have been concerned with local government as one way of administering the National Health Service.

The second perspective sees local politics as part of a national political system. The local authority is one amongst many places where political activity takes place. In one sense the overall political system is an aggregation of political behaviour in the localities of the country; but in another one can detect the operation of factors which are influences across the whole country – for instance, variations in national party fortunes produce similar effects in all the large cities of the country. Thus, such general factors as loyalty to the regime, class conflict and freedom of association will influence local government and perhaps be influenced by it. Those concerned with the differential impact of these factors might look at variations in the Labour-Conservative conflict, the different roles of the Liberals, the rise and fall of ratepayers' associations and similar movements and the activities of local branches of national pressure groups. In short, local political behaviour is part of a much larger system of politics. That this is so has led some to use local election results as an alternative guide to the standing of national political parties.

Third, each individual local authority is a miniature political and administrative system in its own right. Just as the nation state is abstracted from the international system of which it is a part when its system of government is studied, so a locality may be abstracted from the national system when it is treated as an individual in its own right. Most political scientists will be extremely familiar with books on France, America, Russia and other countries which treat each as an individual with its own characteristic features. Indeed, a substantial new tradition in the study of politics and government begins by rejecting the conventional picture of a political system, derived by generalizing from the familiar Western democracies, as a guide to understanding the politics of developing countries.

If each local authority is treated as a miniature political administrative system the whole apparatus for studying political systems can be brought to bear on the subject matter, and such concepts as *environment, social structure, socialization* and *culture,* to give a few examples, can be imported into the study of local government.[10] The remainder of the national system of government becomes part of the environment of the individual local authority, just as the international system is part of the environments of the British, American and Russian systems.

In this perspective consideration is given to such questions as the nature of a local party system, the influence of local social structure on the composition of councils, or the effect of pressure groups in a particular locality. On the administrative side there are case studies of the internal organization of individual authorities. Much of this type of analysis is basically comparative, that is, it seeks to compare two or more authorities systematically in order to throw light on the factors which produce variation between different individual systems.[11]

As can be seen from the above brief examples and references, each perspective is associated with a series of typical problems. Formally, the questions should be about the same thing but in practice this is not so. It is easy to confuse one perspective with another and to answer questions in terms of the wrong frame of reference. Discussion of *apathy* illustrate this very clearly. Both *turnout* and *competitiveness* are characteristics of the individual local authority, yet as will be seen they are often treated as though they were characteristics of the overall system.[12] The real difficulty is of course that two perspectives have been confused, and what is appropriate to the study of individual local authorities is ascribed to the system of government.

In a formal sense, however, the questions in all three perspectives should be related to each other; it is only in practice that they form such a disjointed set of problems. As was remarked earlier, the student may find himself at one moment engaged in the baldest type of moralizing and the next using the most refined statistical techniques. He may go from an emotional demand for more regionalism immediately to a consideration of the model of area delimitation proposed by the Local Government Operational Research Unit to the Royal Commission on Local Government in England.[13]

What then is required is a framework which will make these three perspectives consistent with each other and enable the student to relate the ideas and findings in one to those of the others. It is as much a matter of transformation as anything.

Traditionally, the first of the perspectives mentioned above has dominated local government studies. Textbooks on local government are written in a stereotyped way – almost as though there is a pattern of chapters which it is mandatory to follow. A start is made with the overall pattern of local government and eventually the internal organization of the individual authority is reached towards the end of the book. The study of individual political and administrative systems is thus based on the characteristics of the overall system, and, where facts are relevant, use is normally made of national averages. Internal organization is often divided up into separate compartments labelled 'committees', 'departments', etc., each one described in terms of national law regulating it, and presented as though the fact that each one is a dimension of the same body is unimportant.

The approach adopted here is to reverse the traditional procedure and to base the study of the overall system of local government in a country on the study of individual local authorities. There are certain direct advantages in doing this, in that it enables the student to avoid many conventional mistakes in local government studies which arise from confusing the characteristics of the individual with those of the overall system. But it is also the most promising social science approach, in that it has a number of distinct intellectual advantages.

These advantages arise mainly from the fact that there are a large number of local authorities, but also partly from the fact that the miniature system provides a more easily manageable amount of data. The use of statistical techniques and the testing of models of social behaviour are much easier when there are large numbers of cases and great 'natural' experimentation. The concepts of both *comparative analysis* and *political sociology* are particularly easy to apply in the context of local government.

Thus it is claimed that the third perspective listed above should be made the basic one; only it can provide the foundation that is needed to bring all local government research into significant order. Discussions of the national system of local government and politics must be based on the concept of a locality as a miniature political and administrative system. For instance, if it is proposed to allocate new local taxes to local authorities as a substitute for the income of central grants, then the effects must be analysed for each individual authority, making reference to its decision-making structure, and therefore to the values and perceptions of members and officials, and to the forces in their environment.

To a large extent, therefore, the incorporation of an understanding of local government into the main field of political science involves the use of concepts that have become commonplace in other spheres. Local councils are miniature legislatures, the processes of recruitment and socialization can be seen among council members, and local authority departments are formal organizations or bureaucracies, depending on personal preference.

The new approach is more than a perspective. It is also a framework of concepts which are used rigorously. A conceptual framework in this context is simply a set of ideas which are closely related to each other, which serve to identify important facts and factors in the field of study, and which point to significant relationships between them. Usually the framework embodies a special vocabulary and sometimes a special syntax, but this is not necessary. Conceptual frameworks vary tremendously in their sophistication and, like tribal lays, there are many different ways of constructing them. The only real test is of their usefulness in bringing together distinct and diverse discussion and research into a coherent and justifiable perspective.

The new approach is *behavioural, rigorous* and in the long run *quantitative*. *Behaviour* simply means what people do, as opposed to what they say they do or what they are supposed to do, in legal and institutional terms. *Rigorous* simply means that a deliberate attempt is made to meet the ordinary standards of intellectual discourse – to get things right. Rigorous methods are basically quantitative in the long run, but at the moment there are strict limits to what can be achieved. It therefore remains very much one of the background aims in this book.

All the considerations outlined in this chapter combine to provide a persuasive argument for a special language of analysis in terms of which an understanding of local government can be developed. Before this is set out in detail (in Part Two) it is necessary to master the language of the two local government systems which provide the illustrative material for the book.

Chapter Two

Traditional and New Systems of Local Government

The basic concept on which an understanding of local government must be founded is that of a miniature political and administrative system. But before the process of abstraction by which such entities are identified can be undertaken, it is necessary to appreciate the main features of the local government system in which they are found. In other words, what a local authority is will depend on the system of government which surrounds it and of which it is a part.

This chapter, therefore, is a characterization of local government systems in general, illustrated by reference to the traditional and the new systems of England and Wales. No attempt is made here to define every technical term used in the description of these two systems and a reader totally unfamiliar with the language and law of local government may find it desirable to have as a reference book one of the standard works on local government or local government law.[1]

The description of local government systems

To characterize a system of local government is to place it in an exact category by successively narrowing the more inclusive fields to which it belongs.[2] First, local government belongs to that sector of the machinery of government that is normally called *decentralization, area administration* or some variant of these. These mean simply that there is a governmental body with a jurisdiction limited to only a part of the total territory of a country. But to say that a public authority is part of the system of decentralization is to say nothing about the nature of the authority exercised by those who hold office in the area, nor about the nature of the area itself.

It is at this point that some of the difficulties of providing an exact description of local government appear. For, at different times and different places, various types of area authority have been regarded as local government which would not have been so treated at others. The complexities encountered here can best be explained by looking first at the type of authority that has been seen as the paradigm of local government for over eighty years. This I shall call *primary* local government.

PRIMARY LOCAL GOVERNMENT

Primary local government exists wherever the members of the authority or body corporate are directly elected by the people of the area itself, under a system of elections that is counted as free and fair by the people of that time and place, without the direct intervention of any other public body, other than through the administration of elections. It does not matter what the electoral system is, provided the electorate is limited to those living in the area or having some recognizable and accepted connection with it. The ownership of property, for instance, has often been so regarded.

It is, however, necessary to modify the above in two ways. First, primary local government has for a long time been regarded as necessarily multi-functional – that is, comprised of authorities responsible for a range of services. This is more than a matter of being responsible at a given point in time for a number of distinct activities; it must be the case that the body is regarded as suitable for both the addition and removal of functions, as national policy dictates.

Second, the area for which the authority is responsible must be relatively small. A province, such as Northern Ireland, and a Principality or Kingdom, if Wales and Scotland were to be given elected assemblies, are not to be regarded as part of the local government system. There is a large element of convention in what is regarded as local government; it is not entirely a matter of square miles (or population) and many of the problems of local government are shared with devolution.

Primary local government today therefore consists of a set of local authorities whose members are directly elected, whose jurisdiction embraces a range of disparate services, and whose area is relatively small compared with the major geographical divisions of the country. But at other times this characterization would not have been acceptable in that it would have excluded forms of local administration that were regarded at that time as local government.

Prior to the late-nineteenth-century reforms in England, many local bodies were in practice independent local taxing authorities but were appointed, as were the members of quarter sessions governing the counties, or co-opted, as were the members of some of the closed corporations before 1835. As both of these levied rates and provided a number of public services within their locality they filled the same role in the system of government as primary local government does today.

Also prior to these reforms there were a large number of directly elected authorities which were essentially responsible for only one public activity – school boards, highway district authorities, boards of guardians etc. As the local government system relied so extensively on these they must also be regarded as part of the primary system of that time, but they have now all disappeared, their duties being transferred to the reformed multi-functional system.

SECONDARY LOCAL GOVERNMENT

The local government system, however, does contain more than the primary authorities. *Secondary* local government consists of authorities, with independent powers of decision making and the power of taxation, who are indirectly elected by members of primary authorities. Secondary authorities are thus derived from primary ones in whose areas they are located. Each contributory council has the right to nominate a specified number of members of the secondary body, but once they have been appointed, the members corporately constitute an authority in its own right. They have a fixed term of office in the way that directly elected members of primary authorities do.

One modification on the principle of direct election of all members of primary authorities occurred in boroughs and county councils, where a fixed proportion of members were indirectly elected. These were the aldermen, who also had a fixed term of office and whose electorate was composed of all the directly elected members. One of the 1972 reforms consisted of abolishing this office outside Greater London and providing for it to be phased out in that area also.

Most secondary authorities differ from the primary ones in another way; like many of the nineteenth-century directly elected bodies they are basically single-purpose or *ad hoc.* This means simply that they are responsible for only one public service or a very closely related group of public activities. Amongst the best examples of these were the joint water boards established in many parts of the country after 1945 to administer the water undertakings of a number of local authorities. Another good example is the Inner London Education Authority, established by the 1963 Act to carry out educational functions in the area of the former London

County Council, which consists of the councillors from the 12 relevant Greater London boroughs, who are also members of the Greater London Council.

ADMINISTRATIVE BODIES

Though primary and secondary local government exhaust the list of local *authorities,* there are a number of other bodies which, though not actually authorities in the above sense, are permanent and important parts of the local government decision making system. These are the area bodies established as part of the internal machinery of a local authority, but which are responsible for only part of the parent body's territory. These are created by a process of multiple or repeated decentralization; any individual local authority may have its own field administration and its own form of appointed lay authority.

The simplest form of these is the area office which an authority establishes as its field agency for a portion of its total area. This is usually part of the ordinary departmental organization and hierarchy, and differs only by the fact of geographical separation from headquarters.

More interesting are the committees established to oversee aspects of administration within the separate areas of the authority. These may be called 'boards', 'executives', 'subcommittees' or 'committees', but basically they are all either subcommittees of a headquarters committee or joint committees with other authorities. They vary in the degree to which their existence is protected against the changing will of the parent body. Some have no status other than that conferred by the administrative decision of the originating council, and can be abolished or reorganized at will; others owe their existence to a scheme of administration which has been approved by the relevant minister and needs his approval for modifications.

Finally, there are the bodies which govern institutions. These are groups of laymen who are given some powers of control and influence over a particular institution, such as a school, a children's home or a welfare hostel. The best known of these are the managers or governors of schools in the public sector. These also vary in the extent to which their position is protected against action by the parent body.

It must be stressed that field offices, area committees, joint committees, and institutional government are not authorities because they do not have the power of taxation or of independent decision making. But because of their public prominence and operational significance in the local government system of an area they must always be borne in mind when the question of understanding local government arises.

OTHER LOCAL BODIES

The above exhausts the list of the types of element of the local government system. Because present times operate with much clearer and strict conceptions of local government, other local administrative bodies are usually excluded from the category of local authorities. But there are a number of bodies which are closely related to local government and which interact frequently with the local government system. These are all appointed bodies, and some of them contain members nominated by local authorities as well as those appointed by the central government or some other local body.

A striking example of such a body in the traditional system was the standing joint committee which controlled the police service in the administrative county. The county council and quarter sessions each appointed half its members and despite its name it was legally a joint *board*, not a joint committee, because it had the power of taxation and its decisions did not need the confirmation of either the county council or quarter sessions. The reform of the National Health Service[3] and the reorganization of the administration of the water cycle have both created patterns of authority which depart even more markedly from the model of local government set out above. The system of decentralization now contains two sets of local (and regional) bodies to which local authorities contribute a part, but only a part, of the membership.

Because these new local administrations are responsible for some of the traditional local government services (the personal health services and water supply, sewerage and sewage disposal), and because they have this organic connection with local government, it is well worthwhile always having their existence in mind when trying to understand local government. But for the rest of this book attention will be concentrated on that part of the local government system proper which has been called *primary local government*.

TYPES OF PRIMARY LOCAL GOVERNMENT

The next step is to distinguish different *types* of primary local government. A local government system may contain only one type of local government, or it may contain several. What, then, is a type of local government?

The classification of local authorities into distinct types is based on the number of levels of local government there are at a particular place. A level in this context is usually called a *tier*. The number of tiers is therefore the first factor to be considered.

Though in principle it is possible to distinguish one, two, three . . . n-tiered systems, in practice it is worthwhile simply contrasting single-tier with all the multi-tier systems. This is because in practice only two- and three-tier systems have been important in the multi-tier category, and partly because all multi-tier systems can best be understood as *complex* types of local government. Multi-tier local government is complex, in contrast to single-tier, because the existence of different levels creates a structure of relations between them. As has been recognized in much of the discussion about local government reform, the single-tier type is relatively simple.

The paradigm of the simple tier of local government was the county borough in the traditional local government system. The county borough council was responsible for all local government services, other than those allocated in that area to a secondary authority, within its boundaries, and corresponded originally to the large and geographically distinct town or city. There is of course logically no scope for the existence of distinct species or types of simple local government.

The latter is not, however, true of the complex type. The existence of distinct levels of authority within the same area allows varying patterns of relationship between them. Though many aspects of local government could be used to differentiate species of complex system, probably the best is that of *balance*. The balance of a complex system depends on the relative importance of the two levels, or their 'weight' as measured by such factors as impact on the citizen, tax demands and expenditure. The 'weight' of a type of local government may be such that it is top-heavy, bottom-heavy or evenly balanced.

The languages of local government

One of the difficulties that the student of local government always faces is that understanding local government involves at least three distinct languages and vocabularies. The previous discussion has set out part of the language of analysis – a set of terms which systematically encompass a great variety of circumstances within a few logically ordered categories.

There is, however, the distinct language peculiar to the law and practice of each local government system, which is interpreted on analysis in the terms of the former language. The system of government of a country will assign names to each type of local authority, which in fact designate legal categories of authority, and will allocate public services, which themselves are the names of legally created groups of activities, to them. What an urban district was under the traditional system was precisely defined by the statutes regulating local government.

The difficulty arises because there is a third language which is confused and inconsistent. This is the language of everyday life or of the layman, which is used when talking about local government outside the academic study and the lawyer's office. This language contains two types of terms which are often confused with the legal categories and the analytical types mentioned above. The first are geographical expressions and the second are historic and ceremonial titles.

Words such as 'town', 'village' and 'region' are primarily geographical expressions. They refer to types of social development or to patterns of land use; some are used simply to refer to different sizes of area. They are *not* the names of types of local authority and although there are some conventional and partly fictitious relations between types of authority and types of geographical unit, the relations must always be established empirically; they cannot be assumed. Sometimes, for instance, the geographical town of Exeter coincided more or less with the county borough; on other occasions there were substantial parts of it outside the latter's boundaries. One could also pass through rural England and find neighbouring large villages or small towns having respectively parish, urban district or non-county borough status, even though they were geographically indistinguishable.

Words such as 'shire' and 'borough' (without a prefix) were terms of historic and ceremonial significance. There was of course a time when shires, hundreds and tythings were units of English government, and were in fact the primary local government of the time. But though the geographical county corresponds to the shire the latter has long since ceased to be other than a quaint expression.

The word 'city' belongs to both geography and ceremony. Urban geographers have analysed the patterns of behaviour within and between those densely populated areas they identify as cities, without reference to legal status of their local government or, indeed, to the country in which they are situated. But 'city' is also a title – 'a status and dignity' conferred by the monarch, which does not affect the organization or legal powers of the authority in any way. Thus in the traditional system, the urban district of Ely, the metropolitan borough of Westminster, the non-county borough of Bangor and the county borough of Birmingham were all cities; in the new system this is true of the metropolitan district of Manchester, the non-metropolitan district of Winchester and the successor parish of Wells.

The word 'county' is equally confusing. Traditionally counties were basic units of English government (and Welsh, Scottish and Irish) and their boundaries remained unchanged for many centuries, so that their shapes when the earliest county maps were made were still recognizable in the atlas maps of administrative areas in the 1950s. The traditional county, now referred to as the 'geographical county', began to lose its importance and significance as an area in the nineteenth century, and the reforms of the 1888 Act meant that it ceased to have any role in the system of government, apart from a statistical one and very minor functions in central government and *ad hoc* bodies. This was because the geographical counties had many of the large towns removed from their ambit as 'county boroughs', and some of them were divided into two or more administrative counties. Boundary changes between 1888 and 1972, and in the 1972 Act, have rendered the geographical county even less important in the system of government.

But many social activities did not change their territorial organization as the pattern of local government areas changed. This is most strikingly true of cricket which has never taken note of these changes. County boroughs have always belonged to the surrounding county, the divisions of Yorkshire and Sussex into three and two administrative counties respectively were ignored and Middlesex County Cricket Club continues even though there is no longer such a county. Many other sports are based on the old counties, as are many political and religious organizations. With the recent local government reforms, however, the disparity between local government areas and those of other bodies has grown so great that some are seriously considering adapting to the former.

'City' and 'county' then are ambiguous words in everyday speech and as such have no role in either of the systematic languages of local government – the language of law and the language of analysis. It can easily be seen from the above that those who would understand local government must learn to drop the vernacular and substitute the rigorous languages. This is true not only of the names of authorities and types of local government; it applies also to services, such as education, public health and consumer protection. In local government these have precise and different meanings, though related, compared with those they have in everyday life.

Any local government system can therefore be reduced to a set of individual authorities, that is, a set of territorial and functional jurisdictions. The bodies that control and exercise the powers of these jurisdictions are the entities that are construed as local political and administrative systems in the main part of this book. If an extensive definition of local government is needed then all that is necessary is a list of the types of local authority that exist within the system and perhaps a statement of the jurisdictional relations between them.

In the next two sections the traditional and the new local government systems are described in terms of the analytical concepts developed above and the legal categories the system recognized.

The traditional system in England and Wales

The basic features of the traditional system of local government were laid down by three important Acts in the late nineteenth century – the *Local Government Act, 1888*, the *Local Government Act, 1894*, and the *London Government Act, 1899*. These Acts created a comprehensive pattern of directly elected multi-functional authorities for the whole of England and Wales. Though the conventional picture is to the contrary, this pattern evolved in a number of substantial ways during its existence. It will be described as it was in the late 1950s and early 1960s, with statistics taken from the Census of 1961.

The system drew no legal distinction between England and Wales, but it did have slightly different arrangements for London as it had been defined in 1888. Outside London the whole of the country was divided into two different types of local government. The first was the administrative county which was a complex system, consisting of a mixture of two- and three-tier local government. The county borough was a simple system – an area governed only by the county borough council. The London system was a variant of the administrative county but with sufficient distinct features to merit a separate category of its own.

In the last thirty years of its life the traditional system received a very bad press and was assailed from all sides – from within and without – as irrational, outmoded and inefficient. Many of these criticisms were ill-founded in as much as they claimed that there were no principles underlying the system. As will be seen, the real difficulty was the incomplete way that they were implemented in practice.

PRINCIPLES OF STRUCTURE

Two of the principles underlying the system have already been described. These are first, the direct election of all local authorities, and second, a complete coverage of the whole of the country by multi-functional authorities. These two have never been seriously challenged as principles and they remain important in the new system.

The source of most of the difficulties lay in two other principles on which the system was based. The first of these may be called the *community* principle and the second the *technical efficiency* or *service* principle.

It was and is generally believed that every distinct community, defined in terms of spatial patterns of living, should have its own council. If one examines a map of population distribution, or flies over a country in an aeroplane, one soon becomes aware of the differing socio-geographical patterns the distribution of settlements makes. There are tracts of scattered dwellings, tracts with small nodes – hamlets and villages – with larger groupings – small and medium-sized towns – and so on up the scale of size until the sprawling conurbation is reached.

Each of these was given its own council, except those at the two extremes of the size range. The very smallest communities were given a form of direct democracy – the parish meeting, at which all qualified citizens were entitled to attend and contribute to decisions made. Outside London the conurbation was not recognized at all and the long established urban agglomerations, such as the West Midlands and Greater Manchester, were governed by a mixture of types of local government.

Villages and even some large hamlets were given a parish council; small towns were either non-county boroughs or urban districts (the difference between them was almost entirely ceremonial) and medium-sized and large towns were either one of the latter or were county boroughs. As the differences between non-county boroughs and urban districts were so minimal a collective name of 'town districts' has been stipulated for them, though it must always be remembered that this is not one legal category but two.

The basic local authorities of the system were therefore the parishes, the town districts and the county boroughs. At this point, however, the second principle becomes operative. It is widely accepted that local authority areas should be suitable for the provision of the services for which the authority is responsible. At the very least they should not be positively harmful or handicapping. *Suitability* in this context has been widely interpreted to mean that they should have large enough populations to benefit from economies of scale and that they should correspond to large socio-geographic areas.[4]

Only large towns were judged populous and extensive enough to pass both these tests, and county borough status was the result of a decision to allow one council only to administer all the local government services within its area. The county borough was therefore a single-tier, simple type of local government. But perhaps more than any other type the county borough suffered from a tension between the form of local government and the principles of structure.

The first problem was how large was large enough for this status, and over the years a general conviction grew that many of the historic boroughs could not provide all local government services properly. In some cases they found it necessary to purchase services from the surrounding county council rather than directly provide them themselves. The second problem was that suburban growth was repeatedly producing a divorce between the area of the geographical town and the area of the county borough. In the conurbations, where many county boroughs were located, urban development had obliterated the socio-geographical lines between what had been historically distinct towns. In short, the simplicity of the county borough as a type of local government was not matched by a simplicity of society.[5]

Outside the large towns the basic units – parishes and town districts – were all deemed to be too small and geographically inappropriate for the provision of many local government services. This led to the creation of aggregate units – areas of local government containing two or more (often many) basic units. These aggregate units were the upper tier in structures whose lower tier was comprised of basic units.

This was most strikingly illustrated with parish government.[6] Most parishes corresponded to villages and hamlets; many of them had populations of less than 500, including an appreciable number with less than 300. Though the parish was one of the most satisfactory units from the community point of view, it was quite inappropriate for the provision of any but the most minor public services. Parishes were therefore grouped into rural districts, whose council was responsible for providing a number of services for those living in its parishes. The rural district was therefore itself a type of complex local government, with the rural district council as the upper tier and the various forms of parish government as the lower tier.[7]

Though town districts were generally much larger than parishes and therefore suitable for the provision of many more services – in fact as many or more than was the rural district – they were still small by the requirements of many local government services. Together with rural districts they were also aggregated – this time into administrative counties, whose council was responsible for the rest of the local government services. Thus a second type of complex system was created, having the county council as its upper tier and county districts (rural and town) as its lower tier.[8]

The local government system of London was a variant of the administrative county, and was therefore a type of complex local government. It differed from the provincial administrative county in a number of ways. Some local government services had been removed from local authorities and given to either central government, as in the case of police, or to *ad hoc* bodies as in the case of transport and water supply. The system was universally two-tier; there was no equivalent to the rural district, and all the lower tier authorities except one were called 'metropolitan boroughs'. The exception was the City of London, which still retained its historic (and anomalous) form of local government. The lower tier generally in London had fewer functions than did the town districts of the provinces.[9]

The traditional system of local government, therefore, contained three distinct types of local government – the county borough, the administrative county and London – the latter two being both complex systems. The administrative county also contained within itself a smaller complex system, the rural district.

This local government system was often presented as an organizational chart, for instance by the Central Office of Information in its reference pamphlet. But this was quite erroneous. First, the relations between central government, which was at the top of the diagram, and local authorities were never ones of hierarchy; they could not be assimilated to those found in large scale commercial and industrial firms where the organizational chart originated. Second, the relations between upper and lower tiers in the two complex systems were also presented as hierarchical; this was equally misleading as the elements of super- and sub-ordination that this implies were negligible. Thirdly, the same is true of the relations between rural district councils and their parishes. These were not hierarchical in any sense.

This is not the place to enter into a full discussion of the nature of the relationships between central and local government, and between upper and lower tiers in complex systems – these are reserved for the last part of the book – but it is worth remarking that the law created substantially independent authorities within a circumscribed sphere, which were subject to external control and influence only in specified ways. The pattern is therefore best represented by a different sort of diagram, one which contains no element of hierarchy in its presentation. Figure 1 describes the local government system of England and Wales as it was in 1961.

Local government law created the possibility of constituting joint boards for a long list of local government services, provided the relevant minister or Parliament agreed. These included public health, personal health, food and drugs, education, town and country planning, water supply, police and fire services, rivers and coast protection. These powers were used sporadically; they were more important in water supply, the police force in Wales, and port health than in education in England or the personal social services. For practical reasons it is impossible to give a list of these and the importance to be attached to them in understanding the local government of a part of the country varied from one place to another.[10]

The position in relation to joint committees was even more obscure. Local authorities had a very general power to form joint committees with one or more other authorities, provided all part-

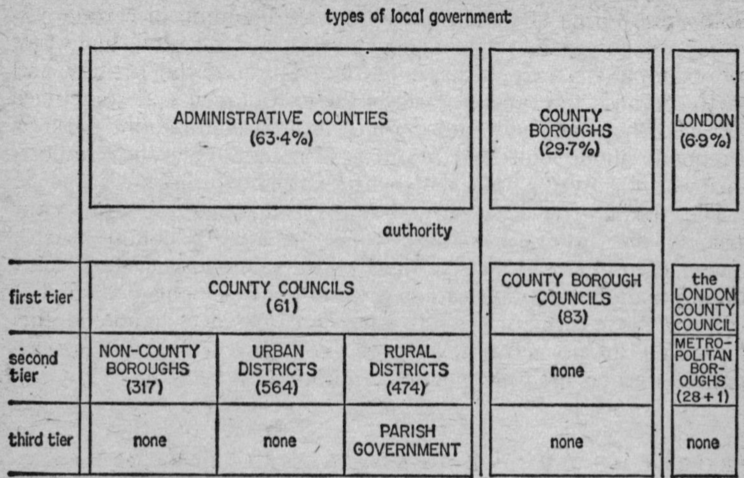

Fig. 1 **The Structure of Local Government in England and Wales in April, 1961**

ners judged this to be in their interest. This power was used extensively but sporadically; some of the joint ventures were short lived because they fulfilled the purpose asked of them, whilst others became permanent. Their importance in a given area could also only be determined empirically.

Finally, there were the bodies created by local authorities for the governance of parts of their territory. Outside the extensive administrative counties the most important of these in terms of geographical distribution were committees to manage individual schools, often called 'the board of governors'. These were found in county boroughs as well as counties, but the forms that they took and their importance in local decision making varied so much that generalization is impossible.

County councils with large areas tended to carry out their functions through various forms of decentralization. Obviously the most common of these was field administration, much of which was inescapable in the light of technical factors within the service itself. But some counties were favourable towards delegation to area committees or subcommittees, sometimes in collaboration with the relevant district councils, or delegation to the district council itself.

Both these forms of decentralization were common in certain services – planning, the personal social services, education, highways, for example – partly because of the nature of the activity and partly because the central government encouraged and sometimes enforced their use. The same point must be made about these as was made about joint boards and joint committees: their importance within a given part of the country varied enormously.[11]

The traditional local government system was therefore constructed on certain principles, which created a comprehensive system of primary local government with joint boards, joint committees and area administration providing an element of flexibility to be deployed wherever individual circumstances rendered this desirable. But no account would be complete without an assessment of how far the principles were followed in practice.

PROBLEMS OF THE TRADITIONAL STRUCTURE

Several factors combined to produce a situation in which in many parts of the country there were both major and minor departures from the principles. First, the pattern as it was created in the late nineteenth century embodied many anomalies. Many of the areas were small in populaion and acreage even by the standards of the time, and their boundaries were ones that were accepted as they stood, without much attempt at rationalization of the old pattern. Second, since that time increasing specialization within many local government services has led to the perception, justified or unjustified, that for technical reasons larger and larger areas are required if they are to be provided properly. Third, the spatial pattern of communities has changed in a number of ways. The free-standing village, town or city is no longer so independent of areas at some distance from it. Individuals are more mobile, diurnally and residentially, than before. This last factor is at its most prominent in the conurbations, and these were becoming more significant in the social geography of the country. But as was remarked before, this form of spatial 'community' was not recognized in the primary system of local government outside London.

None of these points would have mattered, had it not been for a fourth factor – the resistance, much of it effective, of individual local authorities to piecemeal change which related adversely, as they saw the matter, to their interests. Those familiar only with the period 1945 to 1964 were apt to exaggerate the stability over the long term of the structure of local government, but there was no doubt that in many instances there was a growing divorce between what the principles dictated and the existing structure.

One of the simplest ways of illustrating this point is to look at the distribution of sizes of population of the different types of primary local authority in 1961. Table 1 (p. 289) presents this information in comparative form. It shows how each legal type of local authority contained some very small authorities and how their ranges overlapped in that there were numbers of lower-tier authorities much larger than some upper-tier ones. Another way is to look at the pattern of local authorities in one of the conurbations – for instance, the Greater Manchester area. This conurbation in 1961 was governed by a great variety of local authorities. At the centre was the large county borough of Manchester and alongside it the substantial one of Salford. To the north, and at some distance, was an arc of mostly smaller county boroughs – including Bury and Rochdale – and to the south the county borough of Stockport. In between these were a large number of town districts (and one rural district) some in the administrative county of Cheshire and others in Lancashire. Many decisions relating to the conurbation were therefore taken in Chester or Preston. It could also be argued that the above standard conurbation was inadequately defined and that it should have contained parts of south-central Lancashire to the west and parts of Derbyshire and Yorkshire to the east.[12]

A different picture was obtained from an examination of mid-Wales or Devon and Cornwall. Here the problem was not so much that local authorities are too small but that the communities were – certainly too small to be easily fitted into a new local government system. In fact over large parts of the rural areas of England and Wales the traditional structure looked more reasonable than it did in the conurbations; it could be and was argued that for the most part deficiencies were not attributable to the pattern of areas as such.[13]

ALLOCATION OF SERVICES

To complete the picture of the traditonal system as it was in the late-nineteen-fifties and early-nineteen-sixties it is necessary to describe the services for which local government was responsible and their allocation between the different levels of local authority in complex systems.

The services or functions which were in general the responsibility of the local government system can be grouped into five main headings: protective; environmental; personal; cultural and recreational; trading. This classification is not completely rigorous but it serves to indicate the main spheres of activity of local authorities.

The *protective* services were those which attempted to safeguard the citizen against the traditional dangers to life, liberty and property. They were the police and fire services, civil defence, the inspection services (including weights and measures, factories and workshops, diseases of animals, food and drugs, and shops) and licensing (including motor vehicles and drivers, and a host of minor licences).

The *environmental* services controlled and improved the physical environment (and thus had something in common with the protective services). They were highways, town and country planning, street lighting, housing, water supply, burial grounds and mortuaries, and public health (including refuse collection and disposal, sewerage and sewage disposal, street cleansing, river pollution and clean air).

The *personal* services were those that were given to individuals as part of the welfare state. They were education, the children's service, welfare (including care of the aged, blind, handicapped etc.) and individual health services (including health visiting, mental health, home helps, midwifery etc.). Local authority health and social services were much more complicated than the above lists indicate and education was itself an elaborate set of functions.

Cultural and recreational services were those for leisure time as conventionally defined. They were recreational facilities (including swimming baths, sports stadia and grounds, and parks and open spaces), entertainment, and libraries, art galleries and museums. Some of these had other elements within them, for instance, of education and of commerce.

The *trading services* were those that were bought by citizens in a transaction that was to all intents and purposes an ordinary commercial one, except that often the price was determined in part by non-monetary factors. They were smallholdings, allotments, markets, civic restaurants, aerodromes, municipal transport and a variety of miscellaneous activities such as beach undertakings in seaside resorts. Some local authorities had taken special powers to run unusual trading undertakings.

All these services and activities were the responsibility of one council in the areas of the county boroughs, except for those which had been transferred to a secondary authority or which, as they were permissive functions, the council had not chosen to provide.

But in complex systems they were necessarily divided between two or more levels of authority.

To understand the division in the administrative county it is necessary to group local government services into four categories. First, there were the services which were the responsibility of the county council alone. These were police and fire services, motor licences, the children's service, smallholdings and most parts of civil defence. Second, there were those services which were primarily the responsibility of the county council but which were subject to provisions for the compulsory delegation to (or for claiming by) particular types and sizes of district council. This category comprised education, highways, individual health services, town and country planning, weights and measures and welfare services. The third group consisted of services that were the responsibility of district and parish – allotments, entertainment, housing, markets, water supply, burial grounds, etc., civic restaurants, public health, factories and workshops, and some parts of civil defence. The fourth group was a residual one, consisting of those services whose allocation was variable or complex. These included aerodromes, street lighting, swimming baths, parks and recreation grounds, libraries, museums and art galleries, animal diseases, unclassified roads, food and drugs and shops inspection.

The situation was further complicated in rural districts because some of the functions were the responsibility of parish government. Parishes had a whole host of very minor powers (minor in relation to cost and importance to the outside world, not necessarily to the parish itself) in respect of open air and sporting recreation, social and educational projects, the appearance of villages, public lighting, common pasture and allotments, health, housing, communications, inns and clocks and the dead.

The distribution of functions within London differed in a number of important respects from that found in provincial administrative counties. First, a number of services were the responsibility of other governmental bodies – particularly police, water supply, transport, ports. Second, there was the City of London, 'a small island of obstinate mediaeval structure in the midst of a sea of modern local authorities', which in some respects was subordinate to the London County Council like a metropolitan borough and in others equal to it like a county borough. Thirdly, the County Council had more functions or a share in a greater number – for instance, civic restaurants, entertainment, housing, parks and recreation grounds, public health, main sewers – though the lower tier had a greater role in some, such as libraries and highways. Fourthly, the County Council had more tutelage powers over the lower tier than was the case in the other administrative counties.

A straightforward description of the local government system would now proceed to discuss the internal pattern of organization of each local authority and the powers and influence of the central government over it. To do this properly, however, requires the special and elaborate conceptual framework that is the central part of this book. As this conceptual framework applies to the new system as well, before it is expounded and justified, a parallel account of the pattern of local government just created, and now searching for a more permanent form, will be given.

The new system

The new local government system was created by a series of Acts Parliament passed in the period 1972-74, and their associated regulations. There was thus a transitional period of one year when the old and new existed side-by-side, the latter being shadow authorities only. Together the Acts redistributed public services, mainly by removing some from local government control, created a new pattern of local authorities, and introduced some additional institutions into the system.

However, the reorganizations of this time were prefigured in the reform of London Government which took place in the early 1960s. It has been remarked that in the traditional system London, as defined in 1888, was governed by a special form of county government, and in the metropolis the general problems of the traditional structure and the special problems of complex systems had been particularly prominent. The Greater London system, created by the *London Government Act, 1963*, thus acts as one sort of link between the traditional and the new.

Even in 1888 the boundaries of London had been drawn rather narrowly, and the process of population growth had produced a situation where most of those who were to all intents and purposes Londoners lived outside the administrative area called 'London'. This had different effects on the surrounding counties; Middlesex had become entirely a part of London, whilst Kent, Surrey and Essex contained large perimeter sections which were part of the conurbation.

Within each of the counties there were problems of relations between upper and lower-tier authorities which resulted from the particular circumstances of the urban area. Though the usual difficulty associated with widely varying population sizes within each legal category were also encountered, the main problem was created by the fact that district authorities, including those in London itself, were very large by the standards of the British Isles, yet had in general fewer responsibilities.

Partly this was because of the existence of *ad hoc* bodies controlling some local government services, but mainly because the law allocated fewer services to the lower tier in London and discriminated against it in delegation provisions in Middlesex. The result was that many urban authorities in this region were both larger than county boroughs and had fewer responsibilities than town district councils in the rest of England. The law relating to local government in the postwar period had thus significantly discriminated against the components of the greater London area.

In 1945 an attempt had been made to deal with the problems of the administrative county of London separately from those of the rest of England and Wales, but this was almost immediately recognized to be a nonsense by the appointed committee itself. When reform again became a distinct possibility in the mid 1950s it was at first intended that London should be treated by the same machinery that was to be used in the rest of the country, though with certain restrictions on what could be proposed. The absurdity of these was eventually recognized by the Government, and a new area specified – that of Greater London – which was to be the subject to a special investigation by a Royal Commission. This procedure had several advantages, though these were not always articulated at the time. It prevented the ordinary machinery for the rest of England being overwhelmed by the pressing problems of London, and it was a more rapid and direct form of investigation and decision making.

The Commission under the chairmanship of Sir Edwin Herbert took only three years to complete its work and publish its report.[14] It proposed the creation of a new type of complex local government to administer the whole of the area commonly thought of as 'London' (though there has always been argument about its exact extent), in which the lower-tier authorities would have a significantly enlarged role. Though the Government made some changes in the details of the proposals in principle the ideas underlying it were embodied in new legislation and in 1965 this new structure came into full operation. The extent to which it is regarded as satisfactory may be judged from the fact that it was excluded from the reorganizations of the early 1970s, whereas those that had been made in some parts of the rest of England had to be redone.

The new system, however, did contain one reminder of the past, for the City of London was left in existence as a traditional authority, despite the protests of the supporters of the London and Middlesex County Councils. Though their boundaries were judged to be anachronistic and their populations of millions too small, this tiny authority, with its form reminiscent more of mediaeval than of post-industrial revolution England, was allowed to remain, and has survived the most recent reorganizations also.

The whole of the remainder of the area is within the jurisdiction of the Greater London Council and of one lower-tier authority, now called 'Greater London Boroughs'. There are thirty-two of these, ranging in size from 139,000 to 334,000 population, but they are divided into two groups for the purpose of educational provision. The twelve inner London boroughs, who govern the area of the former London County Council, do not have responsibility for education themselves but have it provided by the Inner London Education Authority, which is a joint board whose members are the Greater London Councillors *ex officio* from those boroughs. The twenty outer London boroughs are education authorities in their own right. There are no statutory third-tier authorities within the Greater London area but the neighbourhood council movement has received considerable support here and some voluntary ones have been established, with varying success.

One of the main consequences of the new system has been that London Government has ceased to be top-heavy and become a bottom-heavy structure. The weight of the system, particularly in the twenty outer London boroughs, has been transferred to the district level. The underlying rationale of the division is that the basic operating and service providing unit should be the lower-tier authority, whilst the area wide council should be responsible for those activities which can only be properly treated over the whole area and for strategic planning and related long term roles. As is always the case, the actual division is controversial.

Another remote consequence of the search for means of reforming local government in the 1950s occurred in the separate treatment for Wales and England that the new system embodies. At the same time that London was being given its own royal commission, Wales was being given its own local government commission, separate from that of England.[15] Whilst the English Commission was able to bring about changes in local government areas in some parts of the country, the Welsh Commission was adjudged to be a complete failure and its proposals for the Principality were totally rejected. Thus whilst the English Commission continued on its piecemeal way, it was necessary to find a new procedure to put in the place of the ruins of the existing one in Wales. The process of local government reform thus began to take another course in Wales from 1963 and when, finally, a Government was determined to bring about structural change in local government outside London, it was faced with the results of two different procedures for generating proposals.

The effect of this was seen in the way that the Welsh provisions of the Act are now embodied in separate parts, instead of being submerged in general provisions covering both England and Wales. This should not however conceal the fact that local government in Wales is very similar to one of the types of local government adopted in England.

Welsh local government is now almost uniformly three-tier, with the third level being called *community* instead of *parish* government. In practice it is an adaptation of the administrative county with a slightly different distribution of services between tiers and with much larger district authorities.

In England outside Greater London a distinction is drawn between the largest urban areas and the rest of the country. The former have been given a form of complex local government very similar to the Greater London system. There is a council – called the 'metropolitan county council' – with responsibility for some functions over the whole area, and a number of district councils responsible for the bulk of local government activities. These councils serve relatively large populations, ranging from 172,000 to 1,087,000. The system is almost entirely two-tier but there are a few parishes and successor parishes, accounting for only a minute proportion of the population under metropolitan government.

The territory of the metropolitan areas corresponds more or less to the boundaries of the traditional conurbations except that in some places it has been significantly extended to take in neighbouring urban areas which had not usually been counted as part of it. Thus Sunderland has been added to Tyneside, Coventry to the West Midlands and Southport to Merseyside. In addition, the West Riding conurbation has been divided into two, West Yorkshire based on Leeds and Bradford, and South Yorkshire, based on Sheffield. But in the years to come there will be pressure from other areas to be granted this status because it is advantageous to a large town to be a lower-tier authority in a metropolitan rather than a non-metropolitan county.

In the rest of England the balance of the complex system is quite different. It has been divided into non-metropolitan counties, all of which are a mixture, in varying proportions, of two- and three-tier local government. But the system is top-heavy in that the major part of the responsibilities of local government are allocated to the area wide authority – the county council – whilst the second level has a number of substantial activities and the third, where it exists, a diverse collection of minor permissive powers.

There are in fact two major and related differences between metropolitan and non-metropolitan counties. The first is that in the latter lower-tier councils serve on average much smaller populations; the range is from 24,000 to 421,000, but the bulk are concentrated between 75,000 and 125,000. Second, education, the personal social services, youth employment and libraries are the responsibility of the district in the metropolitan areas but in the rest of England are county council powers. Metropolitan district areas have been made large deliberately to permit them to be substantial authorities in terms of service provision.

The previous brief discussion of the new local government system can be summarized in Figure 2, which is comparable with the figure presenting the traditional structure. Indeed the figure expresses the structure much more clearly than does the text. Notice that the system now contains *four* types of complex local government and that the relationships between these and within them are *not* hierarchical, as is suggested by the diagrams produced by the government and by the conventional textbooks. An attempt has been made by varying the sizes of the elements of the diagram to indicate the weight of each type of local government and each type of local authority within the system.

The remainder of the discussion of the structure of the new system will be reserved for the chapter on complex systems of local government, but there are a number of ancillary matters which have helped or will help to mould the pattern of the future.

First, there has been some redistribution of services between local government and the rest of the system of public administration. Primary local authorities have lost control of some services which have traditionally been theirs. But in the new administrative machinery which has been created local authorities have some role as sources of individuals who comprise their membership. There is also a close relationship between the boundaries of the new bodies types of local government

level	ENGLAND NON-METROPOLITAN AREAS (55·7%)	ENGLAND METROPOLITAN AREAS (23·8%)	GREATER LONDON (15·0%)	WALES (5·5%)
	authority			
first tier	NON-METROPOLITAN COUNTY COUNCILS (39)	METROPOLITAN COUNTY COUNCILS (6)	GREATER LONDON COUNCIL (1)	COUNTY COUNCILS (8)
second tier	NON-METROPOLITAN DISTRICT COUNCILS (296)	METROPOLITAN DISTRICT COUNCILS (36)	GREATER LONDON BOROUGH COUNCILS (32+1)	DISTRICT COUNCILS (37)
third tier	parish government (in some areas only)	none (except in a minute number of areas)	none	community government

Fig. 2 **The Structure of Local Government in England and Wales from April 1st, 1974**

and the structure of local government.

Local authorities have thus lost control of the personal health services which they had developed in an erratic fashion before the creation of the National Health Service from the old poor law. These are now the responsibility of area health authorities – appointed bodies, some of whose members are local authority nominees, which are also responsible for the services previously administered by the executive councils – and the regional hospital boards. The area health authorities have boundaries corresponding to those of social service authorities, except in London, and they are grouped into regions under the control of a regional health authority, which has mainly strategic, planning and co-ordinating roles. The reorganized National Health Service also contains other administrative arrangements but space forbids a description of them here.

The other main loss by primary local authorities has been in what it is now common to call the water-cycle set of services. Previously some of these were the responsibility of river authorities, others of joint boards (water boards) and yet others of local authorities. The new regional water authorities are based on a reorganized system of river authorities, reduced in number to create nine regions in England. A majority of the members of the new authorities are appointed by the local authorities of the area. They are responsible for water supply and conservation, river management and pollution control, sewerage and sewage disposal, fisheries and land drainage, and the use of water space for recreation and amenity purposes. As with the health services, there are complications in the administrative arrangements for which there is no space here.

In contrast to these losses there have been some gains for the primary local government system. In the metropolitan areas the county council has taken over control of the passenger transport executives created by the *Transport Act, 1968*, and the responsibility for the police has been handed back to county councils, except in the metropolitan police district and in ten areas where the combined police authorities have been retained. The youth employment service has also been made a general local authority function instead of being in some areas directly administered by the Department of Employment.

The new system also contains a whole host of administrative bodies and administrative arrangements which complete the operational structure of complex systems. As most authorities have larger areas and populations than their predecessors it is not surprising that area administrative structures have played an extensive role in the internal organization of county councils. It may be surmised in the absence of systematic evidence that in future field administration and area committees will play a larger part in county government than they did previously.

The situation in respect of delegation is more complicated. Most of the provisions for compulsory delegation or claiming of upper-tier services have been abolished and replaced by a general power to enter into agency arrangements with other authorities except for some specified services. These arrangements are in the discretion of the county council, but the district could appeal during the transitional year to the minister against a refusal in a specific case to make such arrangements. The evidence suggests that in the early months of the new system the central government was generally on the side of the county council and few appeals were allowed.

A minor source of confusion in respect of the new system is that some of the ceremonial titles for local authorities have been retained, though care has been taken to stress that these are honorific only and do not have any operational significance. A district council may have the title of 'borough' conferred on it by royal charter, in which case its chairman is called 'mayor' (occasionally 'lord mayor'), and additionally the monarch may designate it a 'city'. A parish or a community may resolve to adopt the status of 'town' in which case its chairman is known as the 'town mayor'. None of these titles has any effect on the provision of services or on the powers and duties of the authority.

One major development must be mentioned in the context of the new local government structure. In the past the territorial pattern of local authorities has been relatively rigid for long periods partly because there has been no suitable machinery for adjustment and reorganization at reasonable intervals. The *Local Government Act, 1972*, attempted to remedy this by creating two permanent boundary commissions, one for England and one for Wales, whose function it is to review all areas and boundaries within the local government system from time to time, to try to ensure that these change with the changing society.

They are responsible for all areas and boundaries, including those for elections. The English Commission must conduct reviews and make proposals in the interests of effective and convenient local government for the alteration of local government areas, the creation of new areas by amalgamation, aggregation, or separation, the abolition of existing areas, the conversion of metropolitan areas into non-metropolitan ones and *vice-versa*, and all similar actions necessary for structural change.

The Commissions are bound by a long list of procedural requirements and they may be brought into action by the initiative of other bodies, such as a local council or the central government. The English Commission has a duty, unless directed otherwise by the Secretary of State, to hold a general review not less than ten years or more than fifteen years after a previous general review.

The intention is thus that all areas and boundaries should be reviewed at reasonable intervals and whatever changes deemed necessary for effective and convenient local government be made, after investigation by an independent and experienced body, with ultimate political responsibility in the hands of the Government of the day. The English Commission has already played a part in the transition, for it advised on the pattern of districts in non-metropolitan counties and on claims to successor parish status by small boroughs and urban districts. It is now at work on more permanent electoral arrangements, to replace the temporary expedients used for the first elections in 1973. The Welsh Commission did not have to consider district boundaries as these were set out in the Act itself, and it has likewise started work on electoral arrangements.

It should be stressed that structural changes were not the only ones made by the series of Acts affecting local government in the period 1972-74. The introduction of a new system of attendance allowances for council members may have substantial effects in the long run on several aspects of local government, as may the creation of local ombudsmen in the form of local commissioners for administration by the *Local Government Act, 1974*. But an understanding of these factors requires an understanding of what a local authority is, and how it should be approached in analytical terms.

The purpose of this chapter has been to give the reader an understanding of one of the two major languages of local government study – the technical language by which authorities are described within a given legal framework. It is necessary to understand this language before going on to the intellectually more important language of analysis. The next chapter is devoted to a detailed examination of the ways in which the behaviour of local authorities must be understood. Because the language of the legal system was presented first it may be thought that this is the most significant one, but this is not so. It is necessary to understand what a local authority is in legal terms in a particular governmental system only as a prelude to understanding what all local authorities are in behavioural terms.

Part Two

Local Political Systems

Introduction

The purpose of Part Two is to set the scene for the substantive analysis of local authorities as political systems, which in its turn provides the foundations for understanding local government.

First, it is necessary to grasp the concept of a miniature political and administrative system. It may be felt by some that the presentation here of the elements of a systems analysis is unnecessarily elaborate, but such a criticism involves a failure to appreciate that the basic ideas must be understood in detail and with precision. Though some progress may be made with the everyday expectation that government contains intricate relationships between various factors, unless this belief is made more rigorous and exact the level of understanding will remain lower than acceptable. The behavioural patterns called *system-environment interaction* require a detailed, consistent and comprehensive language if any sense is to be made of their structure.

Secondly, it is necessary to have a generalized picture of what sort of factors are likely to be important in the environment of the individual authority. Though the main emphasis of this book is on the internal structure of local authorities as political systems, it is vital to see the behavioural patterns *within* the system in their environmental context. Systemic behaviour is neither free-floating nor intelligible in its own terms alone. The factors listed in Chapter Four are those which have been found to have a widespread importance in local government, but it is of course an empirical question how far they are significant in any particular local authority's environment.

In this Part, therefore, the individual local authority is treated as a black box – something whose parts are not being inspected directly – in order that those who wish to understand local government can gain an overall picture of a system within its context – social, economic and political – which is called an *environment* in the language of analysis.

Chapter Three
Miniature Political Systems

The fundamental concept of this book is that of the *miniature political system.* This serves as the basis for the rest of the analysis; other concepts are derived from it or expressed in terms it implies. One consequence of this is that the expression 'local authorities' tends to be used instead of 'local government'. The latter is a source of misunderstanding because characteristics are ascribed to the whole structure which can only be attributed to individual local authorities. There can be no *apathy* in local government, only apathy towards one or more local authorities; to speak of high or low *quality of councillors* only makes sense in relation to a given set of individuals. The truth of statements about local government is often only to be decided by adding up the experiences and behaviour of all individual authorities.

No special point is intended by referring to 'political' in the fundamental concept – the word has the sort of meaning that students of government now generally accept – but the idea of *system* is basic. At least three related but distinct means of 'system' can be found in social science, but they all depend on a process of *abstraction* from a wider reality.

Abstracting the local political system

Each local authority is a miniature political system, and therefore a miniature social system – a concept of much wider application than the study of local government, or even political science in general. It underlies the study of individual countries in comparative government, it is the basis of community studies in sociology and social anthropology, it is the starting point for the analysis of formal organizations and it is used in theoretical and applied economics. States, regions, tribes, primitive social systems, firms and industries all involve the same process of looking at something as an entity in its own right, apart from but within the wider social context which surrounds it.

At the most general level to call something a *system* is simply to say that the elements constituting it can be treated as a set with a degree of internal coherence arising from their interdependence. Often this amounts to no more than an expressed determination to seek out complicated patterns of interaction within a chosen set of events, facts or behaviours. A second meaning is to be found in the social science approach known as 'functionalism'. In this case behaviour is described and explained in terms of its contribution to the performance of functions within the system; sometimes the functions are ascribed to all social systems.[1]

The third meaning of *system* is the one that occurs in systems analysis proper – where it is related to such subjects as *operational research* and *cybernetics*. To analyse something as a system in the technical sense is to construct a model or picture of it using abstract symbols and combining them through the rules of deductive logic. Thus the chosen segment of empirical reality is said to be represented by the abstract model, and its behaviour is said to be a guide to the behaviour of the world.

A fully developed systems analysis is clearly an exercise in applied logic or applied mathematics (the two mean the same in this context).[2] Such an end-product is only a long run ideal at this point in time, but it can serve as an inspiration and guide at the present. What it does is provide a way of looking at local authorities which avoids the errors and misunderstanding that were found in traditional approaches.

The division of reality into systems is like the division of territory into *regions* and *areas* in geography and time into *periods* in history; it is done in order to facilitate understanding and in no sense are the artifacts themselves real or part of reality. Therefore the test of such an analysis is not its descriptive accuracy – it has none – but its usefulness in explaining what is happening, and thus in promoting understanding.

Processes that can only be properly understood as systems are familiar in everyday life. For instance, the ordinary thermostat which is used to keep a tank full of hot water links the temperature of the water, perhaps through a bimetallic strip, to the source of heat input, so that when a pre-selected temperature is reached this activates a switch which stops the heat input, and when the temperature falls, because hot water has been drawn off, the switch starts the heat input again. Whilst the temperature of the water and the source of heat input are linked in this manner the former can never depart from the pre-selected value for more than a short period.

If an engineer wishes to build a machine which behaves in the desired manner, he will have to work out the exact form of each of the relationships between the parts of the system. When these are taken as a set and presented in abstract form a model of a thermostat will have been created.

In order to illustrate this point and the concepts associated with a systems analysis a general purpose abstract diagram (Figure 3(a)) has been prepared. This diagram contains four variables represented by *a, b, c* and *d*. Changes in *a* affect *b*, changes in *b* affect *c*, changes in *c* affect *d* and changes in *d* affect *a*. In the case of the thermostat, *a* would stand for the temperature of the water, *b* for the shape of the bimetallic strip, *c* for the position of a switch and *d* for the amount of heat input into the water. But it could also be interpreted as a governor to regulate the speed of an engine, in which case *a* would be the speed of the vehicle, *b* the angle of the speedometer needle, *c* the size of the valve-opening controlling the input of energy and *d* the speed at which the engine axle rotates.

The fact that the same model can be interpreted in two different sets of data illustrates its representative function. The process could be continued and instead of physical factors being substituted, social data could be used. For instance, *a* could be interpreted as a percentage of party members who were of a certain social class, *b* as the percentage of candidates who belonged to that class, *c* the percentage of councillors and *d* the percentage of aldermen likewise. Whether this model helped to explain the observed facts of council composition in a given locality could only be determined empirically.

Not only is this diagram useful in showing the artificial nature of systems, it also helps in the understanding of the nature of *environment*, which is one of the key concepts associated with *system*.

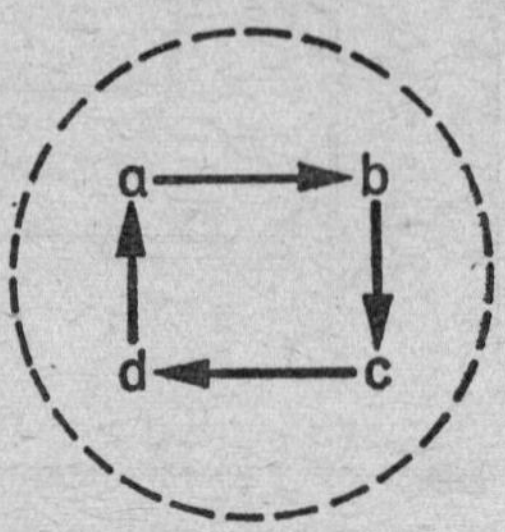

Fig. 3 (a) **Diagrammatic Representation of System and Environment**

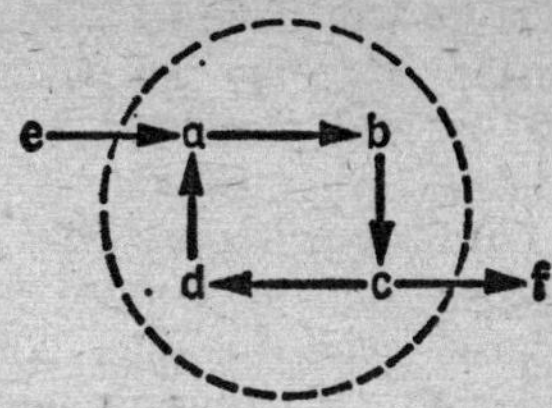

3 (b)

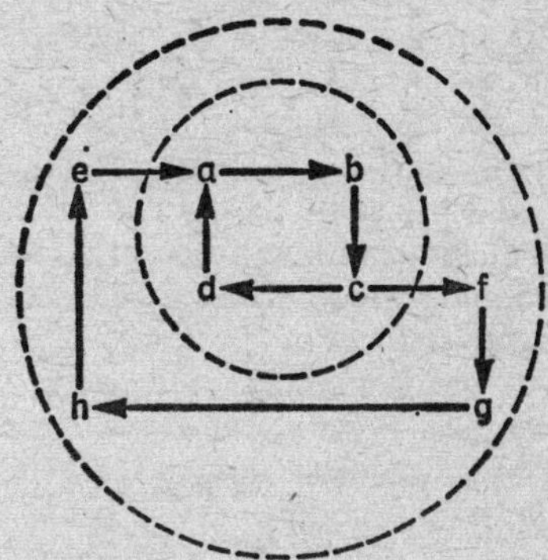

3 (c)

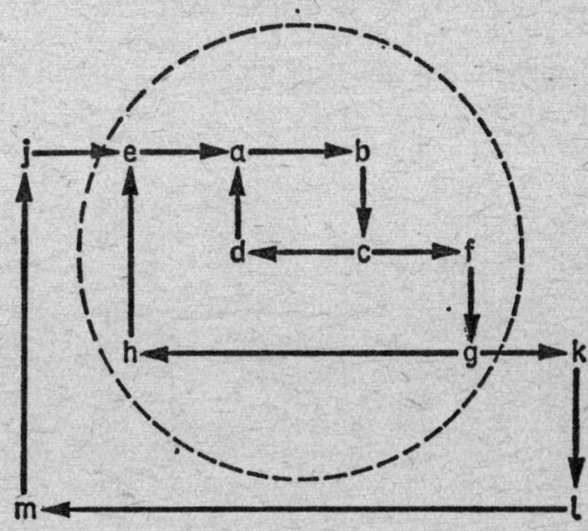

3 (d)

Figs. 3 (b) – (d) **Diagrammatic Representation of System and Environment**

ENVIRONMENT

If the concept of *system* is analytical then so must the concept of *environment* be. If a line is drawn round the four variables in the original diagram then the enclosed space represents the system itself, but there may be two other variables, *e* and *f*, the first of which is an influence from outside on *a* and the second something influenced by *c*. *e* and *f* clearly belong to the system's environment. This is shown in Figure 3(b).

Suppose then that two further variables, *g* and *h*, are discovered to stand in the relations shown in Figure 3(c), so that *c* is additionally linked to *a* through *f*, *h*, *g* and *e*. There is then no reason why the new relationships should not be regarded as another more inclusive system, of which the original four variables constitute a sub-system. But equally, a person interested only in the first four can continue to regard them as a system. If then another four variables are discovered, linked in the manner of *j*, *k*, *l* and *m* in figure 3(d), then a line can enclose them as a sub-system or as a separate system with the original variables as part of the environment. Systems are like chinese boxes, extending indefinitely in both directions, inwards and outwards.

Thus the only possible definition of *environment* is *not-system*. In practice, however, it is important to distinguish between *proximate* and *remote* environment. The former consists of those factors which have direct contact with at least one variable in the system, either as input or output: *e* and *f* in Figure 3(b). The remote environment consists of all those factors which have some definite connection with factors in the proximate environment. Of course it is logically wrong to dichotomize the dimension of proximity/remoteness, which is continuous, into two categories, but this helps to facilitate understanding in the short run.

CULTURE

Those who study groups and organizations empirically soon become aware that each one develops its own *culture*. A culture is made up of several types of element: a set of values; a set of beliefs about the past; a set of symbols; and a set of standardized ways of behaving, usually called 'rituals'. This culture is created through the interaction of members and endures through time. It need not be homogeneous; indeed, it is likely to contain diverse strands.[3]

Though the notion of culture is used as an explanatory variable in some social science approaches here it is treated as a source of misunderstanding. When participants talk about the social system in which they exist they are offering a sample of its culture; this is true whether they write textbooks or answer questionnaires. The relations between culture and behaviour are complex, and there is always the difficulty of deciding which of competing accounts by participants is true. In fact the best way to treat culture seems to be to regard it as a dangerous and insidious phenomenon, a source of error in matters of fact and the cause of much misunderstanding.[4]

The key to understanding local government is not what participants say about it, but a grasp of the ways in which local authorities can be interpreted as local political systems. The first steps in achieving this are to appreciate the two meanings of *locality*.

Localities

In the list of disciplines in which the notion of an abstract system has been used the most fruitful one for local government studies is that which studies the division of the earth's surface into separate parts; aspects of the subject of this book have long been a central problem in geography.[5]

Various words have been used to describe the end result of this process of dividing any chosen piece of land into parts – *area, district, region, division, territory.* These words are not exclusive nor is any single one of them authoritative. As the process of abstracting the local political system from its national 'parent' is basically the same as occurs in regional geography when a particular area is studied, *locality* has been chosen as the technical word because it has the right connotation of size and functional relevance; but it is not one sanctioned by use elsewhere. It does not have a different *meaning* from the others.

First, therefore, *locality* is an analytical concept in social geography. An examination of the spatial patterns of life reveals that there are both clusterings and discontinuities in human activities. This spatial differentiation of social life is the basis of the definition of geographical *localities.* Within a locality people have more in common, in terms of important characteristics or in terms of behaviour, than they have with people outside. For instance, they may interact with each other more frequently and more intensely.

The study of these discontinuities is part of the discipline of human geography.

In some areas there correspond to these behavioural patterns sets of perceptions or attitudes in local people – which constitute a sense of *belongingness*. This is a belief that they are a part of one area and not part of others. It is possible, and in fact has been observed, that people's perceptions and their behaviour do not always coincide.[6] Where the pattern of interactions is particularly intense and closed, and people express a strong sense of common identity, the word *community* is often used. It is to be expected that in the long run in stable situations people's behaviour and perceptions will in fact cohere but in the short run they may not.

Though concepts of *locality* and *community* are easy to understand in a general way they are much harder to identify in an unambiguous and authoritative manner. Mapping the behavioural patterns of life and discovering the attachments of local people both involve technical problems for the social geographer and the sociologist. A variety of techniques have been developed to try to delimit in a satisfactory manner the social areas here called 'localities'. These techniques vary in intellectual difficulty and in meaningfulness.

The simplest is to equate locality with *distinct settlement pattern*. This definition has the merit of easy intelligibility and usability. For instance, as has been remarked, a person flying over England and Wales soon becomes aware that the social landscape shows a varied visual pattern. In some areas houses are scattered, only occasionally being grouped into small nodes, usually called 'hamlets'. If the nodes are bigger they will be called 'villages', and if bigger still small 'towns'. Next in the size scale are large towns and cities and finally the type of development known as the 'conurbation', with its varying densities and types of building. Most of this visual pattern can be reconstructed imaginatively from experience of travel on the ground. There is a clear difference between the hamlets and villages of west Devon, the small market towns of south and mid-Devon and towns such as Plymouth and Exeter, and these are quite distinct from the Greater Manchester or Merseyside conurbations.

A second way is to take some social activity or characteristics and to draw a boundary around those areas which are dominated by the same activity or same characteristics. This is essentially a classificatory approach as the previous one was a visual one. For instance, the activities often used are economic ones, leading to the identification of mining, heavy industry, retirement or agricultural areas. In anthropology, racial or tribal characteristics may be used and in some countries religion. This method is used widely in geography and leads to the series of maps at the end of large atlases, showing, for instance, vegetation regions identified by means of dominant plant life.

The use of both the above methods makes a simple assumption about the consequences of homogeneity and residential proximity. It is often assumed, for instance, that there is a community of interest based on economic circumstances and that similarity of economic activity promotes interaction. It is also usually believed that residential location influences the interactions of individuals. The two methods therefore may be regarded as providing indicators or proxies of the behavioural localities which may also be detected by more sophisticated methods.

The best way to identify localities analytically is to study the spatial aspects of social and economic life directly. It is possible to detect in daily, weekly and monthly mobility, and in residential change, both concentrations and discontinuities which form the basis of the delimitation of localities. The pattern of concentration and discontinuity is shown in work, recreational and shopping activities.

The method can be illustrated most easily by considering the pattern of life in the most uncomplicated areas – rural areas with scattered market towns well away from the large centres of population. First, the market town is identified as a centre of a locality and the boundaries of the locality identified by a pattern of *isopleths.* When the analyst has chosen an activity which involves spatial mobility – say work or shopping – he calculates the proportion of the relevant population resident at any given point that moves in the chosen time period (each activity has its own characteristic time period) to the centre. An isopleth joins all points of equal value to produce the characteristic contouring familiar in physical geography.

Such an analysis may be supplemented by examining some central institution, such as a church, a newspaper or a bank and drawing a map of its clientele. Studies have been done of these and many others.[7] In uncomplicated areas it may be expected that the results of all these studies will be sufficiently similar to allow the identification of the *sphere of influence* or *hinterland* (both words have been used) of a central point and the boundaries of this hinterland are the boundaries of the locality.

Unfortunately, this analytically most useful meaning of locality is also the most difficult to apply in practice, both for technical reasons and reasons of the nature of the phenomena studied. There is no space here to discuss the problems of what must always be a sophisticated process of analysis. Before it can be used many decisions have to be made – the choice of centres, the choice of activities, weighting them when they conflict and untangling the relationships of a hierarchy of centres.

The fourth method of identifying localities requires more sophisticated techniques and is more open to criticism than the one derived from human geography. The study of people's perceptions of where they belong – the locality or community in which they see themselves living – is part of the subject of social psychology. The main difficulty arises because attitudes and perceptions have to be studied by means of interviews and questionnaires. The design and interpretation of such studies is a very difficult matter requiring sophisticated knowledge and skills.

Despite its superficial appeal, the identification of localities by means of questions of *belongingness* has proved to be unsatisfactory. Partly this is a result of the general weaknesses of interview and questionnaire methods. For instance, it is very difficult to avoid the self-answering question; whatever word is chosen it is likely to have connotations for the respondent which tend to determine the sort of answers received. It is not surprising that those who asked about areas in which people felt 'at home' found communities of very small areas – a few streets or a neighbourhood.[8]

A locality in political science may be identified in either of two ways; in terms of commercial, recreational and occupational patterns or in terms of political activities. In the first case it is assumed that political activities are not distinct in themselves but are aspects of social activity. For instance, commuting creates political interests and being a satellite of a major centre creates a political structure. Residential change has marked political effects. In the second case it is an empirical question how far the pattern of social life mirrors the pattern of political activity that identifies the locality.

It may be that because of the 'nationalization' of economic, social and political life, the concept of a locality or region is of less use than in the past, but this can only be established by the failure of attempts to use it in particular cases. Changes in society have undoubtedly made the process of spatial differentiation harder to study, but any attempt to understand local government must make the effort.

In fact, it is both easier and more rewarding to abstract a locality in local government terms than in most others. Local authorities have more easily identifiable boundaries, both spatial and legal, than other abstractions. This is a result of the nature of public administration systems, which at the operational level are mainly patterns of localities.

LOCAL AUTHORITY AREAS AS LOCALITIES

Most public services have to be provided through a system of local offices responsible for only a part of the total area of country. Typically, therefore, all countries except for the very smallest, are divided into elaborate systems of areas and the machinery of government reflects this in a very detailed way. The reasons for this division lie partly in the nature of the individual public services and partly in the demands for efficient and convenient government by both governors and governed. By dividing up the country for the purpose of public services the central government (or those responsible for the systems of areas within the country) is in fact creating *localities* of a special kind. Every area circumscribed by boundaries for the provision of public services is a *locality* in this sense.

Local government is only one form of the local administration of public services but it is the most important in Britain and in many other countries, in some of which it is referred to as 'local self government'. It is important partly for traditional reasons and partly because reasons can be adduced to show that it is a desirable part of a democratic state. These reasons are often referred to as 'the theory of local government'.[9]

It is not usual to think of a local area of administration, public or private, as a locality, unless it is a local government area. Area administration other than local government has relatively low visibility and salience for most of the time; there are several reasons for this.

One of these is that local government is a cause of territorial inequalities which soon become apparent to individual citizens. All systems of decentralized administration are sources of inequality but the potentiality is more likely to be realized in local government than anywhere else. Citizens' tax demands, educational provision, chances of a place in an old people's home, choice of library books and a host of other features are related to the local government area in which they live. The existence of local taxation each year reminds many citizens of where they live, and local elections make local councils appear much more the 'property' of the people of the area than does the appointment of other local bodies. In fact, local authorities can be looked upon as organizations of consumers, and certainly they are often regarded as pressure groups on other public bodies and representatives of their citizens against the outside world. This is a role which was not envisaged in any of the legislation creating local authorities but, as in the case of parish councils, it has become a fairly major one. For instance, local newspapers often report the efforts of parish councils to modify or change the actions of the post office, electricity boards and the local offices of central ministries.

Some countries have a system of general areas for the territorial organization of government and the provision of public services. The French system of *departments, cantons, arrondisements* and *communes* is a good example of this, though in recent years it has proved hard to maintain its scope against the demands of individual services. Colonial government was based on a similar pattern of areas. Britain, however, does not have a system of general purpose areas for state organization, but local government areas come nearest to fulfilling this role. This is because primary local government is multi-functional, and thus its areas are to some extent general.

The significance of local government areas is enhanced by the fact that other boundaries tend to bear a definite relationship to them. When governments are creating areas for other purposes they tend to take as their starting point the local government structure. Though in the end the new areas may in fact depart radically from those of local government, in many cases the latter's boundaries, or some combination of them, are used. Local government areas are also areas for general statistical purposes and thus 'the state of the nation' is presented in terms of facts relating to them. Considerable difficulties of comparison and analysis are caused when other public bodies depart from the pattern of local authority areas.

A further factor enhancing the status of local government areas is the tendency for many private bodies to adapt their own territorial organization to the structure of local government. This is most obvious with political parties; the basic units of party organization are usually the electoral areas of local government units – wards – and these are brought together into borough and county organizations. Constituency parties are related to the structure of local government indirectly as Parliamentary boundaries are drawn with regard to it. Pressure groups and voluntary bodies are usually also organized on a local authority basis, something that is both convenient and prudent – an example of the way political actors adapt to the distribution of political power, spatially as well as functionally.

Local government areas have had a permanence which has been lacking to many other areas of public administration, with the sole exception of the courts. Proposals to make changes have often failed and have always been accompanied by considerable public controversy – partly because it does matter exactly where the boundaries are drawn.

Another reason is that local government boundaries still have a considerable force derived from history; originally local areas were derived from traditional divisions of the country and the names of many authorities have a striking ability to conjure up English history. Cornwall and Devon, for instance, even after the recent reorganization, are recognizably the same areas as have been used for state purposes for centuries. The relative permanence of boundaries since the end of the nineteenth century has also contributed to this state of affairs.

In the light of all the factors mentioned above it is justified to ascribe to local government areas the status of *locality*. Its meaning here is not the same as its meaning in human geography but it is the same sort of concept – an abstraction, in this case from the overall system of government and politics rather than from general social life.

The two distinct meanings of locality need not coincide in practice; the boundaries of geographical localities need not be the same as those of local authorities. Indeed, the two types of area may bear little relation to each other. But there are in fact forces which bring them together.

Probably the most important factor tending to bring about a coincidence of the two is the widespread belief that the territorial pattern of local authorities should reflect the pattern of social life very closely. The spatial distribution of localities is therefore one of the criteria used to create and modify the structure of local government. It is not the only one but, as the evidence to the Royal Commission on Local Government in England, 1966-69, and its Report testify, it is one of the most powerful. The Royal Commission thought it sufficiently important to commission special research to supplement the evidence of interested bodies and private citizens. The Report in fact only repeats, in this respect, a widely stated academic and non-academic view that the structure of local government should have a 'community' basis. The use of the vague notion of 'community' may have confused some of the issues but the fundamental idea has had a traditional as well as a contemporary importance.

For instance, when the Poor Law Commissioners in 1835 set about creating their administrative areas by unions of parishes, they used the market town and its hinterland as the basis in many parts of the country. In Devon, the pattern of urban and rural districts still reflected this process of the 1830s, as the unions became urban and rural sanitary districts in 1872 and then urban and rural districts in 1894, with boundaries that were largely maintained until 1974. After the traditional system was established the extensions of county boroughs by the inclusion of the suburbs developing outside their original boundaries was justified on the grounds that the suburbs were part of a social unity with the borough in their centre. The new system created by the 1972 Act also bears a testimony to the belief in the importance of the pattern of life as a foundation for local government structure – particularly in the creation of the six metropolitan areas and in Humberside, Cumbria, Cleveland and Avon.

There is another factor which tends to bring human geography and local government areas together. In the previous paragraphs consideration has been given to adapting local government structure to geography, obviously the most important process. But to some extent the establishment of a local government unit will affect the pattern of life in an area. The offices themselves will act as central places, drawing people into them for public purposes and thus affecting the pattern of daily and weekly mobility. Likewise the authority will provide employment which again will involve people in daily mobility. This increase in activity will create a social as well as an economic multiplier in the place where the offices are located and thus modify the pattern of life.

One should not overestimate the importance of this factor but there are circumstances where a noticeable effect is likely. For instance, local government in Devon employs a considerable number of people; one can easily envisage what would have happened as a result of reorganization, if, instead of an increase in the role of the county council, it had been divided into four parts and threequarters of the upper-tier staff sent out of Exeter to other centres.

There are several factors which limit the extent to which the two types of locality coincide. First, the spatial pattern of life is changing continuously and the machinery for adaptation works much more slowly and erratically. Under the traditional system boundaries and authorities were changed by private bill or a provisional order system, both of which required one of the interested parties to set them in motion.

The procedure between 1958 and 1965 was more effective but even this had a piecemeal effect and was subject to modifications for political reasons, and to the vagaries of those operating it. If one looks at the arguments and evidence used by the Local Government Commission for England it is not hard to see how a divorce between local government areas and the pattern of social life can arise.[10]

Underlying the last point is the view that not only is the machinery of adaptation slow and uncertain in operation, but its effectiveness is limited by the imperfect ability of those concerned to perceive the nature of social life correctly. *Locality* in human geography can only be properly identified by means of difficult technical operations and thus the nature of the social geography of a particular area is often not perceived. Unfortunately it is too easy to be confident in an impressionistic view of what is a very complex phenomenon, especially in the light of the next factor, created by the tendency of institutional arrangements to create their own interests.

When a system of local government is set up by the central government each individual local authority soon acquires a set of interests on the part of both members and officers – a concern with the maintenance of the *status quo* and a reason to oppose change except in certain specified directions. Citizens may also form historical or sentimental attachments to the areas as they exist. The result is that there is a considerable force against change and these are reinforced by the absence of general authoritative identifications of *localities* in human geography.

A good example of this was found in the case of Rutland which maintained its existence in the most unpropitious circumstances. Likewise the case of Cornwall shows how historic factors may still have operational significance. The evidence to the Local Government Commission and to the Royal Commission showed literally hundreds of examples of the pursuit of self-interest by officers and members, as reflected in the submissions of individual authorities.

It should not be thought that it is in any sense wrong for officers and council members to follow their own interests and the interests of their area as they see them. On the contrary, in the absence of authoritative identification of geographical localities throughout the country they are entitled to trust their own judgements rather than accept those of their apparent enemies. At least, no start will be made on understanding individual local authorities unless the reality of these interests is recognized.

The above discussion may be summarized by saying that each local government area, when it is treated as a local political system, is regarded as a locality and abstracted from the rest of the country. The local political system is the set of political activities within and relating to the locality. The local government area stands in a variety of empirically determinable relationships to the localities of human geography, but is rarely identical in spatial terms with them. In fact the relationship between the legal and social entities are a source of differences of behaviour in different parts of the country.

The political system of the locality is therefore defined in the first instance as the pattern of political behaviour within a local government area. But it is necessary to take the process of abstraction one stage further. Political behaviour in the locality includes all sorts of activities that are not part of local government. The local authority itself is only one part of the locality's political system, though an important one. The local council and its administrative appartus must be abstracted from the locality; the remainder of the local political system becomes part of the local authority's environment.

It should be noted at this point that *local authority* is not given its legal meaning, where it refers to the body that has the power to take the decisions collectively that are those *of* the authority. The local authority as local political system includes also the staff of the authority, and the aggregate organization that both elected and appointed elements create.

To summarize therefore: a local political system is a miniature political system created by abstracting local political behaviour from the national political system in the way the latter is created by abstraction from the international political system of which it is a part. But in the case of local government it is necessary to go one stage further in the process of abstraction. The first stage establishes the locality's political system – the political system of a particular geographical area. The individual local government unit is a miniature political system *within* the locality and is created by abstracting local government activities from the general political activities of the locality (Figure 4). The remainder of the locality's system is part of the local authority's environment.

The main concern of this book is with what happens within the local authority, because this is the foundation of understanding local government. But systemic behaviour, as it is sometimes called, itself needs to be understood within its context, the system's environment. Though each local authority has an environment of its own, it is possible to characterize very generally many of the features that will have some importance in each locality. This is the subject of the next chapter.

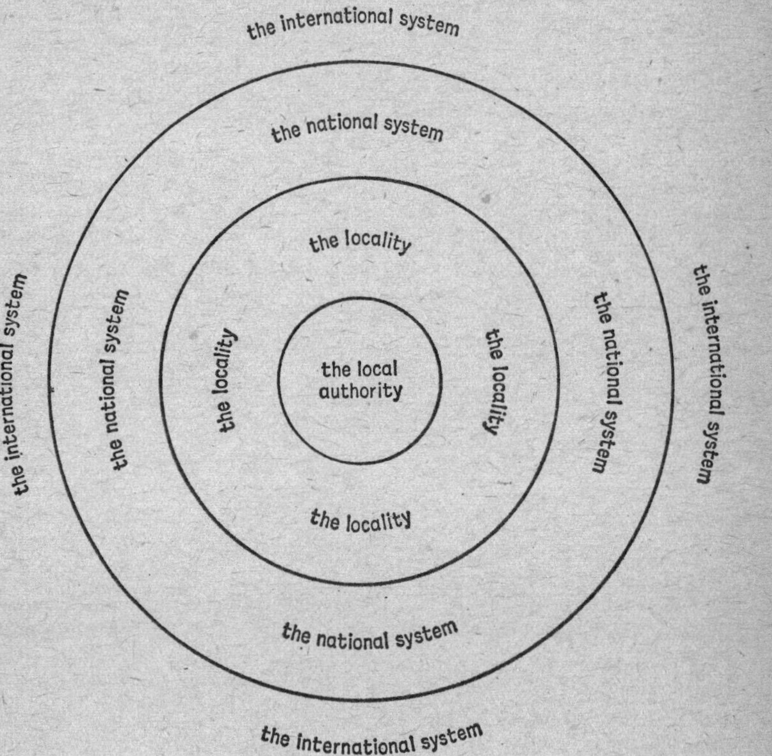

Fig. 4 Nation, Locality and Local Authority

Chapter Four

The Local Environment

Though the major concern of this book is with the behaviour of individuals and groups within the local authority, this cannot be understood solely in terms of factors internal to the organization. The actions of council members, officers, committees and departments are not free-floating, but are set in a specific context which exerts a wide influence on all that happens. Though there are limits of the extent to which generalizations can be made about local environments in total, it is useful to approach the individual authority with a knowledge of the sort of factors which are likely to be of some importance. There are potentially infinite numbers of influences and effects in the environment of a local authority, but considerable advances can be made in understanding by looking at a limited number standing in fairly immediate relationships to the system. In this chapter, therefore, the local authority will be treated as a 'black box' and attention focused on the *not-system.*

The environment of the local authority consists of factors which are in such close relationship with a part of the system that possible intervening variables are ignored, and factors which, though obviously having an influence, operate only through some intermediate mechanism. The former are counted as part of the *proximate* environment and the latter part of the *remote.* To illustrate both the difference between the two, and the way system-environment needs to be conceived, two semi-hypothetical cases are presented below: what might happen to an individual authority first when it becomes the site of an overspill housing scheme and secondly, when there is a devaluation crisis in the national economy.

If the area of a local authority is chosen as the site for an overspill housing scheme, as this is implemented the character of the locality will change and this will in turn produce changes in the behaviour of the council and its administrative apparatus. New types of social and economic activity will appear, the scale of existing ones will change, with consequences for composition of the population and the relations between individuals. Within the local social system it will produce 'insider-outsider' and 'cosmopolitan-local' conflict. The council will be faced with demands for new types of service and the provision of old ones in new ways, requiring new techniques and new types of official. Eventually political parties may be affected; if predominantly one type of housing is built then the balance between them may be changed and their internal composition altered, leading to different types of elected representatives chosen. The town may have its position in the regional hierarchy of urban centres raised, with further changes in the commercial and social activities of the area.

The changes in the local environment brought about by overspill can be seen to have immediate and direct effects on the local council; for instance, the changing social structure may make it much easier for women or lower middle-class men to be elected, and the pressure of redevelopment problems may bring about the use of more managerial administrative techniques. But not all factors are of this order. For instance, changes in the state of the national economy will affect this council through much more indirect mechanisms.

A devaluation crisis, for instance, will affect central policy towards capital and current spending by all local authorities, and this policy will have different effects in different areas. It may affect the rate of interest payable on overdrafts so that treasurers in some authorities have to worry about the size of the balances at the end of the financial year. It will also affect the standing of the government party adversely, and if the revulsion from it is very great, the next elections may remove half a generation of councillors. Strengthening the 'economizers' against the 'spenders' on local councils will be only one type of effect; in the long run, by decimating the council representation of the leading political party, it may produce a radically different sort of local authority.[1]

Notice that the remote environment is shared by all local authorities and that its impact will vary from place to place and will occur through mechanisms that are part of the proximate environment.

It is much easier to specify the features of the proximate than the remote environment, for in principle anything can be part of the latter, including events in foreign countries, provided only a causal chain can be traced out linking them with what happens in the local authority. The proximate environment, however, derives mainly from the characteristics of the socio-economic geography of the locality. What follows is a list of the sort of factors that are likely to be found of importance in the environment of most local authorities.

The proximate environment

No attempt to understand local government can be adequate unless it takes into account two factors, or rather dimensions of all other factors, which fit into the pattern of analysis set out below somewhat awkwardly. *Location* and *history* have an influence diffused across the board, an influence on the way all other forces affect the local authority and on the relationships between system and environment.

Where a locality is situated determines who its immediate neighbours are and the degree to which events in other areas affect behaviour within it. For instance, if a locality is remote from the large centres of population this fact will modify many environment-system interactions. The spread of new ideas about organizational forms will be slower, the pressure for co-operative venture less and the nature of the local community different. It will produce effects on other factors, and thus should be thought of as a dimension of the local environment.

An authority's *history* has a similar effect in that what was gone before creates forces which continue to modify behaviour and interactions within the area. Conflict between two groups or organizations may continue to pervade relationships long after the original cause of the trouble has disappeared. Accidents and other rare occurrences may have consequences in the locality long after they have happened. Disasters such as occurred in Lynton in 1953 and Aberfan in 1966 are of this nature.

Most of the forces, factors and influences which constitute the environment of the local authority derive from the geographical characteristics of the locality. Though physical geography could in principle be important at the present time its influence is likely to be felt through its past effects on economy, social structure etc. – the factors of socio-economic geography.

A good starting point for an appreciation of a local authority's environment is a picture of the statistical characteristics of the local population – size, density, mobility, change and social composition – all considered in comparison to other local authorities. These are not necessarily significant in their own right but often stand as proxies for the other theoretically more important factors.

The latter may be grouped under three main headings: the local economy, the local social system and the local political system. These may be studied as systems in their own right and they are closely related to each other, but to understand local government it is necessary to examine only those complexities that affect behaviour in the local authority.

THE LOCAL ECONOMY[2]

The starting point for a study of the local economy must be the nature of economic activities in the locality. Many of the publications relating to economic affairs do not present data on a local authority basis, but the volume on occupations in the Census gives an indication of the sort of area it is in terms of basic activities. For rural areas the annual agricultural census is extremely useful. Though important factors, such as those derived from the one firm or one industry area, are missed in statistical publications, these are often immediately apparent to the citizen.

Personal wealth is often approximated by domestic rateable value per head, which has the advantage of being known for local authority areas and is directly relevant to local authority decision making, but is imperfect for various reasons. Personal income per head and the pattern of distribution between individuals can only be estimated, though reasonable guesses may be made on the basis of other economic variables.

The state of employment in an area is a complex factor, consisting of male and female unemployment, numbers of unfilled vacancies, level of female employment and proportion of retired persons. The information on these matters is not generally available for local authority areas, though this also may be estimated from other sources.

If the information on all these economic factors is gathered together it is possible to characterize the local economy in simple terms which will provide insights into the relations of the environment to the local authority. Upper-class retirement areas, new light industrial locations, and depressed mining areas all differ from each other in significant ways, and have little in common as environments with traditional farming areas. The local economy will also provide insights into the realities of the next heading – local social structure.

THE LOCAL SOCIAL SYSTEM

The local social system is the set of interactions between individuals in their everyday life. Because of the difficulty of characterizing these directly, they are often approximated by *class, status* and *stratification* patterns. These words are sometimes used indiscriminately and interchangeably, and sometimes with distinctions drawn deliberately between them. They all refer to a person's position in society and the ways in which the positions of all individuals are combined. A local society may therefore be characterized as homogeneous or heterogeneous; traditional or modern; hierarchical or egalitarian, or in many other similar ways. Many of the descriptions of local social systems will overlap with the description of the local economy.

Social differences based on occupation, which is what the above largely are, may not be the important or only factors in local society. In some areas religion is a significant basis of social differentiation, whilst in others society is structured on a local-newcomer distinction. These factors often interact with the class structure and give local society its distinctive personality. Likewise in some of the largest urban areas race and immigration have added another dimension to the local social system.

In the case of both the local economy and local society it is important to take account not only of a static picture at one point in time but also of the way they are changing. Two areas may have the same population on Census day, but one may be declining and the other growing rapidly, with many consequences for the local social system.

The accounts of both local economy and local social system have been very brief, and do not do justice to important subjects, but this can be excused here because both economic and social factors tend to influence the local authority through the local political system. That is, they are one stage removed in the environment from the internal processes of the local authority; local political institutions and processes provide mechanisms whereby their effects occur.

THE LOCAL POLITICAL SYSTEM

A local government area may be a single Parliamentary constituency, but it is more likely to be either part of one, as were most county districts, or a grouping of several, as were most administrative counties. Parliamentary constituencies have boundaries which are drawn with regard to local government boundaries, so that there is almost always some degree of coherence between the two. But party organization for national elections does not stand in any simple relationship to local authorities; a particular local authority may have party organization corresponding exactly to it, it may be part of a larger area body, or it may be a federation of several basic units. The political structure of a locality must be described under several headings, one of which is national party organization.

LOCAL POLITICAL PARTIES

British politics has a class basis in that the party identification of individual electors is strongly influenced, though not completely determined, by the compound of factors known as *social class*. As the class composition of the electorate varies considerably from one locality to another, the relative strengths of the two major parties does also. The first aspect of the local political system is the relative strength of Conservative and Labour in the long run.

In some localities other national political parties are important. The role of the Communist Party is limited to the occasional seat won in heavily working-class areas, whilst the role of the extreme right is even less. The Liberals, however, have consistently won at least 4 per cent of borough seats since 1960 and there are localities where they either control the council, are the largest party, are the major opposition, or control an enclave within the area. But Liberalism is not only a sporadic phenomenon in local government generally, it has waxed and waned in dramatic fashion in the postwar period. A Liberal 'revival' may have had striking consequences within a particular authority, and the existence of an important third party is usually a distinctive characteristic of a local political system.

In some areas and at some times regional parties have played an important part. The Scottish National Party won dramatic victories in local elections in Scotland in 1967-69 and took control of some councils. Plaid Cymru was less successful but it also intervened in Wales during this period. The rise of nationalist parties, like that of Liberals, can have striking effects within a local political system, which through the changes in the major parties, outlasts the challenge of the 'interlopers'.

A major dimension of a local political system is created by the local branches of national and regional political parties, but the form that each branch takes and the nature of local organization varies greatly from place to place. These differences give a locality part of its distinctive political flavour.

Most branches of the major political parties have a body at the local government electoral area (ward) level, at least in principle. But it is not always possible for a party to achieve a complete ward organization for the whole of a locality; in some places ward parties are active political and social organizations, with plenty of people to fill roles, whilst in some the ward is essentially one person, and in others repeated attempts by the party agent to start a proper organization fail.

The difficulties of the major parties in this respect are much greater in the case of other parties. There appears to be a relationship between Liberal electoral success and strength of ward organization, but what determines the latter is not clear. Probably for all parties the growth and decline of ward organization reflects changing fortunes at national level; in 1969 it appeared in many areas that the Labour Party as an organization was withering; when the Liberals gained dramatically in the opinion polls in the early 1960s this was accompanied by a growth in ward activity, and support for the Scottish National Party was reflected in the rapid spread of its local organization.

Above constituency and locality levels the major parties have regional organizations but for most areas these are remote, even if they are conscious of them. It is between ward and region that most variation is found. Some local authorities have a party organization corresponding exactly to them, whilst others are part of a constituency. Glossop had a borough Labour Party and two Conservative associations, affiliated to the respective High Peak Divisional organizations. Wolverhampton had a borough Labour Party but two Conservative constituency associations. In Exeter borough and constituency organization coincided exactly.

Some localities have purely local political parties, that is, parties which do not contest national elections and which are formed for political purposes in the locality only, though they may later join a loose federation of similar groups. They include council tenants associations and ratepayer organizations. Not all of them contest elections; some are local political movements coming to prominence very suddenly and then fading away, after engaging in a variety of political activities, of which electioneering may be one. The occurrence of these parties is hard to explain. There are localities where long established ratepayers' or citizens' parties play a major role in the system; in some they may on occasion hold the balance between the major parties and in others they are simply an interesting fringe group. In other places they have never existed.[3]

It is also important to consider the relations between parties as well as the parties themselves. One factor that tends to have a considerable background influence is the extent to which one party dominates the local political scene.[4] Some areas have been basically one-party for very long periods; others are multi-party, whilst competition between the two major parties is the characteristic feature of others.[5] But from the outside it is impossible to generalize about the relations between parties in a locality; the same numerical strengths may conceal widely different political structures. Relations between parties may also be altered by the rise and fall of local political movements, a Liberal 'revival'[6] or dramatic changes in the national fortunes of the major parties.

LOCAL PRESSURE GROUPS

In each locality there are likely to be social and commercial organizations with a large political content in their activities, and these are similar to the pressure groups with which the student of national government is familiar. But many local groups have a largely non-political existence, becoming politically active only on rare occasions.

In urban localities both working-class and business sectors of local society are likely to have their own general purpose organizations – on one side the trades council and on the other the chamber of trade and/or the chamber of commerce. These are more likely to act in relation to a range of matters than are the individual unions and firms that make up their membership.

In contrast to the above, recent years have seen the growth of 'altruistic' local groups, often part of a national organization but inevitably operating to a considerable extent at local level. Bodies such as Shelter, the Child Poverty Action Group and the Conference for the Advancement for State Education, as well as organizations in the field of race relations, may be an important part of the local political scene. The bodies vary a great deal in the amount of attention that they devote to the local council; obviously a claimants' union will scarcely ever pressure a council, whilst CASE will deal with little else.[7]

There are, however, in local government different types of relationship between outsiders and the council which constitute an equivalent to pressure group activity in the centre but which arise from the special nature of local *government*.

First, because a large part of the work of central government is concerned with the framing of general rules, whether statutes or statutory instruments, pressure groups have adapted to the distribution of power to make such rules. Campaigns on behalf of individuals are rare compared with the sustained activity of trying to influence the general framework in which the organizations live. In local government the balance is reversed; most decisions have a particular applicability to a piece of land and to a particular individual or individual organization. Councils do make general rules but what they do usually has immediate and obvious implications for only a few people.

Secondly, some of the activities are contractual or semi-contractual. The sort of economic relationships in which local authorities are involved are of the sort that create power relationships between those concerned. The local council is usually in a monopoly position, either as a provider or a consumer of services and this creates an indeterminate economic situation. In the latter each side has some power from the relationship itself against the other.

The important fact is the directness of impact of local government. Central government is insulated from the citizen by layers of organization and deals with the general rather than the particular, whilst individuals and individual organizations have a continuous effect on local authority operations through feedback arising from daily relations.

For local government it is probably better to think of interest *sectors* rather than interest *groups*. A sector is comprised of all those who share broadly similar interests or concerns; these may give rise to one or more formal groups or organizations representing those who belong to the sector. An interest sector may be important not because it is formally organized to exert pressure on a council but because it members are widely dispersed through the decision-making process and may speak vicariously for others.[8]

To understand a local political system it is not sufficient to list the political parties and pressure groups found in the locality. Each locality will combine these in different ways; the relationships between groups and parties can take many forms. Sometimes it is believed that there is a local elite or ruling class which dominates the system of parties and pressure groups but though the notion of a small group of people controlling all events in their own interest is attractive, little evidence has been produced that such a political structure exists in any locality. Most recent research has tended not to discover a local ruling class but a diffuse process of decision making involving a plurality of groups and interests.[9]

NON-PARTISANSHIP

Some localities have been and are dominated by non-partisanship in local government affairs. This is only partly the absence of political parties; in many cases 'independence' is a positive belief, even a doctrine. In national politics partisanship is a fairly uniform phenomenon; when electors turn against one major party they turn to the other, or to the Liberals or nationalists – they do not turn against party politics in general. This pattern is repeated in the politics of the large urban areas, which are often replicas of national politics, except for the relative strengths of the parties. But there are areas which are equally partisan in national affairs but which have non-partisan local politics. It is clear that in these cases some people behave differently at the two levels.

It is often thought that independent council members in local government are disguised Conservatives. But at best this is an oversimplification and it may be seriously misleading. A comparison of national party strengths in general elections with the distribution of non-partisanship makes it clear that in most non-partisan areas the Conservative Party is the dominant one but in many areas the Liberal Party is strong and even the leading party, whilst there are other areas where the Labour Party has considerable strength. In the case of north and west Devon and central and north Cornwall many of the Independents are Liberals rather than Conservatives, whilst in parts of Wales, where the Conservative Party is very weak, independents are likely to be Labour, Liberal or Nationalist in national political orientation.

It is hard to doubt that most independents do have a national partisan allegiance; most people vote in British elections and it is difficult to believe that those conscious enough of government to serve on a local council are amongst the minority of non-voters in national elections. But voting for a party is quite different from openly proclaiming membership of it and seeking political support because of that fact. If a candidate does not have the tangible support of his party and does not announce his allegiance publicly (for instance, in his electoral address and electoral speeches) and does not belong to a party group on the council when elected, then he must not be treated as 'concealed Conservative'.

In fact in the areas of genuine non-partisanship there is likely to be a hostile attitude towards national party intervention in local government which extends to the Conservative Party; this attitude thus legitimises the status of 'independent' and provides a justification for rejecting or denouncing national political allegiances. This phenomenon has been observed in other countries. It is well known in America and often embodied in state and local constitutions; it is epitomised by the well-known statement that there is no Republican or Democratic way of building sewers or paving roads. A similar phenomenon has been found in France and India. Thus non-partisanship must be regarded as an important element in local politics in some areas. One of its consequences is to create open political conflict between members of the same national political party; another is to make membership of a political party no more or less significant than membership of social, commercial and sporting organizations.

There is some evidence that non-partisanship is on the decline. It is reduced by greater geographical mobility, by an increase in the size of local authorities under reorganization, and by the merging of urban and rural areas which eventually spreads the former's political style to the countryside. But in the remote parts of the country, particularly at district and parish level, it is likely that 'independence' will survive for a long time.[10]

To conclude this discussion of the local political system, it must be stressed that any understanding of local government behaviour must be based on an appreciation of the *variation* in the environment in which a local authority is located. The factors described above may be combined in a variety of ways to produce recognizable types of local political system. Some localities are one-party Labour systems, in others the local political system is largely non-partisan and dominated by commercial interests of a special sort – for instance, hoteliers and seaside resorts. Sometimes the conflict is between locals and cosmopolitans and in other places there is a traditional leadership based on the possession of land. In some cases a local political system shows a marked contrast to those on either side of it – it may be a Labour island in a sea of non-partisanship or a Conservative enclave in a predominantly Labour region. What the combination of factors produces can only be determined empirically for each individual area.

THE REST OF THE SYSTEM OF GOVERNMENT

To complete the picture of the local authority's environment it is necessary to include the rest of the machinery of government within the locality. This interacts with local society and with the local council. Each local authority may expect to have contact with a great number of other public bodies, some of which are also purely local, some of which have a significance for a larger area and some of which are national in scope. It is as easy to forget that the local authority is only one of many local bodies belonging to the system of government as it is to forget the locality's social system.

First, under the traditional local government system most local authorities were parts of complex systems of local government. The other authorities in the particular system were obviously very important parts of the individual's environment. Now all local authorities belong to one of the four types of multi-tier structure of which the new system is composed; it is therefore even more important to see the complex system as a whole as part of the environment of individual local authority. The nature of the structure of complex systems is explored later in the book.

Secondly, in virtually all parts of the country secondary local authorities will be of some significance. The relationships between these and a primary local authority are often particularly direct and immediate – through the precept and the mode of composition of the governing board. In some areas the secondary authority assumes a much greater significance. For instance, in rural areas where water supplies are still to be modernized the activities of the areas' water board have been of considerable salience; water boards also became parties to the fluoridation controversy. The police may also be of significance, for instance, in relation to traffic management in congested urban centres.

Any local council may also expect to interact with other public bodies outside the local government system itself. Public services are not as easily divisible in practice as they appear in Acts of Parliament. Recent legislation has tended to give more recognition to this fact by providing for statutory consultation between different bodies in an area.

The departments of central government are frequently organized as a set of local and regional offices. Good examples are the Department of Health and Social Security, the Department of Employment and the administration of taxation, (Inland Revenue and Customs and Excise). Not all of these necessarily have an impact on a local council, but as most large localities have several of the local offices of the centre the possibility is often turned into an actuality. It is particularly noticeable in the field of the welfare state services where the law has created a large number of legal distinctions between types of problem which do not correspond to differences in reality. A good example recently arose with a conflict between housing authorities and the Supplementary Benefits Commission in some localities over the assessment of payment due to the same persons – council tenants in receipt of public assistance. Occasionally also there have been difficulties between the local valuation officers employed in the Inland Revenue Service and the local council, over the assessment of ratable values in the locality.

A second category of public body is comprised by the public corporations including the nationalized industries. Many public corporations are also sets of local and regional offices – the post office, the electricity supply industry, transport services, including the National Bus Company and British Rail. The machinery of the National Health Service, both traditional and new, must also be included here.[11] Each of these bodies gives rise to typical modes of interaction with the local council.

Many examples of these can be found – the question of rail closures and rural electrification bring in obvious commercial considerations which are strongly influential with the public corporation but clash with the consumers' interest which weighs heavily with the local authority.

Finally, there are other public bodies such as the armed forces, universities and research establishments which may be of importance in some areas. No local authority can be unaware of the armed forces if part of its area is used for artillery practice or manoeuvres; all the armed forces have a relatively concentrated location and where big naval bases or airfields exist they are likely to be of significance to the local council if only because of their local economic importance.

Two examples of the general significance and operation of local council-other public bodies relationship can be given, one a relatively trivial organizational problem, the other involving more fundamental problems behind the superficial issue.

Local authorities are generally responsible in a variety of ways for highways, roads and parks within their area, though the degree of responsibility varies for a number of reasons. They are also, irrespective of their formal powers, the representatives of the day-to-day users of the routes. But there are also other public bodies who are called 'statutory undertakers' (the public utilities) and these have well-defined and powerful rights to dig up highways for their own purposes. As traditionally they did not collaborate with each other there arose situations in which a stretch of highway was dug up and replaced several times in a year with the consequent waste of money and irritation to its regular users. In order to try to avoid this local authorities have been forced to foster the development of *ad hoc* informal consultative arrangements whereby statutory undertakers in an area exchange plans and try to co-ordinate their activities.

A more substantial instance arises when local councils are brought into conflict with other public bodies over the latters' policy of closing local offices or modifying local administrative arrangements. Examples can be found of opposition to the closure of local police stations, post offices, supplementary benefits offices, railway stations (as opposed to lines) and in a slightly different context, local schools. Though at first sight these might all look like internal organizational problems for another public body they are of vital importance to local authorities, both individually and jointly. For these are the decisions that help to determine what sort of locality it is going to be in the future. Not only are there direct considerations of public convenience but there are local economic effects – for instance, on employment and the profitability of local enterprise – and an impact on the general attractiveness of the locality to present and future inhabitants and the residents of neighbouring areas.

The nature of the local environment

The above presentation of the local environment as a list of headings with sets of factors mentioned under them can be misleading if it is not remembered that the proximate environment is a totality; the factors do not exist in isolation from each other, but are interrelated in ways that may be significant for understanding local government. Sometimes factors are 'end-on' in that there is a chain of cause and effect linking, say, social structure through the local party system to council behaviour. The factors may modify each other and change their impacts on the local authority. Other governmental bodies will be affected by the social system in which they operate, and this will affect their behaviour in relation to the council.

These interrelationships are one of the significant differences between the proximate and remote environments. The remote environment is common to all local authorities; thus the national political system, national society and the national economy are likely to affect all local authorities simultaneously, but the nature of their effects will be modified and transformed by the particular characteristics of the local environment, part of whose personality derives from their reciprocal interaction.

The local environment is therefore a source of demands on the local authority, some of these generated by events at a distance, and some arising from special features of the locality. The next step in understanding local government is to examine what happens when events outside enter the local system itself – in other words, to open up the 'black box'.

Part Three

Local Authorities

Introduction

The elements of a local authority are people, some of whom are elected and some of whom are appointed. The former – *the council members* – are organized as a council, a committee and sub-committee system, and informal groups, such as cliques and party meetings; the latter – *the paid employees* – are organized as departments, sections, area offices, depots and institutions. Opening the 'black box' consists of investigating the behaviour of these elements, both individual and collective, and the structure of the miniature political systems consists of the relationships between them.

The description of this structure takes place in three stages. First, the individuals who comprise the local authority are described in their 'raw' state, as members of local society. Second, the forms of organization adopted by each type of person for its purposes are outlined. Third, an internal organization creates roles within the system, individuals are considered again, this time in their 'finished' state, as occupants of systemic positions.

Just as each local authority has its own local environment so it has its own particular form of internal organization. Describing the latter in generalized terms is therefore a source of error, because it reinforces the myth of uniformity. In what follows it is important to remember that the characterizations are not of all individual authorities, but specifications of *standardized dimensions,* to be used in describing each miniature system.

A good example of such a dimension is *size of council.* This is simply the number of *members* of the council (distinguishing between number of seats authorized, number of seats occupied at a given time and number present at a council meeting) – including councillors, a presiding officer and aldermen where appropriate. In practice few councils have had less than twelve members and few more than 150, but each individual authority's was exactly determined by statute and an approved scheme of electoral arrangements.

In order to avoid this insidious mistake the point has been expressed in rather formal terms as a *rule of interpretation*:

treat all aspects of the internal organization of individual local authorities as dimensions whose application in each individual can only be determined empirically.

Members and employees

The following description is based on the assumption that the differences between members and employees are vital to an understanding of local government. Membership of a local authority is a legal concept and closely defined by law; employees are appointed by and work for members of the authority acting collectively. Council members are often referred to as 'elected representatives', but this is a contentious phrase, partly because in the past some have been indirectly elected and partly because their 'representative' status is controversial. There is no single word or phrase which is in general use to describe the employees of a local authority. Expressions such as 'local government officer' tend to be given a special meaning, and others are used for particular types of employee.

One of the striking ways in which members and employees differ, in addition to their constitutional status, is in the distinctive patterns of organization that they have typically adopted within the overall framework of the authority. It is much more difficult to draw a distinction between their roles; most attempts in the past have been in terms of some *a priori* dichotomy such as *policy* and *administration*, but these have always failed, perhaps because the activities of participants in organizations do not fall into neat semi-moral categories prescribed in advance.

This, then, is the reason for adopting the form of exposition used here. As *role* is largely a function of the organizational system, differences between the two will not be considered until the pattern of operating arrangements has been described. This in its turn depends on the formal differences between the two as types of individual.

Chapter Five
Dramatis Personae: Council Members

In the traditional system there were three legally distinct types of council member – councillors, presiding officers and aldermen. Every council contained councillors and a presiding officer, called in boroughs the 'mayor' and in all others the 'chairman of the council'. The presiding officer was elected by the other members of the council and served for one year unless re-elected. In borough and county councils there was also a class of member, indirectly elected by the body of councillors, called 'aldermen'. The main difference between the old and new systems in this respect is that the aldermanic office has been abolished, and all councils consist only of the other two categories of member.

As councillors provide the electoral colleges for both presiding officers and aldermen they are the natural starting point for a description of the lay element in local government.

Councillors

All councillors are directly elected under an elaborate system of local electoral law which is modelled on the law of Parliamentary elections and resembles it in general terms; there are also some significant differences between the two. Though these are few they play an important part in understanding local government.

There is an elaborate apparatus for administering both national and local elections, designed to ensure that the elections are as free and fair as administrative devices can make them. The machinery provides for the systematic registration of all potential electors, the announcement of elections at the the proper times and the publicizing of procedures for nomination, the scrutiny of proffered nominations, and publicizing of the date, time and place of polling if the election is contested, clerical arrangements to ensure secrecy of ballot on election day itself, provisions for order within polling stations, counting and declaring the results, paying the expenses of electoral administration, and finally, the right of appeal against the decisions of election officials. The similarities are enhanced by the fact that generally the same people and the same buildings are used for both national and local elections.

The means of electioneering – the methods by which candidates can compete against each other – are also regulated in some detail. Certain types of electioneering have been proscribed by law. Electioneering is also controlled informally by custom; the differences between local and national elections are scarcely noticeable here also. In other words the actual conduct of an election by a candidate and his agent (if he has one) is likely to be the same – the organization of canvassing and related activities, the sort of advertising used, the appeals to the voters. The differences between distinct types of local election are likely to be greater than those between national and local elections in general.

The right to vote, which is equivalent to the right to be placed on the electoral register, is governed by the usual set of qualifications and disqualifications. For instance, electors have to be British, at least 18 years old, of sound mind and must not have been convicted of felony or of corrupt electoral practices.

The same document is used as the electoral register for both national and local elections and the process of registering is identical. It is in fact not possible to choose to register for one set of elections and not the other. The electoral register is produced annually and everyone has to register at the place of residence on October 10th of the year; the register is subject to various checks in draft form and becomes operative from February 16th of the next year until February 15th of the following year. There are in fact in each area a few people who can vote in local elections but not in national elections and these are indicated by an L against their name on the register. The registration officer has to present the register so that it is ready for both Parliamentary and local elections.

Lunacy, imprisonment, bankruptcy and electoral corruption disqualify from service on a council. Members must also be British and over 21 years old. Thus local government shares with national government a set of disqualifications for office which are quite common in other countries with free and fair elections.

Some of the differences between local and national elections arise from the application of the same principles to the different circumstances of local government.

It is not surprising that the maximum amount of expenses allowable to candidates is much less in local elections, to take account of the reduced scale of local government elections. Prior to 1969 the rules provided that a candidate should not spend more than £25 on election expenses, unless the number of electors on the register exceeded 500, in which case he could spend an extra 2d per extra name. The *Representation of the People Act, 1969*, changed this to £30 plus 1/- for every six electors on the register (in Greater London Council Elections £200 plus 1/- for every four electors). This had to be modified to take into account decimalization. The maximum has been raised again in 1974 by the *Representation of the People (No. 2) Act, 1974*, to £45 plus 1p for every elector.

The equivalent to nationality as a qualification to vote in Parliamentary elections is obviously an *attachment to the locality* in local elections. This is largely provided automatically by the registration procedure, which restricts the franchise to local people. However, before the Second World War this attachment was defined in terms of property owning and, whilst national elections had universal suffrage, local elections were based on a ratepayer franchise. Thus wealthy individuals might well have several local government votes. The ratepayer franchise has died hard in local government for still today some council members and candidates, including those who do not belong to a ratepayers' organization, refer to the ratepayers in general as though they were the sovereign body of the locality.

The disqualification of council employees from serving on their own council obviously parallels the disqualification of civil servants and other holders of 'offices of profit under the crown' from sitting in Parliament. But a council employee may serve on the council of another authority if he lives outside the area of his employing body. This is not uncommon in county government and sometimes occurred between county and county-borough. Civil servants may also be council members but like local government officers they are governed by extra-statutory rules of prudent behaviour, which regulate the extent to which different types of public official may take part in controversial and partisan activities.

The most interesting qualification has been that which states that council members must be local persons. There is no simple definition of *localness* comparable to nationality in Parliamentary elections and there has been considerable controversy over the years as to what constitutes a local person. There is no doubt that those who are entitled to vote from residence are local persons and this provides the basic qualification. Likewise those who have been resident for twelve months or more in the locality, but who are not on the electoral register are 'locals'. This provides a safeguard against accidental non-registration and against the disbarment of recent movers caught by the provisions of the annual registration system.

Traditionally ownership and occupation of property of a certain rateable value within the area were thought to provide a definite and justifiable connection with the locality. The property qualification was abolished by the Labour Government in 1969 but re-introduced by the Conservatives in 1971. At the same time the opportunity was used to adopt the widest conceivable definition of 'local person' by introducing 'principal place of work' as an additional qualification.

Underlying the original controversies were differing views of the nature of local democracy and of property as a base for political participation. Today the acceptance of a very wide definition of eligibility reflects the changing relationships of local government boundaries to socio-geographical facts – such as mobility of population and patterns of living.

For a long time electors had to find out for themselves about contested local elections, as there were no official notices of poll cards issued by the returning officer. Nor did candidates have the right to send one electoral communication free to each elector by post, a facility worth a considerable amount in large wards. The former has been changed in the new system but local government candidates are still at a disadvantage compared with their Parliamentary counterparts.

Perhaps one of the penalties Parliamentary candidates have to pay for free postage facilities is the deposit which they lose if they do not achieve a minimum level of support from the electorate. This has occasionally been demanded for local elections in order to discourage 'frivolous' candidatures. But frivolity is much harder to define in local elections and demands for the restriction and regulation of these have so far been resisted.

The local electoral system

The most important difference, however, between national and local election law lies in the local electoral system itself. Though the voting system – first-past-the-post or simple plurality – is the same, and some local systems resemble that of Parliament, many of them depart markedly from the national model. Whereas members of Parliament are elected for a maximum period of five years (less at the discretion of the Government of the day, and particularly its leader), each councillor is elected for a fixed term of office. In other words there is no equivalent to the power of dissolution of the House of Commons in local government. Traditionally every councillor elected in an ordinary election served for three years; the period has now been increased to four years. In each case exceptions arise only in respect of casual vacancies, when the successful person serves out the unexpired term of office, 'clean sweep' elections in partial renewal systems, when some successful candidates serve only a proportion of the normal time, according to the order of votes in the poll, (this is in order to make partial renewal work in the future) and when tenure is shortened by government order, usually following boundary changes or ward redistricting.[1] On certain occasions also terms of office have been extended, for instance in wartime and before a major change in the structure of local government (as in 1973-74). The first of these of course occurred with Parliamentary elections also.

On a very few occasions co-option has replaced election as the means of selecting councillors. This occurred during both world wars when elections were suspended for the major authorities and casual vacancies filled by vote of existing council members. It has also been a feature of parish elections. Serving councillors chose people for casual vacancies; in the new system these may be filled through either co-option or by-elections.

Another unusual feature of local elections is the 'deemed re-elected' procedure which provides in certain circumstances for the election of someone who was not nominated as a candidate. This occurs when insufficient candidates are nominated to fill all seats. Those validly nominated take their seats and the remainder are filled, if possible, by retiring councillors who did not seek re-election, in order of votes in the previous election or by lot if the latter was uncontested.

The main features of each electoral system, however, are created by the application of general rules for the timing of elections and for division into individual electoral areas (usually called 'wards') to the locality's particular circumstances. The combination of rules and circumstances are embodied in a scheme which creates a system of electoral divisions, assigns a number of councillors to each and fixes the timing of elections, as far as statute allows a discretion. Though each authority has tended to prepare its own scheme and to initiate changes it has never had the final word. In the past central approval from the Home Office or Department of the Environment has been needed; in the new system all electoral arrangements are to be monitored by the Local Government

Boundary Commissions, though final say still rests with the central government.

The timing of local elections may be based on either of two patterns: *simultaneous retirement* or *partial renewal.*

The simultaneous retirement system is easy to understand – the term of office of every councillor comes to an end at the same time and if an individual wishes to continue he must seek re-election. County councils have always had this system; traditionally all councillors retired together every third year, but in the new system the term of office has been extended to four years. Parishes have been affected in the same way; previously they had triennial and now they have quadriennial elections.

Partial renewal needs to be described in more detail. The basis of it is the division of all council seats into three groups (let them be called A, B and C). All occupants of seats in the same group come up for re-election at the same time; for instance, if in group A, 1955, 1958, 1961 . . . ; if B, 1956, 1959, 1962 . . . ; if C, 1957, 1960, 1963 . . . Under this system, whilst each councillor experiences an election only every third year, the council has elections each year. In the case of boroughs and many urban districts each electoral area was awarded three or a multiple of three seats, one each in groups A, B and C, so that each ward had an election each year. Rural districts that had partial renewal on the other hand tended to divide their wards (which were also usually coterminous with parishes) into three groups, A, B, and C, so that each electoral area experienced elections only every third year whilst the council had some of its seats, approximately a third, coming up for re-election each year.

All boroughs, except those in London, had to have annual elections by law, but urban and rural districts had a choice. In fact most urban districts had partial renewal whilst most rural districts had simultaneous retirement; this was the result of the exercise of discretion by the county councils of England and Wales. In some urban districts the situation was complicated by the fact that some wards had elections in the manner of boroughs whilst others had simultaneous retirement. In the new system all metropolitan district councils will have a variant of partial renewal, and non-metropolitan districts may choose this system or have simultaneous retirement in 1976, 1979 and every fourth year after that. Partial renewal has been changed so that it entails an election each year except in the year in which the county council elections are held. Electors thus have a 'holiday' from district elections, but no respite because there is a county council election in that year.

The relative simplicity of the new system contrasts with the traditional one where some electors had an election every year, some had two elections every third year (where urban districts and county council elections coincided), some had one election in two successive years and no election in the third, some had two elections in one year and one election in the other two years, some had three elections in one year and none in the others, and others had one election in one year, two elections in another and no election in the third year.

The division of the area of the locality into wards (which is the name for constituencies in urban areas) shows a similar degree of complexity. The simplest system was that of the county council, which had to have single-member electoral divisions, and which usually created a sufficient number of constituencies to satisfy most of the diverse interests within its boundaries. County boroughs were constrained by partial renewal; as each of their wards had to have a multiple of three members on the council, the number of wards tended to be much smaller. The most common system gave each three members so that in each annual election there would ordinarily be only one seat up for election in each ward.

Small towns and rural districts had the greatest choice. Boroughs could divide their area into wards or leave it as an at-large system, with four or more seats coming up for re-election each year. Or they could divide into two or more wards with two or more seats at stake in each election. Urban districts were able to have wards of different sizes and to mix up wards with partial renewal with wards with simultaneous retirement. Rural districts could retain the parish basis of local government by having electoral areas with one, two, three or more seats, depending on the size of the parish.

In the new system county councils are still required, after the transitional period, to have single-member electoral areas, but it is to be presumed that some of the same variety will be observed at the lower-tier level as authorities devise schemes which suit the social conditions of their areas.

The complexity of the above discussion of the main features of local electoral systems creates a good opportunity to introduce the first example of more rigorous analysis of local government. It was conventional to distinguish between annual and triennial systems, and between warded and at-large systems, giving a four-fold classification of local electoral systems. Unfortunately this was both misleading and inaccurate in certain respects, by concealing much of the variation described above.

It is possible to represent all local electoral systems by their positions on four dimensions. Some can be represented very simply, by four numbers, and these are called 'consistent' systems, whilst others require two or more numbers on one or more of the dimensions; in which case they are described as 'inconsistent'.

The first dimension is *number of electoral divisions* into which the total area of the local authority is divided. This is an integer variable, with minimum value of 1 (often referred to as the 'at-large system') and stepping by 1 indefinitely upwards.

The second is *number of seats per electoral area at each election* (ignoring by-elections in partial renewal systems). This again is an integer variable, with minimum value of 1 and a practical maximum which varies from type of authority to type, stepping by 1 upwards.

The third is the *percentage of the councillor seats* at stake in any one election (again ignoring by-elections). This is logically a continuous variable, ranging from some very small percentage up to 100 per cent. In practice, however, in the traditional system it took either one of two values – 33.3 or 100 – and in the new system it takes the value of 100 in the new counties (the new county districts all necessarily have inconsistent systems).

The fourth is the *time between successive elections.* This again is logically a continuous variable ranging from the smallest imaginable time upwards to the longest time imaginable. But in practice it took only two values – one year and three years (ignoring by-elections) in the traditional system and four years in the new one for county councils.

These four may be summarized thus:

dimension	1 (number of areas)	1, 2, 3, 4, . . .
"	2 (number of seats)	1, 2, 3, 4, . . .
"	3 (% up for re-election)	33.3, 100.0
"	4 (time between elections)	1 year, 3 years

Some electoral systems can be represented as a point in this four-dimensional space, the dimensions being those given above and in the order given. Thus Devon CC's position in 1964 was:— 89, 1, 100, 3; Okehampton NCB's at the same date was:— 1, 4, 33.3, 1. Any electoral system which can be so described is referred to as 'consistent'. In such a system the elections look the same to each elector – that is, the space he occupies is identical with the space occupied by all other electors. In another sense the system looks the same from the point of view of the elector as it does from the point of view of the council.

But some electoral systems cannot so be represented in a similar manner because one (or more) of the dimensions does not have a uniform value throughout the system. For instance, the number of electoral areas in which elections are held may vary from year to year; the number of seats at stake may vary from year to year and from ward to ward; the proportion of the councillor seats coming up for election each year may vary from year to year and the time interval may be different for electors in different parts of the system. The result is that different electors may find their experiences of the system are different and the system may look different from the point of view of the council as opposed to that of the individual elector. These systems are referred to as 'inconsistent' ones, for an obvious reason. They can however be represented diagramatically in the same way as the others, except that the diagram is more complicated and difficult to read.

If casual vacancies are ignored it is possible to indicate how many local authorities have consistent and/or inconsistent systems. For instance,

county councils (pre-1974):		x/1/100 /3
county councils (post-1974):		x/1/100 /4
all at-large systems (pre-1974):	either	1/x/ 33.3/1
	or	1/x/100 /3
all annual systems with equal sized wards (pre-1974):		x/y/ 33.3/1

The following are necessarily inconsistent: systems with different sizes of wards; most rural districts with annual elections (usually in two ways); systems with different numbers of wards up for election in successive years.

Brief mention must be made of the law relating to casual vacancies – ones caused by death, resignation or disqualification of a serving member. If a casual vacancy occurs close to an ordinary election then it will be filled at the same time as the latter; thus in partial renewal systems it may temporarily convert a single-seat into a double-seat election. Otherwise the by-election is held in the usual manner – incidentally in a multi-member ward temporarily converting it into a single-member election. By-elections are not frequent – perhaps more so in councils with an aldermanic system for reasons to be explained later – and in partisan situations they are simply minor occasions for testing the relative standing of the parties. In non-partisan systems, however, they may be of systemic importance for they may play an important part in processes of recruitment; new members tend to enter through by-elections or their functional equivalent, the ordinary election where the incumbent does not seek re-election.[2]

What is the purpose of this schematic way of representing the variety of local electoral systems, as compared with the traditional way? One answer is simply that it illuminates the variety that traditional methods did not, thus enabling the citizen and the researcher to appreciate the nature of local electoral systems more clearly. The old approach did not bring to light such important facts as the way the separate provisions combine and how they have been adapted to the varying characteristics of local social structure. For instance, the difference between the annual system in rural and town districts was not noticed. It also led to a wrong classification of local authorities. For instance, Honiton NCB was classified with Exeter CB because it was warded, whereas it had more in common with Okehampton NCB which is at-large (Honiton NCB:— 2, 3, 33.3, 1; Okehampton NCB:— 1, 4, 33.3, 1; Exeter CB:— 17, 1, 33.3, 1).

Equally important is the investigation of the relationship between on the one hand the local electoral system and on the other the local social system and the facts of local geography. As it is the operation of the local electoral system which determines the composition of the council, this is a matter of considerable general importance. Different types of electoral system have different consequences in different circumstances. The existence of a refined classification system enables more sophisticated work to be done on these problems.

It is not hard to imagine the variety of local factors which enter into the processes by which a council decides what it thinks its electoral system ought to be. It is through this process that local social structure influences the behaviour on the council for it will influence the system of electoral areas. This is best illustrated in parish and rural district elections and in bi- and tri-polar towns. And as the processes are in the hands of local politicians having a considerable, but not complete knowledge of local affairs, it is not surprising that on occasions the ward system appears to be gerrymandered or that adaptation to a changing distribution of population is long overdue. Once a system is established there is a considerable force working against any changes, for politicians and local electors tend to get used to a particular structure and to build their own organizations around it. Any change is awkward for individual party officials and councillors and, even if not totally resisted, change is often confined to a modification of the existing system which leaves it recognizably a development of the old.

Aldermen

Aldermen were members of councils who were indirectly elected; they were chosen by councillors only and served for six years (unless elected at an aldermanic by-election). They were divided into two groups as nearly equally as possible, and one came up for re-election every third year. Outside London there was one aldermanic seat for every three councillor seats; in London the proportion was one to six. The aldermanic system was introduced in its twentieth-century form into county councils in 1888 (and borough councils in 1910), and from that time onwards it was a source of controversy,[3] both nationally and in particular localities. In 1972 it was abolished for all English and Welsh local authorities, except those of Greater London where it is being rapidly phased out.

Anyone who was qualified to be a councillor was qualified to be an alderman, whether or not he or she was already a councillor. Though the power could be used to bring on to the council outsiders who for personal reasons could not fight direct elections, after the earlier years it was rarely used in this manner, except in some partisan systems, and the importance of the aldermanic system lay in its position in the status and power systems of the council, not in co-option and the mechanical continuity that six-year tenure and partial renewal gave.

The law did not make provision for aldermen to play a distinct formal role in the work of the local authority, yet it is clear that the office often was an important part of the social and political system of the council. It introduced an extra element of ceremony and ritual in many councils; aldermen sometimes had elaborate robes and more prominent seats in the chamber – the title was honorific. Its desirability accounted in part for the growth of the convention restricting it to the select body of councillors. The quarrels over who was to become an alderman when a vacancy arose, within parties and on non-partisan councils, were testimony to its social importance in the status system of the individual council. It had consequences for the tone of human relations within the authority, both within and between parties.[4]

Though the aldermanic system had differing social and political significance in different parts of the country, in most authorities it became a part of the career pattern of the council member; to become an alderman was to be 'promoted' to a more permanent and honoured position. For most authorities it was a seat for life, partisan fortunes permitting, or at least until great age, ill-health and tiredness conspired to cause retirement. The aldermanic bench also acted as a sort of memory in the council because it carried the results of past elections, and therefore the effects of past social systems and past political behaviour into the present. Aldermen were often the newly elected councillors of twenty or thirty years before.

The reasons for its abolition were partly that the conventional arguments in support of it proved spurious, and partly that its obvious defects were brought home to people in different parts of the country on a large number of occasions. It only survived so long because of the 'fear of local democracy' discussed later, and the discussion of its role in that is reserved for the last chapter.

Presiding officers

Unlike aldermen presiding officers did and do have a distinct formal role within the council's decision-making procedures. The basic feature of the role is indicated by its name – in all collective decision-making processes there must be someone to keep order, ensure that the rules of debate are followed and declare the outcome of the deliberations and voting. But this necessary formal activity is only a small part of the presiding officer's contribution to the working of local government in many areas.

Presiding officers have always been elected by the council itself, for one year in the first instance, but with the possibility of indefinite re-election. Previously a council could choose from outside the council but as with aldermen, councillors were reluctant to use this power. The option has disappeared in the new system.

In boroughs the presiding officer was and is called the *mayor*, and in parishes and communities which have adopted the title of 'town' he is known as *town mayor*. Some long established and large boroughs have the extra dignity of *lord mayor*. In all other councils the presiding officer was and is known as *chairman of the council*. There are no legal differences in powers between mayors and chairmen, but in practice there have been different tendencies in the way the office has been used within the local political system.

The mayoral office is usually one of greater formal dignity and involves symbolic and ritual behaviour – ceremony, entertainment and traditional dress. Mayors are often socially more prominent than chairmen, but this is a reflection of the longer history and different social structure of boroughs as opposed to rural and urban districts. *Mayor* is a more powerful symbolic title than *chairman* and this has meant that the office has been prized not for the power it brings (there is usually none) but for its social significance. Members therefore conspire to make it rotate between them and create an annual mayoral system in which the office is purely ceremonial and the political leaders of the council are found elsewhere. Thus leadership is divorced from headship rather in the manner of British central government with its distinction between prime minister and monarch.

Though some other authorities with chairmen also operate an annual system, there are a considerable number of authorities where the chairmen have served for more than one year in succession. Sometimes there was a convention of two years only, but in other places chairmen continued in office indefinitely, until they died, retired or were deliberately defeated for some reason. It is likely that differences in tenure are related to differences in role.[5] A long service chairman is more like the American than the British Speaker of the lower house, in that he takes an active part in the control and direction of the authority generally, rather than being just a neutral presiding officer. In some partisan areas the notion of a formal ceremonial head is so strong that the mayor during his term of office is expected to drop all party positions and cease to be a member of the council caucus. His impartiality may be protected by traditions of not opposing his re-election if his mayoralty coincides with the end of a term of office and ignoring temporarily his latent party affiliation. In the long tenure system, however, the holder of the office is likely to be one of the party leaders, and in non-partisan situations he may expect to be a leading or dominant figure on the council.

There are two reasons why councils have been reluctant to bring in outsiders as presiding officers. A familiarity with the standing orders, conventions and customs of the council is very important for a person presiding at a meeting, but in addition the office is usually at the top of either the status system or the political structure of the council; council members were rightly hesitant about bringing in someone to take a highly sought ceremonial prize or a powerful position which the occupant normally has to earn over the years. Thus in both types the office is at the apex of the 'career' structure of the individual council.

Where the presiding officer's role is a ceremonial one the same sort of partisan and personal rivalries which characterize the aldermanic system have also marked the mayoralty. In leadership systems these are much less marked; often the party leader or a close associate is the presiding officer and takes an important part in council business. In non-partisan systems the importance of the office is recognized by the need to groom a successor as vice-chairman.

Yet in many systems on rare occasions the role of the presiding officer has changed temporarily. For instance, during the two world wars those councils which operated an annual system tended to change to longer tenure – something which may have reflected the changed role of the office – and occasionally councils have made a point of choosing an outsider. This has been done for various reasons; the person may have been in some sense special, the council may have found it embarrassing to give a particular year's mayoralty to one of its members, or it may have been difficult to find someone to take on the onerous social duties.

Council members as individuals

The description of the formal categories of council membership gives no indication of the sort of people who actually serve on local authorities. The information available relates mainly to the traditional system but there is no reason to suppose that the new is fundamentally different.

Since 1945 virtually the whole of the adult population has been qualified to serve on at least one council, and in many cases on two or more. But there are marked tendencies for certain types of people to predominate on councils and for others to be almost completely absent. The tendencies are often presented in the form of statements about the 'quality' of councillors, but these are usually extremely misleading.

What sort of people become council members? This question can be answered at two levels: first, that of the whole country, and second, that of the individual local authority. There is some evidence that there are powerful social and political forces which operate throughout the country to favour the participation of certain types of people, and the facts of differential involvement may be presented as national averages. But these may not be true of any individual authorities; each council is likely to have special features – the local flavour – which reflect some combination of purely local forces and the effect of national forces on the circumstances of the area.

The only extensive study of the social composition of a wide range of councils is that presented in volume 2 of the Maud Committee Report.[6] This confirmed the findings of individual narrow scope investigations that local councils were male, bourgeois gerontocracies, just as were the majority of local and regional appointed bodies.[7]

There can be no doubt that over the country at large very powerful forces operated to produce councils which were more male than the population from which they were drawn. Though women comprise over 50 per cent of the population in most localities, they were only about 13 per cent of council members. These national averages concealed considerable variation from place to place but the number of councils with over 20 per cent women was negligible. There were many more places which had no female members at all for years at a time. Male dominance appeared to be more marked at the chairmanship/mayoralty level and amongst aldermen.

There can also be no doubt that council members were older than the populations from which they were drawn. The Maud Committee figures showed that council members had an average age of just over 50. There are virtually no councillors in their 20s, and quite a number in their 60s and 70s. This again was something that varied from authority to authority, but generally local government was the province of the middle-aged and old.

Local councils were overwhelmingly middle class. The Maud Committee was able to compare council members with the general population broken down by socio-economic groups, showing which groups of occupations were over- and which under-represented. *Social class* is a concept often used to stand for certain other ideas and is related to many other factors. Professional and managerial occupations were more over-represented, whilst skilled manual workers and unskilled workers were almost entirely absent. It is not therefore surprising that council members were considerably more highly educated than the population from which they were drawn. Even in the areas which were the most proletarian there was a strong tendency for councils to be more middle class than the population they served.

There is one other factor of a different sort. This is the extent to which the individual is a *local* person. Obviously the law requires that members have some definite attachment to the area, but this requirements can easily be met. Many members of councils are obviously 'locals' at the time they first stand for the council; if they are not, long service will make them so. In some areas many candidates seem to be long-term inhabitants of the ward, as well as of the authority, when they are first elected. The importance of this sort of factor is attested by the campaign literature that candidates produce.

These national averages conceal many variations between individual authorities, some of whom have changed substantially over time. But much of the special flavour of a particular council will derive from the operation of local forces – those special to the locality.

The most obvious of these special factors is the way that the dominant, strategic or vocal occupations (the three adjectives mean more or less the same) of an area tend to be very well represented on councils. An example of a *dominant* occupation occurs when there is one major industry or one major employer in a town or village. Mining, steel production and farming are good examples of these. Farming, though, is probably a better example of a *strategic* occupation as is railway employment in the railway towns. A *vocal* occupation is one whose members are in a good position to organize and make their aspirations known. Trade unions and trade associations are often in this sort of position, but one of the best examples is that of hoteliers and cafe proprietors in seaside towns.

A different sort of influence on the composition of councils is found in areas where elements of the deferential society are still to be found. It is hard to avoid the conclusion that in many areas of the south-west, particularly for county councils, in the 1940s and 1950s the traditional leaders of local society were a major source of local council members. By the 1960s this was changing rapidly, partly because there were no new social leaders to replace those who fell ill or died. The new system will probably bring to an end the persistence from the pre-war era of 'extinct' types: partisanship and social change have combined to reduce their influence to a minimum.

Comment in general on the sort of people who serve on local councils has stressed national averages, but these should be only the starting point of the analysis. What is much more important is the relationships between the individual council on one hand

and the economy, social structure and political system of the locality on the other. What is interesting is therefore not the 13 per cent of women councillors in England and Wales but the fact that the proportion varied markedly from place to place. Why was it that two neighbouring authorities had proportions of women respectively higher and lower than average?

It is this fact of variation that is significant because it is an indicator of the relationship between local authorities and their environments. The processes by which local social structure and the local political system affect the council partly operate through the composition of the council, which is the end-product of a complicated set of forces and processes. A deferential society will produce a different sort of council than will a suburban, middle-class overspill development or a traditional working-class area.

COUNCIL MEMBERS AND LOCAL SOCIETY

The previous section stressed the importance of the composition of the local council as an aspect of system-environment relationships. But council members are important in this respect also because they are members of the local social and political systems, and thus by their existence provide links between the outside and the inside of the council chamber. Their role in the larger society may have effects on the behaviour of the local authority and their membership of the council may have effects in external life.

Despite its obvious theoretical importance little proper understanding has been achieved of the political significance of overlapping group memberships, except for those involving political parties.

People who are sufficiently concerned with public affairs to serve as council members are likely to belong to other social organizations. That this is so has been attested by many individual studies, one of which spoke of 'public persons' who made almost an occupation of being on committees, whilst another referred to the 'stage army' of active participants in local affairs.[8] It may therefore be expected that council members will be members of local groups also: the trades council, the chamber of commerce and chamber of trade, the Country Landowners Association, the local branch of the National Farmers Union, Rotary and Round Table, the Women's Institute, local churches, the British Legion and sports clubs. It is less likely that they will belong to the altruistic groups mentioned earlier because the rationale of these is often a strong opposition to the 'establishment', in which they include the local council. Civic societies, the Child Poverty Action Group and Shelter spend a considerable part of their time criticizing the local authority for its policies.

The difficulty of making judgements about the systemic significance of multiple local memberships of public persons is that the folklore of political culture of many localities credits the outside bodies, including the masonic societies, with great political power, and these claims have not been properly investigated. Amongst the questions unanswered are: how far membership of a social organization precedes rather than follows a council membership; how far individuals are influenced by their council membership in the larger society or vice versa; how salient the outside body is for the council member and how far he plays an active role within it; how far an increasing role in council affairs affects participation in other bodies? It might be speculated, for instance, that the occasional intervention in local politics by a social organization has been sparked off by the presence of a councillor at its discussion of the matter.

COUNCIL MEMBERS AND LOCAL POLITICS

Much more is known about council members and local politics, for partisan activities are the basis of most local political systems and may pervade the local authority itself. Partisanship is a phenomenon which crosses system-environment boundaries and links the local council and local society very closely.

Two aspects of the relationship between council member and party are of importance. The first is the extent to which the member is involved in party activities – is he or she a relatively inactive member or a leading office-holder? The second is the position of the party in the local political structure, which depends also on what that structure is. In other words some of the most important personal characteristics of council members derive from the party system of the locality.

The major features of local party systems have been described as part of the environment of the local authority. An area may be competitive or basically one-party; it may have strong Liberal or nationalist elements and it may have purely local political parties playing an important part in its affairs. Some of the latter may turn out to be disguised Conservative organizations or long established Conservative-Liberal alliances against the Labour Party; others are separate ratepayers' or residents' associations, whose activists may or may not also belong to a national political party. Also, council members who are genuinely independent in local government affairs may have national party identifications and may even be office-holders.

There is no simple way of characterizing the party system of a locality in a way which makes an understanding of individual council members' behaviour more straightforward. The best way is to think of the local political system in terms of a number of dimensions. These include the extent to which parties contest local elections, the degree of partisanship shown by the voters, the number of parties represented on the council, the competitiveness of the local electoral system, and finally the nature of party organization on the council itself. Party organization inside and outside the council is interdependent, if only through the personnel of the council.

MOTIVES AND ATTITUDES OF MEMBERS

The characteristics of council members considered so far are all social, in that they derive from their positions in society – occupation, age, membership of social and political organizations etc. But most people with the same social attributes as council members do not seek office; standing in a local election and serving on a local council are very much the activities of very small minorities. To account for participation some have looked for more sophisticated social factors, such as kinship or membership of highly politicized organizations such as a trade union or business association. Others, however, have considered the role of psychological factors, such as personality traits, motivation and attitudes of the individual.

A firm distinction must be drawn here between the individuals who are first considering entering local politics and those who have been councillors for some time. It is not surprising that the latter seem to be particular types of person, for they will have selected themselves through the decision to persist and will have been subject to extensive processes of socialization. Many of their attitudes will have been strongly modified by membership of the council.

Those members who find themselves temperamentally unsuited to service on a council are likely to resign in mid-term or not to seek re-election at the end of their first period of office. Those who do remain for two, three . . . ten terms acquire value systems which are specifically related to the individual council and to service on it. As the processes of self-selection and socialization are well known in many spheres of life, the motivation and attitudes of long-serving council members are less problematical than those of the new recruit.

What follows is partly a summary of published and unpublished research and partly the results of *a priori* speculation. Those who seek election to a local council do so for a variety of motives and in a variety of personal circumstances. At one end of the scale there is the persistent defeatist, who believes that elections should not be uncontested or that the party should have a standard bearer, irrespective of the chances of success. In contrast there are those who believe that council membership is very important because of the range of services that councils provide and the impact they have on the local community. In between are those who see some personal advantage in membership of a particular council; the existence of selfish motives has led to a good deal of general cynicism about local councillors, which has been buttressed in recent years by a number of well-publicized scandals.[9]

Any systematic treatment of the motives for standing for election must deal with at least three dimensions of the processes of recruitment. First, there are the personal advantages and disadvantages which may accrue from membership of a council. These may arise from occupation, the possession of property or some other material factor, or they may be largely ideological in content, such as those that arise from partisanship or the 'do-good' attitude. Secondly, there are the factors of knowledge and ignorance, which will be influenced by occupation, kinship, workplace, organizational membership etc. Thirdly, there are questions of means and opportunity; membership of a council almost always involves surmounting certain obstacles of time and money, and different people are differently placed in relation to these. Release from work is an example of the latter problem.

Much of what is said about motivation derives from assumptions about the effects of occupation on attitudes and interests. Those who deal in land and property, such as estate agents, builders and solicitors, have sinister motives attributed to them. Even if these are correct judgements in general it is still necessary to understand the recruitment patterns of local council members in terms of a context which affects the individual's knowledge, means and opportunity for local government work.

This completes the first part of the consideration of one of the types of element of the miniature political systems that local authorities constitute.[10] Before the second part is started, in which the characteristics of individuals within the system are considered, a similar description is given of the second type of element – the paid employee.

Chapter Six
Dramatis Personae: Employees

Elected representatives are usually described as 'lay', 'amateur' and 'unpaid'; they are thought of as *members* of the local authority, not its employees. But local authorities collectively employ a large number of people (over 2½ million) for whom local government is their occupation and their career. Not all employees are full-time and not all are pursuing a life-long career in local government, but the vast majority expect to work for a local authority, not necessarily the same one, for the whole of their working time.

It is a consequence of the historical development of local government that there is no *one* acceptable collective name for the totality of those who work in local government. All possible descriptions are to some extent inappropriate; words such as 'local government officer' or 'local official' normally refer to white collar staff only and there are large categories of similar occupations, such as teachers and policemen, who are referred to by their occupational name rather than by their employing authority. But they and many others have their salaries or wages and national insurance contributions paid by a local authority, and they are regarded as employees for the purposes of the laws relating to work and employment. An indication of the numbers of occupations involved in local government is given in Table 2 (p. 290).

It is not possible to give an account of employees in terms parallel to that given of council members for three reasons. First, much less is known of them in the 'raw' state because little systematic research has been done. Secondly, because they are employed, a much larger proportion of their time (their working week and their working life) is spent inside the local authority, and thus local government is correspondingly a much larger proportion of their *personae*. Thirdly, as a consequence of this, role differentiation within the organization plays a much larger part in the description of their salient characteristics. It is therefore harder, though not impossible, to present them as individuals apart from the operating structure in which they work.

The description of employees as individuals therefore will be largely in terms of their formal position within the structure of the local authority. The most basic distinction is in terms of *location* of work, for local authorities employ people who work within one of the four organizational 'places' within the overall operating framework. These are *headquarters, area office, institution* and *depot.*[1] These are given semi-technical meanings in order to promote the understanding of local government.

The locations are generally organized into *departments* which is the expression local government itself tends to use to refer to the main organizational unit within the local authority. Departments are known by the name of the activity that is carried out in them, such as education, police, social services, highways, finance and establishment. A department always contains a headquarters staff, which may or may not have attached to it one or more satellites in the form of area offices, institutions and depots. This geographical dispersion is a particular feature of the large departments providing the major local government services.

The most distinct group consists of those who work in an institution. By *institution* is meant a socially recognizable unit or grouping of people, often housed in a separate building, whose members think of themselves as belonging primarily to that body. In local government today this includes schools, police stations, libraries and residential homes. In many cases the staff of institutions belong to separate professional organizations or trade unions. It is not uncommon for members of institutions to see themselves as part of a large national organization rather than as employees of a local authority.

Institutions as such are not usually studied by local government specialists and little reference is made to them in general textbooks on local government. Yet quantitatively they are very important. They have tended to be studied by those specializing in the public service of which they are a part. Thus there is a literature on the police, on schools and teachers and on old people's homes, which does not generally treat them as integral parts of the local government system of the country. Whether or not the 'service' literature would gain from a more explicit local government context is open to argument but there is no doubt that the study of local government would gain by a wider recognition of the existence of institutions.

Within the rest of the department it is usual to distinguish between *indoor* and *outdoor* staff. To a large extent this is also a distinction between non-manual and manual occupations. Typically local authority manual workers belong to the relevant general trade union which may well have many members in non-local government employment. The difference between the two is recognized by the creation of separate collective bargaining machinery.

At one time manual workers were much more important in local government numerically than they are now, because they included the workers in the electricity and gas generation and supply industries, transport staff and those in the water-cycle system. Today those who are employed in depots for highways and property maintenance, as well as those engaged in horticulture and gardening, and refuse collection and disposal, still remain important categories.

The growth in local government employment, however, has taken place amongst the white collar staff, most of whom work indoors, though this is not necessarily so. For instance, the growing consumer protection service and personal social services both involve a substantial amount of peripatetic and decentralized organization. But a large part of the work of the large modern authority is clerical and administrative and this implies a large white collar component. These are the ones to whom the name 'local government officer' is normally applied.

A department may or may not be itself internally decentralized, depending on the nature of its work and the geographical area of the authority. This introduces the distinction between headquarters staff and the staff of a department's area offices. Usually there is one building or group of buildings which is recognized as the headquarters of the department. In recent times it has become more common for all or most departments of a local authority to be housed in the same purpose-built building – 'county hall', the 'town' or 'city hall', even 'the council house' or 'municipal buildings' – as in recent years many councils have built new, or extended old, office buildings.

The area office is a distinctive organizational feature of the extensive authority and the larger county councils have normally carried out their duties through a system of areas, sometimes called divisions, each with its own miniature area headquarters. Social service departments have necessarily had to send their workers out into the distant parts of the authority's territory in order to make contact with their clients. This form of organization is likely to be much more significant in the new system as authorities have become larger in area. Sometimes the same building will be used by different departments within an authority for their area offices but on other occasions different accommodation, sometimes in different towns or villages, will be used. Again social service departments have had to think systematically about the form of organization suitable for the disposal of their duties.

Members of institutions, outdoor staff and the staff of area offices have one thing in common which marks them off from most headquarters staff: they either deal directly with the public or perform their work in a highly visible manner. They are part of what may be called the 'operational state'. These are the people in the front line or at the state/citizen interface, and it may well be that the public image of local government, and the popular stereotypes that express it, derive from the activities of the visible staff – teachers, policemen, street cleaners, active social workers, etc.

Of course some headquarters staff deal directly with the public and some outdoor staff are invisible to the general public, but in writing and research in the local government world itself interest has always been focused on the types of staff who have a structural importance in the overall pattern of local authority operations, whose function it is to bind together the disparate activities which constitute the substantive work of the authority.

This means partly those who are responsible for expediting and monitoring the flow of business within the authority, but above all it means those who deal with council members and council member organization. The council member/officer relationship is one of the fundamental ones within the local authority, and thus officers who deal with members have a greater operational significance overall and a higher status than others. In fact, largely the same groups both deal with the other type of person and have a general role within the authority in making it function.

Local authorities are generally free to appoint whatever staff they wish to enable them to discharge their duties, and to pay them in the manner they deem fit. But this description now needs to be modified in three ways. First, local authorities are legally required to appoint some staff and their power to dismiss staff is restricted by the growth of elaborate collective bargaining procedures which cover a very wide range of staff – indoor and outdoor, as well as institutional – and determine to within a narrow range, subject only to grading decisions, the appropriate salary for a given job. Thirdly, recent years have seen a growth in militant unionism in the local authority occupations, including the traditional generalist union, NALGO, and the teaching profession.

The specialist-generalist dimension[2]

The whole of the local government employment situation is dominated by the distinction between professionals and non-professionals (in the terminology of the sociologist of organizations) or between specialists and generalists (in the terminology of the civil service and the Fulton Committee). A professional or specialist is someone who is recruited because he has, or proposes to acquire, some professional, technical or scientific qualification. Some of the specialisms find a wide range of employment outside as well as inside local government – for instance, law, accountancy, architecture, engineering and planning – whilst others are entirely or largely local government professions – public health inspection, consumer protection and the fire service. The professional, if he has chosen a career with wide employment outside local government, could move away for a time and then return. But those professions which have a use only in local government find that their career patterns and bargaining scope are restricted.

The types of officer that are picked out as especially significant in terms of the framework of this book are those who either deal with elected representatives or else are responsible for the flow of business throughout the authority; they are supplemented by those who are responsible for the integration of one part with the remainder. Most of these are professionals or technically qualified people, even if by the end of their career they have for a long time acted in a managerial role.

Chief officers are particularly important in the local government system. First, the concept of a chief officer defines the concept of a department, the basic form of aggregate organization of employees. Thus the number of chief officers tends to determine the number of departments, and the relations between them may well determine the relations between departments and other staff. Second, most of the relationships between council members and officers are conducted from the employees' side by chief officers; only a few non-chief officers deal with elected representatives, and often in the less important matters. This is a second important structural aspect of the chief officer role. Third, chief officers are often public persons of considerable prominence in their locality; the anonymity of the civil servant is denied to many of them because the system pushes them into public roles. Fourth, because of this, and because by occupation and salary chief officers are members of the local upper-middle-class, they are also prominent in the social structure of the area.

It has already been remarked that in the traditional system almost all chief officers were also professionals. But it would perhaps be more true to say that by the time they become chief officers they are former professionals, as before achieving the highest office the individual will have been increasingly concerned with managerial or administrative duties at a high level in the organization, and may not have exercised professional skills in the strict sense of the words for some years. Even their attachment to professional values may have weakened.

In contrast to the specialists there are the administrative and clerical staff who are usually appointed without definite high level qualifications (some of course have qualifications in shorthand, typing and related skills). In the traditional system administrative staff would normally enter the service of a local authority on leaving school at fifteen or eighteen and expect to spend all their working life within the same authority.

Because local authorities are professional organizations in the sociologist's terminology generalists have restricted life chances compared with specialists, in marked contrast to the situation in the central civil service and many forms of industrial and commercial organization. In this respect local authorities are more like universities and hospitals than most other forms of governmental organization. Thus a generalist may expect to get only half to three-quarters the way up the hierarchy of the local authority, even if he is very successful, whilst the specialist tends to enter halfway up with the chance to reach the highest positions.

The contrast may be highlighted by considering the career patterns of two teenagers who entered local government at the same age, at the same time and with the same basic qualifications, but with the difference that one began to study for professional examinations and the other became a generalist. If the former was successful in his studies he would rise rapidly up the salary scale and take on more and more responsibility, possibly achieving the top position in a local authority, after moving several times between authorities, each time seeking to better his position, whilst the latter would rise regularly within the administrative hierarchy of one authority only and, if lucky, become chief clerk to the department. From the same starting point careers would diverge markedly and the specialist obviously would have the better life chances.

Chief officers

Not all chief officers are equal in informal status nor indeed in formal status as measured by salary levels. Over the country as a whole the clerk to the authority was the highest paid and most important officer within the individual authority, with the treasurer, medical officer of health, engineer and surveyor usually forming a second level of high status officers. Their claims to high status are differently based however – the treasurer, like the clerk, was of structural importance in the local authority because of the systemic significance of finance. The importance of the engineer and surveyor derived from the traditional importance of public works in local government (something which is still true) as did that of the medical officer of health from the traditional importance of environmental health. Chief education officers were usually important simply because of the size of their departments – a reflection of the quantitative importance in local government of the education service. Also the education committee and education department had a special organizational status in many local authorities, probably dating from the time education was administered by an *ad hoc* body.[3]

Traditionally chief librarians, curators of museums, chief public health inspectors and the developing specialisms in social work before the 1970 reorganization occupied a relatively low status. Some were of course finding their place by trial and error. Obviously children's officers and welfare officers were not likely to become leading figures because of the limited scope of their work and its relative financial unimportance. Amongst the new types of officer, the planning officer seemed likely to become one of the leading officers eventually because of the growing general significance of planning. Those specializing in organizational matters, such as personnel, also seemed to be increasing in importance.

There were also professions in local government which rarely achieved even minor chief officer status. Horticulturalists and chemical engineers normally worked under the supervision of a civil engineer, for instance, and housing managers had varying statuses from place to place.

The pattern of chief officer roles was part of the general status system of the local authority. It might be thought of as a 'pecking order', but one in which the ranking varied from authority to authority. In some authorities the surveyor or the treasurer was described as the 'strong man' of the authority. In other places the housing manager was a leading figure. The variations referred to here are variations in influence and operational significance. These are only partly reflected in salary differences. More significant is the question of attendance at formal or informal chief officers' meetings.

It is hard to get direct evidence of the pecking order in many individual authorities as researchers did not look for it and, though council members and officers were well aware of it, in practice they did not always explicitly conceptualize it. Openly to recognize such a phenomenon was to violate some of the myths of local government. But it may be assumed that such variations were related partly to the history of a local authority and partly to its direct environmental demands. A housing manager is more likely to be important in an area with a large stock of council houses. The importance of an engineer may have been due to the fact that he managed to 'seize' the planning function many years ago when it was just becoming fashionable.

It was likely that the clerk and the treasurer would be amongst the top officers, even if they were not necessarily the top. This was because of the special nature of the professions they represented. Law and accountancy both tend to blur the difference between specialists and generalists in practice. Both have had a central place in the development of local government in the nineteenth and twentieth centuries. Because of the roles assigned to them these professionals tended to do a generalist's job from the specialist's point of view. They were thus disguised generalists.

Local government reorganization gave an added impetus to processes of change amongst the roles and status of chief officers in many authorities.[4]

In recent years there has been a tendency to try to reduce the number of departments and this can only be done by reducing the number of chief officers. This is done partly to promote coordination between what are believed to be closely related services. Its consequence is to create 'overlords' or directors of groups of services and thus introduce a more formal status system within the relations between chief officers. This process of differentiation shows how different professions have been valued in local government. In the upper-tier authorities the treasurer, engineer and surveyor, director of social services, and the chief education officer have tended to emerge as overlords of financial, technical, social and educational/recreational services.

The actual working relationships between an authority's chief officers are important parts of the political system of the individual authority. To some extent this will parallel the relationships between council members. Again this is something that commentators have been unwilling to discuss except in very general terms of the need for team work and the lack of co-ordination that obviously exists in some authorities.

In many ways the new patterns of chief officer organization look very much like a formalization of the traditional system, replacing *ad hoc* and informal arrangements with a system which recognizes the position of the clerk as a chief executive, the five or six most influential chief officers as directors of groups of services, and creates a committee system for the officers themselves. In many places the continuity of membership from old to new guarantees that the latter is recognizably the offspring of the former.

Lay administrative officers[5]

The generalist in local government is often referred to as the 'lay administrative officer', following the Mallaby Committee. He normally entered local government at the age of 15, 16 or 18, preferably with O-level or A-level qualifications, and worked his way up the administrative hierarchy by doing his job well, or appearing to do so in the eyes of his superiors and the professional officers in the department. He might also have studied at home for the Diploma in Municipal Administration or possibly the relevant secretarial or business administration qualification.

The particular expertise and skill of the lay administrative officer lies in understanding how his particular part of the organization works, and of helping to make it work. To some extent he acts as the memory of the system because he is aware of precedence, has a knowledge of files and understanding of past problems within a limited area, in contrast with the often short service professional officer. One of his chief qualifications will therefore be experience of a particular system.

However, despite the operational importance of generalists, their life chances are considerably reduced. At any given time a specialist and a generalist may be earning the same salary and have the same formal status, but the former will be very much younger and will be looking forward to a career involving much higher things whilst the latter may be nearing the end of his promotion chances.

Despite this restriction of life chances the lay administrative officer does have a career path within the individual local authority marked out for him. The special roles that a generalist may aspire to are section head, committee clerk, deputy chief clerk of the department and chief clerk. In each case the role will bring him into increasing contact with council members and/or professional officers.

A large part of a local authority's work consists of administrative and clerical operations. This is particularly true of the large departments such as education. Quite often a good generalist will be given responsibility for a block of work under the general supervision of his section head or deputy head. The effective performance of this sort of duty is a recommendation for promotion to greater responsibilities especially if he has discharged a number of similar jobs in other sections equally well (generalists may be expected to be moved around from section to section during their early years – sometimes, when they are junior entrants, to an absurd degree).

The section head's role is an obscure but important one. Individual departments conceptualize the disposal of business in terms of sections and the head of a section has a considerable responsibility to see that the group of activities assigned to him are performed effectively. His job is managerial or supervisory rather than clerical and he will probably be in frequent touch with a relevant professional officer. Also he will play a part in the estimating procedure, as often the only person with the relevant detailed information is the section head. Section heads may expect that if they perform well in a small or non-strategic section they will be moved to a more important one.

The most successful of the section heads will become deputy chief clerk of the department and eventually chief clerk – the highest post to which a lay administrative officer could aspire in the traditional system. The chief clerk in a department is generally the head of the lay administrative staff (all the non-professional staff) and is often an office manager and controller in a real sense. He will be in close contact with the head of the department (the chief professional officer) and he may thus be regarded as one of the key link men in the operating system of the local authority.

Unfortunately, little is known about the real importance of the chief clerk and his deputy in the local government system, despite the research undertaken on local councils and on local politics. This is only partly because officers generally are less visible than council members and local politicians, and have not received the attention they should receive. Few lay administrative officers themselves have written about local government; when committees of enquiry receive evidence they usually receive it only from professional officers, particularly heads of departments; and clerks and treasurers when they recount their experiences do not seem aware of the internal structure of their departments – at least they prefer to look outwards rather than inwards.

An important role within the lay administrative service is that of committee clerk. This may be combined with a section headship or other formal position or it may be in a separate section within the clerk's department. Thus sometimes committee clerks are members of the relevant individual department and sometimes they are all members of the clerk's department, each one taking a group of committees.

The committee clerk's job is as the name suggests. The primary activity is that of attending committee meetings in order to take the minutes, but a committee clerk will also be responsible for seeing that any necessary communication arising from the meeting goes to those who need to know about it and that proper preparations are made before the meeting. This routing operation is a vital one in authorities with elaborate committee systems because a failure in this respect is likely to lead to lack of co-ordination between the different activities a local authority is undertaking. This co-ordinative role is performed both collectively and individually and usually committee clerks work closely with a senior professional member of the clerk's department and a member of the treasurer's department, as well as the head of the individual departments concerned with the committee meeting.

The role of committee clerk may well be a step in promotion in the administrative hierarchy of the department or the authority. In most professional organizations the generalists who have most contact with those at the top of the hierarchy (in this case professionals and council members) are the most important and most likely to progress.

There are other types of local government officers similar to section head and committee clerk in their role within the overall pattern of local authority operations. Little is known about the position of head of an area office, depot manager and director of an institution, even though they are key persons in the overall system of activity. Some have been studied within their organizational location but this usually involves an abstraction from the local authority itself, and it is the contribution to the total system of the latter that is the concern of this book.

The above description of types of individual employee in local government has not strictly paralleled that given of council members because it has had repeatedly to look forward to the organizational forms in which employees work. This is because types of local government employee are specified by the latter rather than by a set of legal categories.

The social characteristics of employees

Unfortunately it is not possible to answer the question what sort of people are local government employees in social terms, as their backgrounds have not been investigated in the ways that those of civil servants have.

The Mallaby Committee chose to study a sample of NALGO members rather than the local government service itself, but within those limits it provides some evidence of the social composition of local government employment. In the sample about a third (31.4 per cent) were female, but women were younger and of shorter service on average than men. They had also tended to serve fewer authorities during their working life. The suggestions in these figures are partly confirmed by an examination of the sex of chief officers serving in local government in the early 1970s. These are overwhelmingly male, even in spheres where women are widely employed. In the traditional professions of law, accountancy and engineering men almost monopolize, but women are less prominent in social service, educational and cultural departments than one could expect. It is fairly safe to assume that the important positions in local government employment are overwhelmingly held by men – and this dominance is greater even than amongst council members.

No general figures appear to be available for the age distribution of staff comparable to those for council members, but the Mallaby Committee provided figures of the pattern amongst administrative staff in the different types of authority. These show a high proportion of over 50s and relatively few under 40s for most types of authority, but it is hard to know what to infer from these. It does appear, though, that as each age cohort moves through the local authority the situation with respect to administrative staff will become increasingly difficult. Unless there is a big influx of young and middle-aged administrative staff, many local authorities could be facing a crisis in the near future.

No survey is needed to report that local government employment is basically middle-class and white-collar within headquarters and in senior posts in area offices, depots and institutions. This is obvious from salary scales and from job descriptions. If only the systematically significant officers are considered then many of them must be counted as members of the local upper (rather than middle) class. There are two reasons for this. One lies in the nature of their present employment and salary. Senior local government officers hold important, public, managerial and leadership positions. In terms of responsibility for staff employed and money spent, they are often the leading managers of their area. The fact that a local authority is only a small one does not usually affect this as small local authorities normally operate in small communities; the *relative* position of the local government officer may not be affected.

There is a second factor however. It is to be assumed that most senior local government officers are aged between 45 and 65. As they are professionals normally their formal training will not have been completed until they are in their early- or middle-twenties. A chief officer of 45 in 1950 may well have finished his professional education in 1930; in 1960 in 1940, and in 1970 in 1950. They were therefore educated in quite different circumstances from those that obtain today. The leading local government professions in those years were the preserve of the children (obviously the sons) of well-off parents. Engineering, law, and medicine either required premiums of new entrants (to be paid to the chief officer) and/or the financial support of parents until professional training was completed. This system of articled pupilage persisted until the 1950s and 60s in some areas and reserved the highest positions in local government to the sons of the middle and upper classes. A similar phenomenon can be observed in education where chief officers are drawn from the school teachers of the 1930s and 40s.

There is one social factor which can be looked at profitably in superficial terms. This is the question of the *localness* of local employees. It may be remembered that local government electoral law guaranteed some definite connection between council members and the area they served. But the strength of the connection varied empirically in several dimensions. *Localism* is a factor which may be looked at in terms of *birth*, *residence*, *workplace* and *social life* (including shopping etc.).

There is no requirement that a local government officer lives within the area of the authority for whom he works; probably many do but some may well choose deliberately not to, to try to divorce work and leisure. Probably also the situation is affected by the relationship between social and administrative areas. Obviously they must work within the area of the authority, but what of birth or pre-employment residence?

Under the traditional system whereby local authorities recruited a large proportion of their junior staff, both administrative and professional, from local school leavers it was to be expected that initially the local government service was also a local service in this sense. People just commencing a career in local government were likely to be either born in or near the area or to have lived there a considerable time as children. The professional may well expect to move during his career to other authorities, thus reducing the connection between local government employment and localism. However the generalist's value lies partly in his knowledge of the system he is in – thus he is likely to serve out his time with one authority.

The mobility of the professional may be over-exaggerated, however, in the conventional literature; it may be that when a professional becomes a chief officer he tends to stay there to the end of his working life. In unusual cases, however, one could imagine that a changing set of professional officers sandwiched between long-serving councillors and long-serving administrative staff.

The growth in employment of graduates as professionals and administrators may well reduce the localness of local government. Graduates belong generally to a national labour market; there is no reason to think that the tendency to seek employment in the area of origin is more than a weak one. The same may well be true of those professions where the person is trained externally, rather than within the local authority.

This completes the first part of the examination of the *dramatis personae* of local political systems. The second part can only take place after a description has been given of the typical ways in which each type of participant is organized within the system. Each type of person is located within a set of institutions and working arrangements which tend to be peculiar to that type, and these create the roles which individuals fill. A major structural feature of the local political system is the interaction between member organization and employee organization.

Any complete account of an individual local political system would of course deal with the *dramatis personae* of the environment who interact with the system directly, without being actually part of it. These will include leaders of local pressure groups, prominent and active individuals and party activists. Lack of space forbids a treatment of these.[6]

Chapter Seven

The Internal Organization of Local Authorities; Part 1: Elements of Structure

The internal organization of the individual local authority is built up out of the institutions and organizational patterns created as a framework for the activities of elected members and paid officers within the system. The work of elected members is structured by a complicated pattern of meetings of the council itself, of committees and of subcommittees, whilst employees work in departments which are basically administrative hierarchies – the sociologist following Weber would call them 'bureaucracies' – whose own internal structure contains sections and groupings of sections, and which often have satellite area offices, institutions and depots attached to them.

The description of the behaviour of the miniature system that a local authority has been assumed to be is complicated by the fact that conventional views about it have been in a state of flux for the last fifteen years. The organization of a local authority tends to be perceived through the medium of a set of prescriptions about what it *ought* to be. These prescriptions include the delimitation of the respective roles of council members and employees, the form of council member organization and the form of employee organization. Many accounts of the internal organization of local authorities have been strongly influenced not by what can be observed of behaviour within the system but by the writer's beliefs about the right and wrong patterns of operation.

Policy and administration

The traditional way to approach the internal organization of a local authority was in terms of a distinction between *policy* and *administration*. Making policy was thought to be the activity that elected representatives ought to undertake (and employees ought to refrain from) whilst administration was the province of the paid element. The distinction had the meaning that those words normally have – that council members should decide what ought to be done in terms of a set of general rules, and officials implemented the rules by applying them to particular cases and circumstances.

Originally the distinction between policy and administration was developed in American government as part of the attack on the endemic corruption of public affairs in the late nineteenth century. In a real sense it was only a new version of the distinction between legislative and executive functions of government made familiar in the theory of the separation of powers.[1] As time passed it became increasingly discredited as greater knowledge of the reality of government showed that it was quite inadequate as a description of the working of public bodies. The result was that there was a search for other distinctions which would serve the same function – of determining the respective roles of council members and officers. Many candidates were suggested in their place: *new* and *routine*, *unprogrammed* and *programmed*, *political* and *non-political*, and *controversial* and *non-controversial*. The Maud Committee attempted to distinguish between *key* decisions and others.

The difficulty with every one of these distinctions is something that has not been recognized either by those who have proposed them or those who have rejected them. It is that if the distinction is to fulfil the function required of it it must be usable *a priori*, for it must determine what the respective roles are *before* decisions have to be made and actions taken. It is often clear *a posteriori* that something was controversial or not controversial, but predicting this is one of the skills of the politician – and the politically sensitive officer. There are no prior criteria which enable an authoritative judgement to be made as to what will be political and what non-political. What council members do and what officers do is in fact an empirical question, to be answered differently for different authorities at the same time and for the same authority at different times.

The Bains Committee, which reported during the interregnum between old and new systems, argued against a distinction between the two respective roles, saying that both elements were involved in all local authority activities, though in differing degrees.[2] The flexibility that this approach entails is equivalent to saying that there is no *a priori* distinction to be drawn.

In fact the respective roles of council members and officers can only be understood by reference to the others' activities. What officers do depends on what council members do and what the latter do depends on the former. But in exposition one needs a starting point; as the behaviour of council members seems to be influenced more directly by exogenous factors this will be treated first. This is supported by a legal point; as council members are collectively the local authority, they can do what they wish, subject only to the law of the land and their own values, perceptions and limitations.[3] Council members appoint officers and create the structures in which they work; in a real sense what officers do is what council members do not do, for reasons of choice or necessity.

It would be wrong, however, to see the council members' roles as being solely determined by the council members themselves. A complicated set of environmental factors, mostly derived from the size and composition of the population directly or indirectly, tends to increase the role and influence of officers, particularly heads of departments. These forces operate through their effects on partisanship, the volume of business, the length of the meeting cycle and the number of committees, and the atmosphere in the council chamber. Other factors include the degree of technicality of the service being provided and the presence of conflict amongst officers themselves.

Once the role of the chief officer has been determined only the principle of hierarchy is needed to begin the explanation of the role of other employees. In other words, below the head of the organization departments can be analysed on more or less the lines used for large-scale formal or complex organizations by the student of organization 'theory'.

The traditional principle of organization

The confusion and ferment about internal organization of local authorities have always encompassed both council member and employee institutions. The traditional system was based on a simple principle which determined, subject to a prior identification of *service* and *function*, the exact form of lay and official institutions.

Briefly, this principle said that for every distinct local authority service there should be a committee to run it, served by a chief officer who headed a department of officials dealing with it. In schematic form this can be represented thus:

one service → one committee → one chief officer → one department.

It is easy to interpret this principle again so that it applies to every distinct function that can be identified, thus:

one function → one committee → one chief officer → one department.

Again it can be interpreted to deal with every distinct part of a service or function, thus:

one part of a service → one subcommittee → one section head → one section.

Thus educational authorities appointed education committees and the latter were served by an education officer and an education department. The authority would also probably have a finance committee to deal with that function throughout the authority. The education committee would be served also by a number of subcommittees, for instance, for primary and secondary education, and also often for finance.[4]

The principle received different interpretations in different authorities so that there was no single blueprint which described accurately the internal organization of all local authorities, but the consequences could be seen in similar phenomena across a wide range of councils. First, there were large numbers of committees, subcommittees, chief officers and departments within each authority, and there was constant pressure to increase them. Despite periodic attacks over the years, especially in the larger authorities, the number of committees and departments had grown until there were serious problems of co-ordination between the different activities of the local authority.[5] These led to the creation of yet more machinery to try to impose consistency and harmony on a fragmented system.

In the 1960s there was a large scale movement to try to simplify the internal organization of the individual authority, and the demands were symbolized by the Report of the Maud Committee. The simplification consisted of merging all committees and departments until there were only a handful of each, with consequent reduction of the number of independent chief officers, and the elimination of the unrestricted communication network between committees which had been a characteristic of the traditional system, in favour of one that channelled everything through a new functional committee, called inappropriately the 'management board'.

The details of this simplification did not find much favour with the local government world as it stood, and its rationale has been rejected for a different approach associated with the Bains Committee. The Bains approach was one of deliberate complexity, but based on different assumptions from those that motivated the traditional approach. A Bains-style organization would have a more complicated committee system than the traditional one, because it would have committees for officers as well as for council members. The principles of differentiation between committees of all types were not to be based on the conventional distinctions between public services and functions embodied in local government law but on facets of the work of the local authority as a corporate body dealing with an individual environment.

Probably the underlying reason why simplification has been rejected is that it is not seen as desirable whilst society makes complicated demands on the system of government. Systems interacting with their environment tend to develop sufficient complexity within themselves to deal with the variety that they experience in the inputs into them. If they do not they disappear or perish.

It has been conventional to present the internal pattern of organization of local authorities in diagrammatic form. The first diagram (in Figures 5(a) – (c) and 10(a) – (b)) is the traditional presentation of the classical form, though the more accurate version is shown in the second diagram. The third diagram is the Maud Committee's proposals for a management board system and Figure 10(b) (p. 255) an interpretation of the totality of the Bains' Committee's proposals. But all these diagrams contain static models of the system; as a system 'behaves' it can only be represented by a dynamic model. In this context 'dynamic' simply means that *time* is one of its dimensions. This is a necessity because activities take time to occur, and when they do they happen in an irreversible temporal order. It is the *sequence* of behaviour which is vital in models of complicated activities.[6]

Before a detailed consideration is undertaken of the pattern of council member and officer activities within the system, it is worthwhile reminding the reader that in trying to understand an individual authority the first step is to find out which of the 'models' or prescribed patterns is supposed to be the basis of the system. Reality may depart from this pattern very markedly but it is important to understand the beliefs of those who are responsible for its construction. In practice a corporate management system may be identical with a somewhat simplified traditional system, but this can only be established empirically.

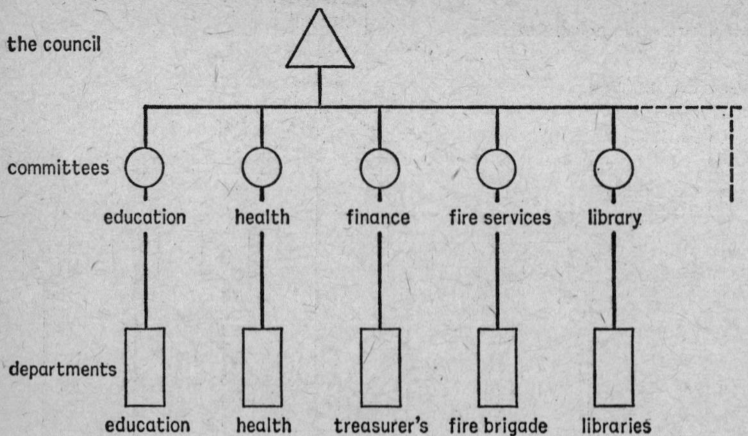

Fig. 5 (a) **Patterns of Internal Organization – the Traditional Presentation**

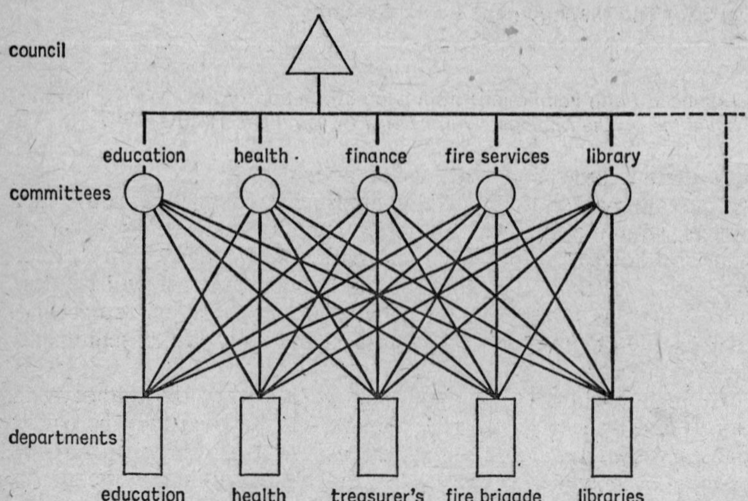

Fig. 5 (b) **Patterns of Internal Organization – Improved Version of 5 (a)**

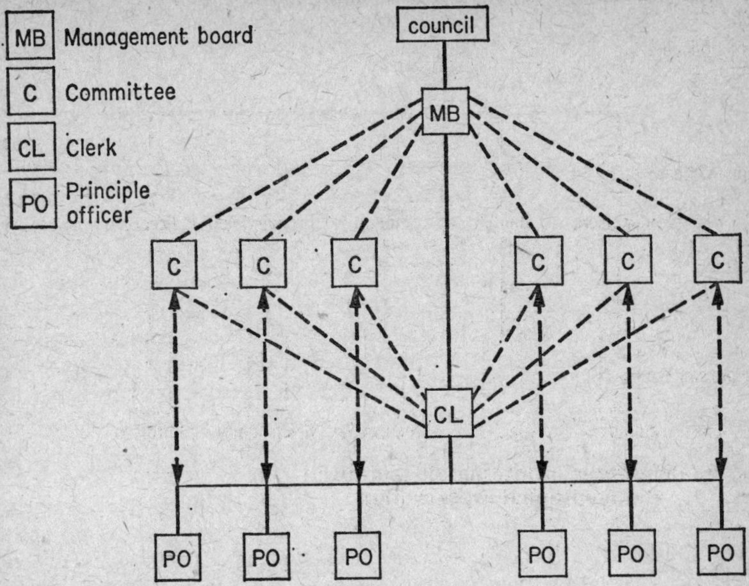

Fig. 5 (c) **The Management Board System**

reproduced (with permission) from page 50, *Report of the Committee on the Management of Local Government*, HMSO, 1967

Information flows and patterns of activities

As an alternative to the static approaches described above the system within each local authority can be analysed as a set of temporal flows of information and patterns of activity with distinct rhythms over time. The 'life' of the council member will be described first, as the pattern of activity amongst elected representatives is one of the dominant factors in the daily life of senior and strategic officers.

Council members find that their work within the authority is dominated by two temporal sequences: that which may be called the *municipal year*, and which has a period of one year, and the *meeting cycle*, which is repeated several times within each year, and thus has a considerably shorter period than the former. In fact the determination of the length of the meeting cycle is an important management decision to be made by the council.

THE MUNICIPAL YEAR

Each council has to hold an annual meeting which formally starts the municipal year. Since 1949 this has usually taken place in late spring or early summer (the law prescribed different times for different types of council). In the annual election system it therefore always followed the elections, which determined who was entitled to attend. The meeting has to take a number of basic decisions. First, it elects the presiding officer for the coming year, and in councils with aldermanic systems it had to elect half of the bench every third year. Then it implicitly or explicitly determines standing orders, particularly those which govern the number of types of committee to be appointed, and allocates members to these. The council then begins its regular working cycle of council, committee and subcommittee meetings, the intervals between meetings having been determined at the annual meeting, again often implicitly.

Many councils experience a lull in activities in August – some even provide for a 'vacation' in the meeting cycle – but in September the financial processes begin in earnest as departments start to collate their estimates for submission to the relevant committee in October and November. At this stage the estimates are in draft only, but when the committee has given a provisional approval they pass to the finance committee with those of all the other committees. The process is closely monitored by the staff of the treasurer's department who are responsible for the collation of the separate estimates. The finance committee considers the estimates along with the treasurer's estimates of revenue from the various sources. If the marriage of the two produces too frightening an offspring in the shape of the rate in the pound, then the estimates will be returned to the original committees to be reduced. Eventually, however, the finance committee has to determine a rate to be recommended to the rate fixing meeting held in February or March.[7] The next event is the holding of elections if it is an election year for the individual authority, and this is followed by the annual meeting for the new municipal year.

THE MEETING CYCLE

Throughout the municipal year there will have been shorter cycles of business which can be referred to simply as the ordinary meeting cycle. Each cycle runs from one council meeting to the next, and contains within it a sequence of committee and subcommittee meetings. Each council's system can be described in terms of a few variables.

The first variable is the length of time between two successive council meetings. Most councils make provision both for regular meetings and for the calling of special meetings if required. The time between the former is determined by each council according to its own values and beliefs. County councils have traditionally met quarterly, whilst county districts and county boroughs tended to meet monthly. A few met fortnightly but in recent years there has been a trend towards five- or six-weekly cycles, often consciously adopted as a result of an O & M survey which sought to balance the officers' need for sufficient time to take action between meetings and arrange the flow of business from one meeting to another with the council members' need for speedy decisions and frequent opportunity to deal with urgent (to them) matters. The longer the cycle the easier it is to fit in a multitude of committee and subcommittee meetings, but the longer citizens may have to wait for a decision.

Meetings of committees are fitted into the sequence, usually with the same period of time between two successive ones, though not necessarily since some may have longer and others shorter cycles. It is usual also to put the vertical or service committees at the beginning of the cycle and the horizontal or functional committees at the end, so that particular aspects may be considered by the relevant committee before they go to the council itself for a final decision. The subcommittee system is fitted into the committee system in a similar way, though it is likely that they meet more irregularly in general than do their parents. However, education committees often look like federations of regular subcommittees, so important are the latter in the education service.

Thus the council, its committees and their subcommittees are bound together into a complicated communication flow system. Figure 6 represents a simplified version of this system and is intended to draw attention to the formal similarities between the meeting cycle and the networks studied in critical path analysis.

The next step is to examine the elements of this network, and the obvious starting point is the council itself.

Fig. 6 **A Dynamic Model of a Simple Committee System**

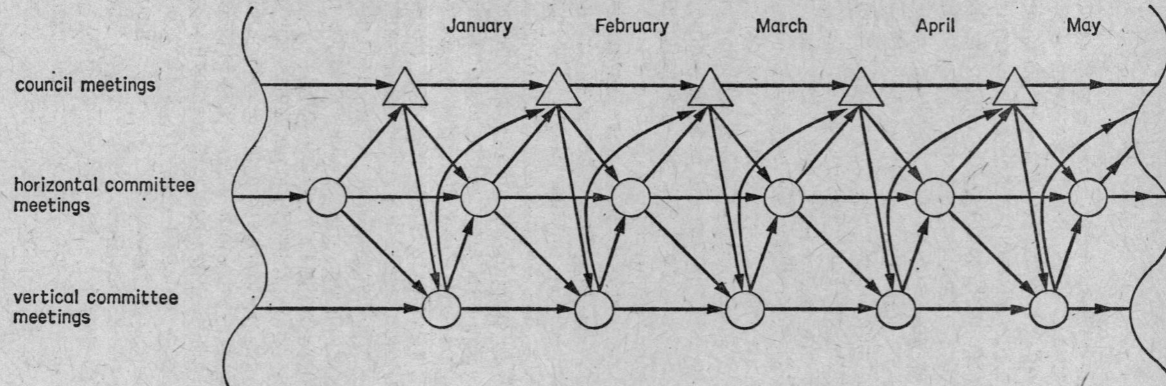

Notes: The arrows represent paths through which information can flow from one meeting to another. The wavy lines at each edge of the diagram represent the fact that the set of meetings shown above are a segment of an on-going process, without a definite starting or finishing point. The diagram can be imagined in three dimensions, with a series of horizontal and vertical committees running parallel to the one drawn here in the same plane.

The council

It is not uncommon for commentators to regard the council itself as a negligible part of the local authority and to treat council meetings as empty farces. This is a mistaken point of view and arises partly from a failure to appreciate what actually goes on at council meetings and partly from the treatment of the council in abstraction from the system of which it is an integral part. Three aspects of the council are important: the council as a legal entity which in a formal sense controls the whole of the decision-making process within the authority; the council as a body of people with definite empirical characteristics; and the council meeting itself.

The council members are collectively the local authority and procedures are laid down whereby they, sitting as the council, make decisions that have the force of law. From this point of view decisions can be divided into three classes: those which the council cannot by law delegate to other bodies or persons; those that are of such importance that in practice it will not delegate; and those it may and often does delegate *de facto* or *de jure*.

The limitations on the power to delegate have always been very few, and they are the sort of things that councils would in general be reluctant to surrender in any circumstances. The main ones occur in relation to finance, the levying of a rate or precept and the raising of loans and, in private bill procedure, the passing of the statutory resolutions. The final approval of major schemes and the ratification of decisions with large financial or social consequences are the sort of matters that councils will not normally delegate. For the rest of the matters that a local authority decides the council may or may not delegate to others; often the formal difference between delegation and non-delegation does not have much effect on the operation of the local authority.

Councils as collective bodies may remain quiescent for long periods. Their meetings may be short, formal and ceremonial, committee members may assume that whether a matter is delegated or not is irrelevant as the committee decision will be the final one, and public interest will be non-existent.[8] But this may suddenly be changed; council meetings become controversial, heated and lengthy; committees may find that their decisions are being questioned and sometimes overturned; the press and public takes a much greater interest. In extreme cases delegated powers may even be withdrawn in order to take power away from a committee.

When these things happen the practical significance of the legal supremacy of the council is forcibly thrust upon the attention of everyone, including officers.

In fact the nature of the council meeting and the role of the council itself is probably as good an indicator of the general state of system-environment relations as any. For changes in the environment which affect relations with the system are likely to show themselves in the place where adaptation can most effectively occur. So that such changes as an influx of new types of people – say 'cosmopolitans' rather than 'locals' – a changing partisan structure in the locality, a social or political crisis in the area, must affect the council itself before they can substantially affect other parts of the system. The council is thus a weathervane of system-environment relations.

The council as a body has a number of attributes which are of importance in the working of the system. For instance, it is the only source of members of committees (apart from the minor contribution of co-option); its composition thus helps to determine, in conjunction with the system's allocation rules, the social and political composition of each committee. The point can, however, best be illustrated by considering the *size* factor as an influence on the working of the system.

The size of the council is a variable which affects many aspects of the operation of the local authority. First, it helps to determine what sort of occasion the council meeting itself will be. Some councils are really small or medium-sized groups whilst others are mass assemblies. This has consequences for the discipline and formality shown at the meeting, and this may have consequences for the level of friendliness and consensus developed amongst members.

Secondly, the number of members of a council determines the flexibility there is in filling the roles that council organization creates. A small council with an elaborate committee system may well find itself allocating chairmanships to those whom it regards as scarcely competent. The situation may be more desperate in partisan authorities, for if the ruling group has a small majority and attempts to control the whole committee system it may find itself forced to load its leading members with double and treble responsibilities, or else risk allowing incompetents to take on responsibilities. All councils experience a 'leakage' in that for a variety of reasons some members will be incapable, unwilling or unsuitable occupants of major roles in the system. As the leakage is a probabilistic process, occasionally factors combine to place a council under stress and threaten the operation of the system in the manner to which it has been accustomed.

Allied to this is a third factor. Filling committee places and systemic roles is only one aspect of the life of a council member; some of the work arises from constituents and groups in the locality. In general the larger the council the more the work is shared around.[9]

THE COUNCIL MEETING

Council meetings are occasions of much misunderstanding by those who casually go to watch a single meeting or even two or three. In part this is a matter of being able to recognize the different types of people present and identify systemic roles, but it is more a matter of starting from the premise that what is being experienced is a sample from a distinct subculture. Equally, it must be realized that one meeting is only a phase of a complex process, not complete in itself.

In order to facilitate understanding of council meetings an account will be given first of the people present and secondly of the business transacted.

The largest single group of people present at most council meetings consists of the council members themselves – councillors, the presiding officer and in some councils in the past the aldermen. Attendance is not compulsory so that at any given meeting some are likely to be absent, some will arrive late or leave early, and some will absent themselves for a time during the meeting. Council chambers show a variety of seating patterns; some are arranged in the Parliamentary manner with the leaders of the parties facing each other, and also cross benches at the back, whilst others show the continental semi-circular pattern.

The second group of people will be the officers of the council. Most if not all of the chief officers will be present, including the clerk to the council who will sit near the presiding officer. Also in prominent positions will be the committee clerks who carry out the administrative and clerical duties at the meeting. Like the roles of the most prominent council members, the roles of officers cannot be understood unless it is realized that they reach out beyond the meeting itself to other parts of the decision making network.

The remaining people present are not members of the system itself but outsiders with various degrees of closeness of connection to the system. There may be a party of school children studying civics, the representatives of interests affected by business before the council, individuals who are hoping to become councillors, and the press. On rare occasions the public attempt to intervene in the meeting contrary to law and they may be removed by the police. This again is a sign of the state of the environment-system relationships.

Some of the business transacted at a council meeting is purely ceremonial or ritual. This includes calling the roll of members present, receiving official communications, standing in memory of a recently deceased alderman, receiving gifts of civic silver and passing resolutions congratulating notable citizens. Many councils also start their meetings with prayers. Many bodies have similar sorts of rituals to start their meetings but it is sometimes felt that council members place greater stress on the ceremony, perhaps at times when the substantive business before the council is slight or uncontested.

Substantive decision making in local council meetings takes one of two forms. The most common and most important form consists of the meeting determining its attitude towards each item contained in the reports or minutes of committees submitted to the council. The consideration of matters arising from the activities of committees is often the only important business before a council meeting. Committee reports and minutes contain several different sorts of items. Some will be for information only, reporting action taken on delegated matters or work in progress. Standing orders vary in the extent to which they permit discussion of such items, but in no case is there any question of the council taking decisions. If however the matter is a recommendation then the council has to do one of several things.

The fate of a committee recommendation may be any of the following: it may be accepted as it is (often 'on the nod'); it may be amended; it may be referred back to the committee for further consideration, with or without definite instructions; or it may be rejected. Rejection or substantial amendment are relatively rare, as the council meeting usually does not have the machinery for substituting its judgement for that of the committee; hostility to a proposal is more likely to be expressed in a reference back.

The second way in which substantive business is dealt with at a council meeting is through the notice of motion, whereby one or more councillors table a proposition which, if accepted, commits the council to an attitude or a course of action. The reluctance of many councils to act at the meeting itself is often illustrated here also, because the motion if passed will be sent to the appropriate committee for implementation or further consideration. Motions, therefore, play little part in the decision-making structure of most councils, but they may have a publicity and partisan role, as do some of the procedural devices of the House of Commons.

To the outsider what goes on at a council meeting often appears pointless or stupid, even though many of the council members would hotly contest this. The reason for this is that much of the form that activities take is determined by the subculture of the council itself, and any individual meeting is a sample of this. In fact the pattern of behaviour at meetings is often a very good guide to the underlying state of relationships within the system – between individuals, between parties and between council members and officers. An appreciation of this point can only come from an analysis of patterns over a period of time of the relative importance of different types of procedure and business, and the structure of moves made by individual members during the course of the meeting. Press reports are unfortunately of little use in this respect as journalists deal with the unique event as it occurs and there is little reflection in the local press on 'the state of the system' comparable to the coverage of Parliament.

A further requirement for understanding the processes at work in council meetings is an ability to identify systemic roles. Some of these can only be properly appreciated when their position in the overall system is understood. To a large extent the business is monitored by a few leading members of the council. In party systems the leaders of the parties carry out general strategic and tactical roles, whilst specific segments of council business are conducted mainly by the relevant committee chairman. Both party leadership and chairmanship can only be understood after the overall pattern has been described.

The role of the presiding officer is more obvious. Procedural matters in council meetings are dealt with in the usual manner and the presiding officer is expected to act like the Speaker of the House of Commons in these matters. But on occasions procedural matters become important and the time of the council will be taken up with controversies about the order of amendments, the closure of discussion etc., in which case the presiding officer's role becomes more significant. In some systems also the chairman is not solely a neutral president, but is also a leader of the council. This is particularly true in the long tenure systems of chairmanship. The role is therefore more akin to that of the American rather than the British

Speaker of the lower house.

Officers and members of the public are not generally permitted to speak at council meetings; it has been remarked that occasionally outsiders disrupt a meeting, and some councils have procedural devices which allow a member of the public in effect to address the full council. These are all relatively infrequent. The participation of officers is more interesting and significant.

Though officers are not supposed to speak at council meetings, except in the case of the clerk advising on a point of law or standing orders, in small councils this is often ignored. In these cases, in effect, the council is more like a committee in its informality and the atmosphere one of discussion rather than debate. But in the large councils, especially those organized on partisan lines, the prohibition is strictly observed. Yet officers may feel the need to participate indirectly. How this is done depends on the seating pattern of the particular council chamber. Some councils place all committee chairmen on the platform, with chief officers sitting unobtrusively behind them. In this case the officer leans forward to whisper to the chairman or the latter turns round to ask a question. If the Parliamentary model is used, however, this is not possible as many of the committee chairmen will be on the front benches. Sometimes a look of agitation is seen on the face of a chief officer sitting at the side or back of the hall and a hastily written note is passed across the council members' seats.

In a large meeting it will often be possible to detect what are in effect self-appointed roles of ordinary members of the council. There will be the perpetual critic, often a backbencher in party systems, those who are more royalist than the king, those who watch only for items of concern to a particular area or a particular functional interest and interpret everything in these terms, the fervent 'economizer' and so on.

The council meeting is, however, only one part of the internal organization of a local authority, and it can only be properly understood in its context. The next step is to examine other elements of council member activity.

The committee system

Local authorities have long had a general power to create a committee to discharge any aspect of their work, with the exceptions mentioned above. In the past councils have exercised this power repeatedly so that apart from parish councils and very small district councils they had a very elaborate committee system. The Maud Committee found in the mid-1960s that it was common for a large authority to have over twenty committees meeting regularly as part of the cycle of meetings. Since that time many councils have made determined efforts to reduce the size of the committee system, and reorganization after 1972 gave an added impetus to this movement. Still, however, council members carry out a large part of their work in and through committees, even if they sometimes give them another name.

The committee system has been regarded as so important an agency for local authority decision making that several central government departments have insisted through legislation that the relevant local authorities each appoint a committee to consider matters relating to a particular service and refer these to it before taking a council decision. These are called 'statutory' committees in contrast to the optional or permissive ones that a council may choose to appoint or not, at its own desire. In the traditional system these included the watch committee, education, health, allotments and children's committees. The new system has reduced the number of such requirements but has left education, social services, police and a number of others as statutory obligations. As will be seen later, there is more flexibility inherent in the statutory 'impositions' than many commentators have believed.

The first aspect of the committee system, therefore, is the statutory-permissive dimension. Committees may be classified in other ways that cut across the above dimension. One of the most important ways is through the distinction between *vertical* and *horizontal* committees. A vertical committee is one which is concerned with all aspects of one service, such as education, fire brigades, smallholdings or police; a horizontal committee is concerned with one aspect of all services, such as finance, establishments, supplies or contracts. The role of horizontal committees has tended to increase over the years as council members and officers have reacted against the special form of fragmentation of decision making that results from a stress on individual public services as defined by the central government. The new forms of internal organization all attempt to promote horizontal functions above vertical services in the working of the decision making framework.

Committees may be permanent or temporary. Most committees are permanent in the sense that they are reappointed each year at the annual meeting of the council and meet at regular intervals in the cycle of meetings, but some are appointed for special short term or non-recurrent purposes, and disappear when these have been fulfilled. These provide a necessary element of flexibility in the system in the face of a changing environment; for instance, they may be used to deal with problems that do not fit into any of the neat categories of the permanent committee system.

In the latter case they are likely also to be a form of joint committee – one formed by two permanent committees – a category which is most important in the relationship between separate authorities. This often occurs when the proximate environments of two or more authorities overlap, or where joint action has certain obvious advantages of economy and effectiveness.

A committee system consists of a pattern whose elements are the types of committee mentioned above, but before considering the pattern itself it is important to examine the attributes of individual committees.

COMMITTEES

Apart from the characteristics that derive from the committee's method of composition and powers given to it by the council, probably the most significant factor is its *size*. The number of members on a committee affects the sort of meetings it will have in terms of formality and friendliness; it affects both the speed and expertness of decision making; and it affects the 'burden of work' laid on council members generally.

Like councils, however, committees only effectively exist when they are meeting. It is the committee meeting that is part of the information flow and decision-making systems of the local authority.

Most of the people present at a committee meeting are council members, one of whom is almost invariably the presiding officer of the committee – the committee chairman. Committee meetings experience the same vagaries of attendance and absence that council meetings do. A selection of chief officers will also be present, including the professional officer most concerned with the committee's business, a representative of the clerk's and the treasurer's department, and other officers whose attendance is dictated by one or more items on the agenda. In attendance also will be the committee clerk responsible for the particular committee. The presence of officers is thus a function of the business coming before that particular meeting, and apart from the committee clerk, none are universally necessary.

Whether press and public are also present is a more difficult matter. Traditionally local authorities did not permit the public to attend committee meetings at all, and the press only if they accepted restrictions on reporting. The tendency of recent years, however, has been against secrecy in public affairs, and it was argued that because *de facto* committees were so important in decision making press and public should both be admitted, at least to some committees and some parts of others.[10] The law now requires the admission of press and public to some committees, and many councils have gone much further than the minimum legally required, reserving only a few types of item for private consideration.

CO-OPTION

The other type of person who may be present is the co-opted member of the committee. This again is a matter on which there is a considerable variation between authorities. In some cases the law requires that certain persons be co-opted and in others it does not permit it at all. In many cases the co-opted member is a full member of the committee, except that he is not on any other committees or the council itself, whilst in others he may have an advisory rather than a decision-making role.

The processes of co-option are often ignored in discussions of local government because it is not a very important part of the decision-making system; but it has considerable significance both as a reflection of the underlying structure of the local authority and as a sign of system-environment relationships.

The two dimensions of co-option are the *statutory-voluntary* and the *expert-representative*. In the first case the co-option of certain types of people on to a particular committee is required by law; it is part of the statutory committee system. Thus there are justices on police committees and education committees are constituted according to a scheme approved by the minister. For other cases the local authority has a choice of whether to co-opt or not, and this power has been exercised in vastly differing ways. Councils have tended to favour co-option in the cultural and recreational fields whilst avoiding it in the environmental sphere.

A person may be co-opted because he or she is regarded as an expert on the subject matter with which the committee deals, and thus has skill and knowledge to contribute to the discussion and decision making. Others are co-opted because they belong to another body or organization judged to have a considerable interest in the committee's work; sometimes the outsiders are permitted to nominate their own representatives rather than have the council itself choose them. Some co-options combine both motives as when a doctor or dentist is co-opted to a health committee and a teacher to an education committee.

But these dimensions say little about what sort of people are actually chosen and how they are recruited. Though there is little hard evidence on this subject, it is fairly clear that co-option in general involves people who are like serving council members. In some cases they are former councillors who have retained their membership of one committee, in effect, after leaving the council itself; some are councillors-to-be, and in some authorities they are actually wives and husbands of members. In partisan authorities they are often party members, because it is easy to find people who combine that with expertise or representativeness.

Co-option was seen as another way of 'escaping' from the consequences of having local elections but, as with the aldermanic system, it must fail in this objective. Only those who are known to serving members are likely to be co-opted (the right to nominate introduces a different factor), thus only those with some organic connection with the existing council, such as family or partisanship, are likely to be considered. What counts, therefore, is the behaviour of the council members, and system-environment relationships are important here as elsewhere.

Some of the problems in the role of co-opted members as conventionally pictured tend to be ignored by those who stress its desirability. The outside expert may clash with the council's own employee; representative co-option may give certain groups a favoured position; and the values and perceptions of the individual have not had legitimacy conferred on them by election. It is easy to see that the co-opted member does not bear the same responsibility for decisions as does the council member, particularly in the financial sphere – and they are excluded by law from finance committees. Co-opted members must therefore necessarily play rather different roles, even if they are full members of a committee, from the ordinary council member.

BUSINESS TRANSACTED AT COMMITTEE MEETINGS

Though the same categories of business may be found at a committee meeting as were found at its council counterpart, the balance will be different and the style of interaction of a distinct flavour. Though there is likely to be some ceremonial and ritual business this will be a minor part, and the stress generally will be on decisions. If the committee has its own elaborate subcommittee system then most of its business will arrive in the form of a report or minutes. Otherwise large parts of the business will be based on officers' reports, surveys and recommendations, or on the previous meeting's business. Committee work has an on-going character that cannot easily be appreciated from the observation of one meeting only.

Other sources of items of business are previous meetings of the council and other committees. Some items originate in a direct action by a member of the public or outside group, or by particular request of a committee member. Committee meetings therefore are occasions on which information may enter the decision-making system of the local authority and are thus important aspects of its relations with the environment. Though often committee agendas are very traditional documents, in times of a changing environment they will reflect this through a rising proportion of new items of business.

Discussion in committee is usually much more informal and often not bound by the elaborate rules of debate that govern many council meetings. The chairman is much more likely to be a leader rather than a neutral presiding officer, and interventions from all present, except members of the press and public, are often more spontaneous. Officers will speak frequently and more frankly, not always waiting for a formal request from the chair to intervene. The interaction between officials and elected representatives, which will begin before the meeting and continue afterwards, is an important part of the operating system of a local authority, and accounts for many aspects of the style of decision making found in many systems under the traditional pattern of council organization. New patterns which reduce the number of committees and the frequency of meetings may have unintended consequences for the tone of human relations within the authority.

SUBCOMMITTEES

Much of what has been said about committees generally applies to subcommittees; their size, number and method of composition will affect the working of the local authority in several distinct ways. This discussion need not be repeated, but there are a number of special points about subcommittees that must be mentioned.

A committee may have an elaborate system of subcommittees reporting to it as many education committees do, but for most the subcommittee is an element of adaptabality and innovation to be used as and when required. The frequency of meeting of subcommittees therefore tends to be more erratic, and a higher proportion are probably temporary rather than permanent bodies.

As subcommittees are even less formal than committees in general, and more detailed in the matters they consider it is likely that both the role of officers and of co-opted members will be more significant. In fact the arguments against a co-opted member becoming chairman are much weaker. But the role of subcommittees is such that it is not to be expected that either press or public will be present.

Some committees use the device of the *visiting committee,* which is usually a subcommittee of two or three whose function it is to make visits to the property and sites controlled by the committee between meetings, and to report back. They are available to be called upon by a chief officer to inspect an installation so that a lay opinion can be expressed at the next meeting. Equally important is their function in the education of members, for the visits enable them to make acquaintance with 'plant', personnel and problems in a way that daily life and the committee meeting do not.

Party organization on the council

It has been remarked that not all councils have partisan members; those that do not lack the informal organization that can be an important part of the life within the system for the individual. It is to be presumed that on independent councils cliques and the like form and disappear spontaneously, but little is known about these, other than that some observers have seen 'sinister' groups as the real power in the authority.

The minimum degree of party organization is the meeting of all members of the party on the council, sometimes with observers from the outside party. The role of this meeting varies tremendously. It may simply meet before a council meeting to discuss the agenda, but its resolutions may be only advisory and attendance may be regarded as optional. On the other hand attendance may be required in the absence of good reasons and decisions are binding on members, on penalty of expulsion from the group.

Some party groups elect a committee of leaders from amongst

their number to monitor the business coming before the group meeting, and generally to act as a sort of executive. In some cases this committee achieves an ascendency over the meeting and provides political leadership which extends throughout the council. In some cases the members of a particular council committee will meet beforehand to discuss the agenda for the next meeting, and similar variation is found in respect of these pre-committee discussions. Finally, council members will expect to discuss council business across the board in meetings of the ward party to which they belong, if the ward is an active one.

It is hard to overestimate the effects of strong partisan organization on the life of the council member.[11] It may also double the demands on his time arising from council membership, by requiring attendance at two parallel sets of meetings. It introduces many different constraints into the ability to behave in different ways – in relations with other council members, with officers, with outside groups and with constituents. But there is no standard form of these effects as each aspect is modified by the overall pattern of partisanship within the authority – for instance, by the extent of party control and by relations between the parties. It is therefore worthwhile considering briefly the nature of party systems in local government.

The earliest characterizations of parties in local government simply compared the local council with the Westminster model of legislative politics and found that very few councils even approximated to the national system. This was replaced by more complicated classifications.

If the differences between individual parties are ignored, a fourfold classification can be produced on the basis of two dichotomies; parties either contest or do not contest elections – parties either do or do not attempt to control the council. This typology is represented by Figure 7.

If parties both contest elections and control the council there is a fully developed party system, which is found in many large cities of the country – Leeds, Wolverhampton, London and Sheffield, for instance. Where parties contest elections but make no real effort to control the council there is a semi-party system, which may sometimes deceive the outsider by the rhetoric of electioneering. This type is illustrated by Glossop, Newcastle-under-Lyme RD and Torquay. If parties do not contest elections but members come together as a caucus or group to influence council decision making there is a 'concealed' party system. There are no well authenticated

parties control the council? / parties fight elections?	yes	no
no	**partisan systems** London County Council Wolverhampton CBC Sheffield CBC Salford CBC Cheshire County Council Leeds CBC	**'secret caucus' systems**
yes	**semi-partisan systems** Glossop NCBC Newcastle-under-Lyme RDC Torquay NCBC	**non-partisan systems** Devon County Council (1945) 'Ashworthy' PC St. Thomas RDC

Fig. 7 **A Simple Typology of Party Systems**

Note: The examples quoted are either to be found in the case-studies listed in the bibliography, or have been studied personally by the author.

examples of this, though it exists in the mythology of some areas. The fourth category is the genuinely nonpartisan system, where parties are absent from both elections and council. This was very common in terms of number of authorities, though in terms of population living under it it was not as significant as the fully partisan one.

It is soon found that this fourfold classification system is too simple for all but the most elementary purposes of understanding. It represents complicated situations too crudely for elaborate analysis and the dichotomization of each aspect leads to the loss of much information. It is often extremely difficult to use because it requires judgement of complex matters of fact and weighting of different behaviours without any proper guidance.

To avoid these problems understanding local government may be advanced by not trying to reduce complicated phenomena to two or three or several categories, but by taking the original facts of behaviour as *dimensions* of party systems as factors in their own right; relations between them cannot be settled by *fiat*, as classification systems imply, but must be established empirically.

To some extent this has already been done when the party system of the locality was considered above. Party politics in the local political system were indicated by such dimensions as *competitiveness* and *partisanship attachment* in local elections. Aspects of behaviour of both electors and activists contribute to the picture of the local party system.

Within the local authority the first aspect of partisanship to be considered is the party composition of the council, and from this the derived patterns of dominance, if any. This dimension must always be given a temporal interpretation; the proportions held by one party may vary dramatically or may be relatively constant over a period of time. Other sets of factors are not so easily measured because they involve the relationship between parties. These are often called the 'conventions' of the local constitution; they are not legal rules but customs which are accepted as important determinants of the behaviour of council members. The conventions which are important are those which govern the distribution of 'patronage' – choice of aldermen, mayor, committee chairmen and outside nominees, for instance – and voting behaviour in council and committee.[12] In multi-party situations there is the possibility of alliances of different sorts; a coalition may in fact dominate the council or there may be a shifting pattern of reciprocal support accompanied by some indiscipline in partisan voting producing a situation not unlike an independent council in terms of unpredictability of votes and consistency of policy.

The party organization itself must be treated in similar manner. The organizational structures that are created on partisan councils vary in a large number of dimensions. Some are extremely simple and have little positive effect, whilst others have extremely complex arrangements, as in Leeds, with party meetings of various sorts, leaders, whips and party discipline throughout the council and committee system. Herbert Morrison was able to give an account of the London County Council under his leadership which made it resemble Parliament, whilst the party groups in Newcastle-under-Lyme RD were themselves affected by the local basis of politics in the area.

One effect that has been frequently discussed in the past has been on the relationships between officers and party organization.

Most people are agreed that the conventions of impartiality prevent officers attending informal party group meetings and generally being active in partisan affairs. But this may have the consequence of removing the influence of experts from direct contact with what is *de facto* the most important single location of power in the authority – or, if chief officers are leading policy makers, of devaluing the party meeting. Individual members can act vicariously for officers, but this places a great deal of reliance on the layman's abilities. Some councils have side-stepped the problem by appointing a policy committee of majority party members only; as an official committee its meetings can be attended by officials with perfect propriety.

Council, committee and subcommittee meetings, and the work of party organization are bound together into a complex structure through which information flows and which dominates the lives of all council members and chief officers, and some of the other officials.[13] This cycle of meetings provides the general rhythm of systemic activities and provides points of reference for many aspects of decision making. It is a major avenue of access to the system from the environment.

Employee structures

The main elements of employee organization have already been mentioned in the previous chapter. As the institutional forms in which they work are those of formal organizations or 'bureaucracy' most of the relationships within the organization are the hierarchical ones familiar in many walks of life – super- and sub-ordination, and equality of rank. To a large extent, therefore, their operations may be analysed in the terms thought suitable in management thinking generally.

In the previous chapter the basic unit – the department – was described in terms of four locations at which work is carried out. This account needs to be supplemented by an analysis of these structures as formal organizations.

DEPARTMENTS

A department was defined as all those employees who are under the hierarchic supervision of the same chief officer. It consists of a headquarters staff and varying numbers of satellites, which may be area offices, institutions or depots. Virtually all local authority departments have the sort of structure which leads the sociologist of organizations to classify them as 'professional organizations'. Much of the general thinking about the differences between these and non-professional organizations is helpful in developing an understanding of local government.

All organizations may and do contain people who have some recognized professional, technical or scientific qualification, or who are in the process of acquiring one. Whether obtained internally or prior to membership the qualification is accepted in the outside world as an authoritative sign of expertise in the specified field. A professional organization is simply one in which those qualified in the substantive field of the organization's activities are at the top and those who have a general educational qualification, however high a status this may have, are in the lower positions. In a non-professional organization the positions are almost reversed; generalists occupy the leading roles, including that of head, and specialists are confined to a group of middle-range positions.[14] The two contrasting types of organization may be represented schematically in the crude but helpful manner of Figures 8(a) and 8(b). Most industrial and commercial organizations are basically non-professional in structure, as are the departments of the civil service, but local authorities have patterns of departmental organization which are based on the supremacy of the professional.

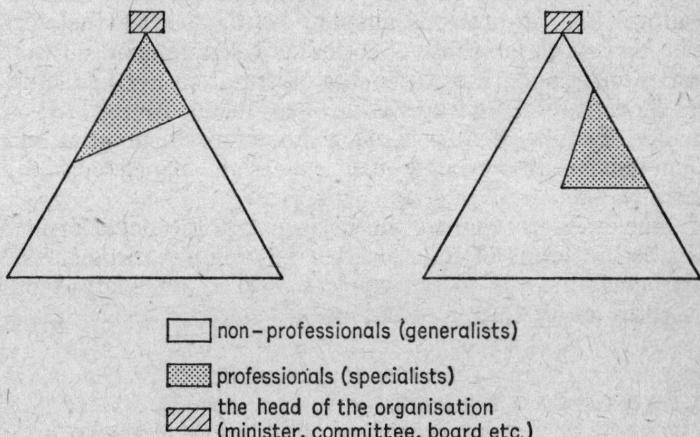

Fig. 8 (a) **A Professional Organization**

Fig. 8 (b) **A Non-Professional Organization**

One important consequence of the fact that local authority departments are professional organizations has already been discussed, when the difference in life chances between specialists and generalists was explained. But not only is the tone of human relations within the organization affected, but the fact has large consequences for the overall pattern of internal organization of local authorities. The number, sizes and types of department are all strongly influenced by the law and practice governing the appointment of chief officers; powerful forces are generated which press the individual council in particular directions.

Many of the characteristics that were important in the committee system are relevant to the study of chief officers and departments. Some statutes make the appointment of a chief officer of a certain type mandatory and this virtually guarantees the creation of a department to work under him. The law relating to such appointments has traditionally been rather complicated because of variations in provisions for approval of the person appointed and for dismissal. In the new system there has been some simplification but a noticeable number of these statutory appointments have been left in existence.

The local government world has often objected in principle to these obligations on local authorities because they pick out certain services for special treatment and because they introduce an element of inflexibility into the internal organization of the individual council. But many individual authorities have shown the same sort of ingenuity they showed with the committee system and exploited the terms of the law in ways that were convenient to them.

Certain other organizational problems are caused for local authorities by professionalism. In the local government context it is highly advantageous to be able to 'prove' that one's occupation is a true profession because this is the way to higher salary, higher status and greater working autonomy within the local political system. The Maud Committee called this 'pseudo-professionalism' because it led to unreasonable claims for professional status, attempts to separate activities from each other and a waste of highly trained manpower – for instance, in treasurers' and public health departments and libraries. It also combined with the statutory obligations to produce administrative systems with a large number of separate departments, especially in county boroughs and in the large authority, with consequent problems of co-ordination and integration of work activities. District councils with small populations and few responsibilities obviously did not have the same number of departments as did Birmingham County Borough.

Departments also differ in terms of size, function, heterogeneity, the use of area offices and the number of institutions and depots attached to them. These factors are not unrelated. For instance, the average size of a local authority's departments depends not only on the size of population served but also on the heterogeneity of the minor professions attached to it. Some departments have typically depended on one major profession, such as civil engineering, and have attached to it a number of professions that are minor in local government terms, such as horticulture and chemical engineering. Under the traditional system the medical officer of health was in charge of quite a large number of distinct semi-professionals and technicians.

Of particular interest are the two horizontal departments usually based on law and accountancy – the clerk's and treasurer's. These two professions are much more organizationally-oriented than many others and they have played crucial functional roles in the operation of the decision-making system. In fact they have frequent contacts with all other departments and with all committees, whereas many of the others are operationally more self-contained.

In recent years there has been a determined effort in many authorities to reduce the number of separate departments, often by a simple policy of merger, to the extent that the statutory chief officer provisions will allow. The most favoured way of doing this has been to interpose a layer of directors or chief co-ordinators, five or six in number, between the heads of each profession within the authority and the committee system. It is not clear at the present moment how far this has worked in the ways envisaged by its originators – how far a new integrated directorate has emerged rather than the old arrangements continued under what is little more than an umbrella name. The retention of the title 'chief officer' for those who are not members of the directorate also indicates a variety of possible working relationships.

SECTIONS

There is a sense in which the section is the basic working group or unit of employee organization. It may be suspected that sections retain their identity throughout considerable departmental re-organizations, being simply linked with a different set of other sections under a new name. It may be that sections tend to be equal in size to the number of people who can be properly accommodated in one room in the council offices, or that other aspects of physical layout of buildings influence the internal structure of departments.

Sections differ amongst themselves in the same sort of ways that departments do. Some have a primarily horizontal function whilst others are vertical groups. Some sections will be of higher status and importance than others. Some will have more frequent contact with sections in other departments. Sections may be grouped into divisions or branches, especially if the department itself is a loose confederation of related activities. Some will be largely composed of generalists whilst others will have a higher proportion of specialists.

Thus many of the things that were said about the department as a whole could be repeated about the section.

THE AREA OFFICE

One of the most distinctive features of the administration of services in extensive authorities is the *area office* – that is, the office created to deal with the problems of a part of the total territory of the council and located away from headquarters. It is an example of field administration within local government itself, and was a marked feature of county government and the government of London in the traditional system. It was found in elementary form in the large county borough. Present evidence suggests that it is likely to be even more prominent in the new system as generally counties have larger populations and wider and more disparate areas to administer.

The area office will vary in size from one person, perhaps operating from home, to a miniature replica of headquarters. The study of Birmingham undertaken for the Redcliffe-Maud Commission showed that in the four chosen departments the degree of territorial decentralization varied considerably, but there was a general consciousness of the need for it and its problems. In Devon before 1972 the county council's area organization ranged from 105 and 61 'outposts' of district nurses and health visitors respectively to the 11, 4 and 3 divisions of surveying, architecture and fire services respectively.[15]

Certain general problems are always likely to appear in field administration. The first of these is the question of the degree of autonomy given to the head of the area office. Geographical separation gives greater scope for some independent action, which may lead headquarters to institute stricter controls, with consequent effects on the speed of decision making, or it may lead to the 'capture' of field administration by the forces of localism. Related to these problems is the question of the pay and status of heads of area offices, which affects the willingness of officials to take a turn in the field and the respect accorded their judgements by headquarters staff.[16]

Secondly, if decentralization within the authority is on a large scale, the problem always arises of the relationship of one department's areas to those of the others. Traditionally each department would settle on its own desirable pattern of areas and locations of area offices, with the consequence that the citizen of a particular part of a county could find himself dealing with local offices in different towns and belonging to one area for one purpose and another for others. In recent years a greater awareness of the existence of area administration within authorities has led to an appreciation of the confusion and inefficiency that an incoherent pattern of areas and offices can create. There has therefore been a movement of opinion in favour of miniature town or county halls to co-ordinate the work of a number of decentralized services.

INSTITUTIONS AND DEPOTS

Some institutions and depots are attached to an area office; indeed the main function of the latter may be to control the former within its area. Others, however, are satellites of headquarters directly. Institutions are so diverse, and depots so little studied, that they will not be considered here at any length. What is important from the overall perspective of this book is the way in which they are fitted into the decision making and operating systems of the local authority.

Both vary tremendously in terms of size – schools for instance, range from the very small to the very large, police stations include the dwelling of the local constable as well as the big urban establishment, and sewage works are sometimes only a field and a hut rather than a massive industrial plant.

The separateness and self-sufficiency achieved by an institution also vary considerably. Schools and police stations probably operate from day-to-day with relatively little contact with headquarters, though they are closely bound by general rules; welfare and children's homes may become very inward looking, whilst libraries, museums and clinics are much more open institutions. The important fact about most institutions and depots is that they exist *between* the parent department and the public, and their systemic importance often derives from their impact on the latter. The public image of a local authority is derived in part from the behaviour of policemen, road menders, firemen and librarians.

The officers of systemic importance in institutions and depots, like those in area offices, are the ones who deal with headquarters. In practice this means the formal leader of the organization – the chief inspector, the headmaster or headmistress, the warden and the curator. Although little is known with confidence about these roles, it is clear that they are of great significance in the overall pattern of operations and at the system-citizen interface. A considerable part of the 'outputs' of local authorities impinges on the environment through depots and institutions, and the positions that link those who carry out the service with the rest of the system are necessarily of strategic importance.

This completes the picture of the *elements* of local authority organization. The miniature political and administrative system that is embodied in each local authority is built up out of people, out of many different types, and out of the characteristic organizational forms that they have developed for their purposes. The system itself consists of the interaction of these aggregate units – the pattern of operations which includes all of them – and itself creates specific roles for the individuals.

In the picture that follows an emphasis is placed on the methods by which the operation of the system is given a degree of coherence and integration of activities – usually called creating *co-ordination* within the system. The complexity of the organizational system described above always has a potential for discontinuity, disruption and failure from the point of view of both insiders and outsiders. The system is basically fragmented and therefore special efforts are needed to keep it together.

Chapter Eight

The Internal Organization of Local Authorities; Part 2: Relationships and Processes

In the exposition so far the individual local authority has been presented first as a collection of different types of individuals, and second, as a set of institutions and organizational forms into which the elements are aggregated. But to see either council members and officers or committees and departments as entities which can be understood by themselves is completely mistaken. For in every case the behaviour that they exhibit at every point in time must be seen within the context of the relationships and processes that bind them together within the confines of the individual political system.

The next step in understanding local government therefore is to examine the relationships between the different parts of the system and the typical processes that give the local authority its form, its characteristic ways of behaving and its individuality. In this chapter, therefore, further vital steps are taken towards an understanding of the main concern of this book – the system-environment interaction which is created by the coexistence of an individual political unit and its own particular context.

The two main structural relationships for most local authorities are those between the council and its committees, and between committees and departments. It is not worth giving separate consideration to the relationships between the council and its departments, as these are mainly mediated by the committee system.

The regulation of these relationships is one of the main functions of a council's standing orders. In principle this is a much more important function than that of regulating the conduct of meetings in strict detail – providing elaborate rules of Parliamentary procedure – but often it is given less attention than it warrants. What standing orders do is provide for the operation of the committee system within the framework of council meetings, and govern the relationships between council members and officers. In modern terminology, therefore, standing orders could be an important tool of management within the authority, and the annual meeting, at which they are renewed each year, an important management occasion.

For both sets of relationships the two most important aspects are the method of *appointment* (of committee members and officers) and the extent of *delegation* of authority downwards.

Allocation of members to committees

Members of the council are allocated to committees at the annual meeting, usually on the recommendation of a committee of selection consisting of the senior members (party leaders where appropriate). The choice of particular individuals for particular committees is governed by a number of factors.

In many authorities one of the most important factors is that of *continuity* – the tendency for members to stay on a committee once they have joined it, provided they do not leave the council. This is a reflection of another factor – the personal preferences of individuals for particular committees – which may well be strengthened by service on that committee. Members may specialize therefore in the work of a particular committee because of original values and because of the socialization that attendance embodies.

Partisanship is a factor about which little need be said. It is obvious that in those councils where parties attempt to exercise control over the business of the authority that some sort of party balance will be maintained on each committee. In fact the composition of committees may be a sign of the degree of partisanship within the system. If this factor is dominant then the others will operate *within* each party.

If continuity and partisanship are important the other factors tend to exert their influence within the framework these provide, that is, when the question of a 'vacancy' arises. In many councils, where committees are informally ranked in terms of status, *seniority* will be important for 'promotion' to the most desirable ones. Personal *preference* also usually plays a part, and is often indistinguishable from *relevance* – occupational, sexual etc. – and *appropriateness* – which often produces committees with a number of members with a qualification in relation to the services administered. Some councils place emphasis on maintaining an *area balance* within each committee, so that matters with a specific locational reference will not be discussed without first-hand lay knowledge being available.

The process of allocation may be influenced by two other considerations. The first is an attempt to ensure that all members have a reasonable burden of committee work. Some councils operate with a rigid formula, but for many it is to be expected that some members will be more active than others. Secondly, there is sometimes an attempt to provide co-ordination between committees by having interlocking memberships of closely related ones, for instance, a health and a social services committee in the traditional system.

Despite the apparent complication of the large number of factors above a committee system in a council with a relatively stable membership will settle down through processes of adaptation of both organization and individual in a pattern which will adjust to small changes in the environment and create a climate within the council which is more than acceptable to the individual councillor. But there is always one source of tension within the system.

The combination of factors listed above is likely to result in committees that are not microcosms of the council itself, even if an area and party balance has been maintained. The differences may be accentuated if council members serve on a committee for a long time. Committees develop their own 'culture' in the way that all small groups do; officers are virtually always more influential in their 'own' committee – provided two or more do not disagree – and they are usually specialists rather than generalists; and the council member will become less and less interested and knowledgeable about the services of committees of which he is not a member. There is the probability that the opinions and preferences of committees will differ from those of the council itself.

There are several ways in which this may be accommodated. Sometimes council members show inconsistent behaviour by voting one way in committee and another in council, where different influences bear on their decision. Another is through a general deference to the opinions of the committee as a collectivity; each committee expects that in return for letting the others get on with their business it will be undisturbed in its work. In some councils the role of interlocking membership and the work of the common service departments will reduce the possibility of conflict between council and committee. But even if all these factors operate the structure will never be entirely free from tension and will sometimes erupt into open conflict, as when a council meeting rejects a health committee's recommendation to adopt fluoridation of water supplies.

Delegation and reference

In view of the potentialities of the situation it is not surprising that there are varying degrees of trust shown by the council for its committees, and therefore varying degrees of discretion allocated to them. This aspect of council-committee relationships is usually discussed in terms of the *delegation-reference* dichotomy mentioned in relation to the council meeting.

If a matter is *referred* to a committee then the result of the committee's deliberations and decision is not action but a recommendation to the council meeting that may be adopted, amended, referred back or rejected.

If a matter is *delegated,* however, the decision of the committee determines what action shall be taken without any consequent authorization from the council itself. It acts in the name of the council, and if it reports its decision to the latter this is for information only, a matter of courtesy or a matter of publicizing its work, and all action, other than comment, by members of the council is prohibited.

Any matter which is not specifically delegated is deemed to be referred to the committee; thus attention focuses on the methods and extent of the former, leaving the latter as a residual (even if it is a residue equal to virtually all the original). It has already been remarked that some things – particularly levying a rate or precept, raising a loan and promoting a private bill – cannot by law be delegated. But for the rest there are two methods by which executive responsibility can be allocated. First, the council may delegate only specified matters, reserving everything not mentioned *de facto* in the control of the council meeting. Secondly, it may delegate all parts of a service, except those specifically reserved for council determination. The latter is appropriate when delegation is extensive, as it often is when councils meet infrequently, and when trust of committees is high. The method reserves to the council meeting only those major matters which have been judged to be too important for committee decision alone.

But extensive delegation may make co-ordination more difficult as it reduces the flow of information through a reduction in the amount of publicity given to committee activities. In practice the balance between *speed* and *openness* of decision making is influenced by a number of factors; in particular, partisanship, the tone of human relations within the council, the amount of work the authority has to do, the meeting cycle, the technicality of the subject itself and attitudes to the public within the system.

Committee-department relations

Committee-department relations are one of the most important aspects of relations between the two types of person involved in the local authority, but only a proportion of them occur in a collective rather than an individual form. That is, many of the individual interactions between a council member and an employee derive from their respective memberships of a committee and a department. The classic example of this is the relationship between a committee chairman and the chief officer of the relevant service department. There are in fact three important dimensions of collective interaction – the committee meeting, which has already been discussed, the appointment, discipline and dismissal of officers, and the delegation of decision-making powers by committee to chief officers.

APPOINTMENT, DISCIPLINE AND DISMISSAL

The question of establishment work (or personnel management as it is often called) in local government is a somewhat complex one.[1] There is no space here to deal with it systematically but attention will be focused on those aspects in which a committee may be expected to play a part.

One point is clear. Though junior officers and other employees low down in the hierarchy may be appointed by other officers, acting as individuals or collectively, this is not possible for the chief officer positions. It would be quite inappropriate for them to be appointed by other chief officers or a chief executive, or by their predecessor in the role. But not only is there no one else to make the appointment, it would be wrong for council members to be excluded. The major part of a chief officer's task lies in dealings with council members and their organizational structures. Thus the degree to which chief officers are congenial and sympathetic to elected representatives (and therefore also the general public) is an important aspect of their qualification for the position.

The difficulty arises as one moves down the departmental hierarchy. For instance, it is from the ranks of deputies or assistants that future chief officers, not necessarily in the same authority, are chosen. They will also deal with council members to a considerable extent. Should they therefore be appointed by the committee?

The extent to which council members are involved in the appointment process will depend to a large extent on the size of the authority, but other factors, including tradition, it may be expected, will also affect the situation. Disciplinary measures and ultimately dismissal must also often involve council members, as they are collectively, the employer, but their involvement in the processes, other than in the most serious cases, will also vary through the influence of a number of factors. Some councils appoint a joint staff committee to consider employee matters throughout the local authority.

The tension in this aspect of relationships between council members and employees arises because the former cannot avoid the responsibility for being *the* employer, yet personnel matters have very large technical elements in them, about which laymen are not qualified to judge. The great security of tenure that officers, particularly chief officers, enjoy means that wrong decisions can haunt a council for many years. Employees also rightly feel that as local government is their career they should be given some guarantee of a stable working environment and a predictable future, both arguments for restricting the influence of elected members.

DELEGATION TO OFFICERS

For many years the question of delegation to officers was confused by its apparent *de jure* prohibition and its obvious *de facto* daily occurrence. Though some very small authorities managed to put a high proportion of the decisions of the authority in the minutes, it was found that the same matters in other authorities, particularly the large ones, were treated as matters of administrative routine. In 1968 the delegation of planning control decisions was permitted to named officers of the council, and this was regarded as a major innovation in local government.

Perhaps in view of the unsatisfactory state of opinion in respect of this question, the 1972 Act has specifically empowered councils, committees and subcommittees to arrange for the discharge of their functions through officers, thus regularizing the ordinary state of affairs.

In schemes of radical reform of local government administration delegation to officers plays an important part, because the only way in which greater speed can be introduced into decision making is by taking out the stages that involve council member organization. Many reformers also see this as a way to change council and committee agendas so that elected representatives concentrate on the things that they are best at or which are important enough for them to consider.

No one can doubt that the decision-making role of officers is of vital importance in the functioning of local authority systems, but the above picture, which presents it as a matter of technical decision making, does not do justice to the tensions between the roles of officer and council member. For ultimately the council member as part of the collective authority cannot disclaim responsibility for any item which pressure groups, the press or constituents draw to his attention. Notice that the discretion to make a matter one of public controversy is not in the hands of the council member but is open to all outsiders: it can and will develop in the environment.

This fact must colour all elected representative-employee relationships. There was in fact much to say for the traditional system in its ability to adapt to changing patterns of controversy; items which were straightforward passed through 'on the nod' whilst those that were difficult or the subject of public debate could be aired at the only level possible – that of council member organization. The price to be paid for this flexibility was a slowing down of the decision-making process – but few are happy with rapid but wrong choices.

The difficulty with understanding member-employee relations is that they are harder to observe, even when compared with intra-party behaviour, than any other aspect. The formal interaction reaches out in both implications and causes to remote events and factors. Nor can the reports of either council members or officers help, as each has little appreciation of the values and perceptions that affect the other's behaviour within the system.

The 'agenda' of local politics

The 'agenda' of local politics consists of the issues that are of concern to the council at a particular point in time. These vary enormously in salience and importance, from trivial (to the outsider) personal cases to questions of what sort of future the locality may have. The sources of items for the 'agenda' are equally varied; they range from international affairs, which may cause an alert of the council's emergency services, through the demands of the national government, which may require the provision of a new public service, to a minor local mishap, such as the dislocation of a sewer. To a large extent the council does not have control over what is on this 'agenda'; items are forced on its attention by the environment.

Little can be said in general about the sort of things that are likely to exist in all or most environments, but this does not matter here because the focus is on systemic response, which must necessarily be adapted to the *uncertainty* that characterises all localities. Eventually choices, problems, controversies, personal crises and the like become items of business in the local authority's decision-making system. The ways they are dealt with constitute a response by the system, and this will be complicated by such facts as the structure of problem – does it fit neatly into the organizational pattern? – and the importance ascribed to it by members and officers.

The flow of business

Up to this point the relationships within the system have been described in structural terms, but the system also operates on a day-to-day basis, when items (for want of a better word) are passed from location to location within it, occasionally coming into and occasionally going out of the formal decision-making apparatus.

It is a consequence of the specification adopted here of the system-environment boundary that items can only enter or leave the system at definite points: at a council meeting; at a committee meeting; at a subcommittee meeting; at a party meeting; and through contact with an employee. Each of these has its own characteristic devices for permitting the entry of business into the system.

Once business is within the system it may be transported in a multitude of ways, and follow any one of an infinite number of paths. It may move from any meeting to any other, provided only that the second is later in time than the first; it may move from meetings to officers and from officers to meetings; and it may move between officers.

As has been seen, some parts of this system can be represented simply and accurately by the use of a few diagrammatic conventions in the manner of the familiar flow chart of network analysis. The example given on page 140 is only intended to show the simplest system in operation; any realistic chart would show several committees of each type and, if the authority were partisan, a sequence of party meetings integrated in the same way in the overall pattern.

In some cases when business passes into the departmental system it creates its only informal temporary committees or working groups, which can be represented in the same manner because they exist only as meetings. If however, an officer works alone on the problem it must be represented rather differently – in fact as a segment of time rather than a point.

In any complicated information flow system several things can easily go wrong. The errors are of two types: those which arise from a fault in a transmission, either in the transmitter, the message or the receptor; and those which arise from a fault of routing, through wrongful inclusion or omission of a stage in the whole process.

The traditional system had regular procedures which dealt in part with these problems. First, there was a tremendous amount of redundancy in the transmission of each message, for it was 'carried' by the minutes of the first meeting and any memoranda generated by these, and in the minds of council members attending both meetings and the officers who service both committees. It is possible to find the effects of 'noise' within a particular authority, but it may be suspected that any 'misunderstanding' this caused was almost deliberate.

Problems of routing are dealt with by the committee clerks and other officers responsible for servicing committees through the minuting and reporting system. To understand how this happens it is necessary to visualize the basic clerical processes used.[2]

Every committee meeting generates its own minutes which are written according to the general rules of minuting. These can only be approved as a correct record of the proceedings by the next meeting of the same committee, but they are the basis of the contact with the council and other committees. If only contact with the council is considered, then there are three distinct ways in which they can be used. First, they can simply be sent *in toto* to the council as part of the agenda for the next meeting, the meeting deciding which items it needs to approve formally and taking the appropriate action. Second, they can be divided into two groups, those which are sent to the council and those which are not. The latter are sometimes called 'private' minutes in contrast to those made 'public'. Thirdly, a special report may be written, based on the committee minutes, which becomes part of the council meeting's agenda.

Each method has its advantages and difficulties. The first system ensures that nothing is not legally done because it did not reach the council that must approve it, but it runs the danger of premature disclosure of business and of libel if confidential matters are discussed in committee. In practice a good clerk should be able to avoid both these quite easily. It can also almost overwhelm a council member with paper, particularly in the traditional system with a large number of committees and a commitment to detailed lay involvement in decision making. This can be remedied in part by symbols which indicate the status of each item and the action that the council meeting can take.

The other two systems may both involve a little extra cost, but their chief difficulty is that by concealing things from the council meeting, they are often concealing them from council members not on the committee and from officers not servicing it, and always concealing them from the press and public.

The problems of routing are basically those of trying to ensure that all (and only) those other committees and officers that ought to be involved in a particular decision-making process are informed of the item and the actions of the previous stages. In many cases, especially in the small authority, this will not be very difficult but as committee systems and departments grow in complexity with the size of the authority a number of general problems tend to appear.

The origins of some of the major difficulties lie in two related phenomena – over-specialization by council members and pseudo-professionalism by officers.[3] Both are encouraged by elaborate subdivision of responsibilities between large numbers of committees and departments, something that has been seen not to be entirely in the control of the individual local authority, resulting as it does in part from central-local relations and the prescriptions of the law, but also from delegation to officers and committees. Fundamentally both are attempts to define a problem in a narrow way so that it is self-contained and within the ambit of the committee or department alone. But the world does not divide up into neat categories that correspond to the artifacts of statute.

Hence the preoccupation in local government with co-ordination. The concept of co-ordination is often misunderstood, because it is regarded as an activity, the process of making things co-ordinated, whereas it is a state of affairs throughout the organization. If it is thought of as the activity then this leads to a search for people or institutions that will co-ordinate; sometimes there is not even a search, as a role is defined hopefully as that of 'co-ordinator'. If it is thought of as a characteristic of the whole organization, not a part of it, then words such a *consistency, coherence, harmony* are the appropriate ones. In fact it is often easier to think of the things that can go wrong rather than of the 'right' state of affairs. Anything that reduces inconsistency or incoherence is therefore a co-ordinating activity.

Matters can go wrong in several dimensions. There may be inconsistency or lack of coherence of activities between different times and different places, between different subject areas, and between different parts of the organization. The actions that are taken to remedy or prevent these are called variously *planning, problem-solving* and *rationalizing*. These tend to fall into two groups: those that require action in or through the committee system, and those that require action in or through the departmental structure. The former tends to be equivalent to what is often called 'policy co-ordination' and the latter 'administrative co-ordination'.

The errors of policy co-ordination arise largely from three factors: isolation of sectors of decision making from each other; the ignoring of relevant facts and ideas; and the lack of a sufficiently long-term perspective. Councils have favoured two answers to these problems. The first is the strengthening of council member organization through the creation of a special committee whose function it is to deal with planning, harmonizing and generalized problem-solving through the authority.[4] The second is to create an officer organization above the traditional departments, or to strengthen the traditional co-ordinating officers (the clerk and the treasurer) so that council members get as good support in this function as they do in questions of professional expertise.

Administrative co-ordination tends to require quite different sort of machinery, and takes place much lower down in the organization. Some of the problems can easily be identified as waste of resources such as land, staff or money. In the case of land something as simple as a register of land owned and/or occupied by the authority, with indications of its future use, including the degree of certainty about its present allocation, can deal with the problem. Staffing is more complicated but it is the province of personnel management – a set of techniques for dealing with the separate aspects of the recruitment, training, promotion and deployment, discipline and removal of staff. Many problems of finance within the authority are the subject of management accounting – another set of techniques, this time concerned with the control and allocation of money. In both cases the existence of the techniques points towards the employment and training of staff in these, and the arrangement of the departmental structure to accommodate them properly.

In fragmented organizations, such as many large local authorities embody, there is always considerable scope for standardized administrative policies and these are the province of other common services, such as central purchasing, filing and information storage generally. If one looks more widely at the problems of administrative co-ordination faced by many local authorities one becomes aware that the vast range of specialized administrative techniques often called 'management services' are highly pertinent.

The discussion of co-ordination has been presented in the sort of terms council members and senior officers themselves use. This is because the subject has become more topical in recent years, but it is still very hard to distinguish reality from pious hopes for a new form of organization. In order to understand an individual authority today the outsider needs to know how it has tried to emerge from reorganization, and what sort of co-ordinating devices it has created. It may have been the victim of the latest fashion in new committees and types of chief officer, or it may have succeeded in restructuring its operating system in significant ways.

A great deal of optimism is often encountered in the literature written by chief officers about these methods of improving co-ordination within the local authority. The problems that the environment generates do not fall into neat categories; nor do all of them have solutions that better organization can guarantee to find. Decision making can only be improved; it can never be perfected. Dilemmas over alternative uses of resources – land for housing or recreation, grants for culture or the needy – and over the interests of the present and the future, for instance, do not permit of tidy problem-solving and co-ordination.

The discussion of co-ordination completes the picture of the structure and basic dynamics of local political systems, a structure composed of people organized into characteristic aggregate institutions, and operating as a system through which items of information and decisions flow. But systems create systemic roles or positions and these must be occupied, if they exist, by individuals. The previous discussion of people in local government concentrated on them in their 'raw' state, but they also acquire personal characteristics which derive from their participation in the system. A fuller understanding of local government can be achieved by examining these roles in relation to the individuals who fill them.

Activities and roles of council members

It is important to stress that in what follows the description is of differentiating characteristics, not universal ones. The question of whether or not a particular individual occupies a given role is an empirical one, and in many cases the answer will be 'no'. Roles are built up out of activities to which participants attach expectations when they occur in stable groups; in the case of council members these are all forms of speaking and voting, though their descriptions will often more appropriately be such expressions as 'opposing and supporting', 'persuading and advising' and 'publicizing'. The concern here is not with the activities themselves so much as the way they are used in the working of the total environment-system interactional patterns.

The first group of activities consists of those that are part of representative roles. The individual council member will have to deal with his constituents as individuals, as components of an interest sector or sectors, as leaders of interest groups and as party members. These would all be called 'input' roles in the strict terminology of systems analysis, for they link the environment with the system. The boundary between the two is drawn, so to speak, through the political life of the individual council member.

The second group consists of roles at the council meeting. Here is found some of the sharpest differentiation between individuals. Though representative roles as above have council meeting phases or facets, the most striking differences are those between leadership and backbench or follower roles. Procedural control of the meeting is largely in the hands of the presiding officer and the leader of the council (in partisan systems) though informal leadership can be achieved by other members who are prepared to use the procedural motions, such as the closure, to expedite business. Leadership in substantive decision making is often largely in the hands of the committee chairman, though his is often a different sort of representational role – speaking for the committee collectively, as other members will be quick to remind him if he places too personal an interpretation on their work.

The third group are those that occur at the committee meeting. In many ways these are microcosms of the council meeting roles, but the structure of interaction will probably be more open and a much more substantial proportion of the ordinary member's life. Committee membership is also the source of other roles – for instance, at the council meeting itself or on some other body. And if one had to nominate one role as the most important over the whole country in local government generally it would be that of committee chairman. This is usually of such structural importance in the system that it will be considered separately at a later stage.

The fourth group consists of the representational roles members have as a result of their membership of the council. Council members formally represent the council on other bodies, such as joint boards, joint committees, local and national organizations, and informally as spokesmen, explaining and defending the actions of the council or a committee. Committee members have similar roles – they may represent the committee on other committees of the same council or on joint subcommittees. Some of the most important ways that such representation occurs is in relation to partisan organization – members 'represent' a committee in the party group meeting and the council itself in the local party.

The fifth group occurs only on partisan councils – those in which party organization plays a part in the political life of the council member. These roles are very much more variable than those described above, because the impact of party within the council is itself so varied.

The major dimensions of party roles within the local authority are: relations with the external party organization, including ward parties; roles within partisan group meetings, which are often replicas of those in council and committee meetings; partisan activities at the council and committee meetings; and roles which relate one party to the others. The importance of each of these varies tremendously from one council to another and from one party member to another.

It is suspected that the host of separate roles described above do not occur independently of each other, that different council members achieve different balances of activities; thus it is possible to identify broad groupings of roles which differentiate individual council members from each other. An American study identified four major types of legislative role in a state legislature – the *lawmaker*, the *advertiser*, the *spectator* and the *reluctant*.[5] Other studies have simplified the categories still further by distinguishing between *leaders* and *led* or *ministerialists* and *anti-ministerialists* (the 'country party'). Ministerialists on a council are distinguished by two facts: they place a greater emphasis on the substantive decision-making role of the council, and the corporate interests of the local authority than on the representation of area, sector, group or party; they also share with chief officers views on the disposal of council business and the policies that the authority should adopt.[6] In some party systems the alliance will be between the leaders of the parties and the officers against sections of the backbenches.[7]

The above description of roles has presented them largely in terms of their location – the occasions at which they occur. This heuristic device can be seriously misleading if it is not realized that the important feature of many roles is the way they penetrate different locations, and help to integrate the separate actions. This is nowhere better illustrated than in the role of committee chairman in the traditional local authority organizational structure. It may be confidently guessed, also, that when the new system settles down it will be found to contain identical roles.

COMMITTEE CHAIRMEN

The role of committee chairmen in the traditional system was extremely important because it brought in its train a host of other activities. The formal basis of the role was the election each year of the individual to preside over meetings of the committee. There is some evidence that committee chairmen did not generally act as neutral 'speakers' in the chair but as leaders of the discussion and decision making. Keeping order at the committee meeting was therefore in practice a very minor activity. Leading the committee discussion and decision making is not, however, and is perhaps the foundation of many of the other roles the committee chairman finds thrust upon him.

First, there is a group of representative roles. The chairman generally represents, or is one of the representatives of, the committee at other meetings – at the council meeting where he explains and defends committee action and recommendations; on other committees, such as the finance committee, and on joint committees or subcommittees; on outside bodies, including party meetings of all sorts.

Secondly, he is a representative in a different sense when he deals with the grievances of individuals, with leaders of interest groups and with the press. The spokesman role for the services for which the committee is responsible will often devolve upon the chairman, though in technical matters the chief officer may play such a role.

Thirdly, he will be in frequent contact with chief officers, both presenting the views of council members to the head of a department, and therefore to employees generally, and in receiving the views of employees through the chief officer. If one had to pick one interaction within the traditional local authority operating system it would be that between committee chairman and the chief officer principally concerned with the terms of reference of that committee. Unfortunately it is more or less completely unobservable.

The fourth role introduces a degree of flexibility into committee operations. Chairmen are often specifically empowered to act for the committee between meetings in determining minor or very urgent matters, and one of the early items of the agenda will be to learn about and if necessary give retroactive approval to the actions of the chairman.

In partisan authorities the chairman will not only represent the committee in party meetings but also the party in committee meetings. There may be considerable tension for the chairman between his partisanship and his other committee roles, and the balance between the two can be resolved in many different ways. The crucial factor is the degree of partisanship in the authority as a whole.

Finally, many committee chairmen will be ceremonial and ritual leaders in the activities for which their committee is responsible – for instance, in making presentations to long service staff, opening new 'plant' and greeting distinguished visitors. Nothing further need be said about these activities.

The picture given so far of the characteristics of council members as occupants of roles has been a cross-sectional one; it portrays the roles as they exist at a given point or period in time. But individuals do not suddenly appear in roles; they have to achieve them over a period of time, and these temporal processes of position allocation can be referred to as a council member's *career*, even though this is only a useful analogy with the career of a local government officer.

THE COUNCIL MEMBER'S CAREER

Some sociologists of organizations analyse behaviour within the individual organization in terms of the existence of three distinct systems. These are *an operating system*, in which the functional activities of the organization are linked together, *a status system*, which allocates prestige to roles and positions, and *a power struc-*

ture, which derives from the influence of individual holders of positions.[8]

In the long run, and provided the environment stays fairly stable, it may be expected that the three systems will be congruent; those with greatest operating importance will have most power and highest status. But this need not be the case in any organization in the short run, and in some types there are structural factors which prevent any full congruence from appearing.

At any given point in time the actions of a council member may be understood largely in terms of his position in the operating system. He is, for instance, a backbench member of two unimportant committees, or he is the leader of the majority party on the council. But changes in his position in the operating system of the council will reflect the force of the other two systems on his long-term behaviour.

It has long been remarked how individuals in organizations experience tension between their own personal needs and desires and the demands of the organization itself.[9] Local authorities are no exception to this conflict but it can be regarded as a positive contribution to the long-term adaptability of the system. The conflict is between the personal preferences, knowledge and abilities of the individual and the systemic structures of power and status, and the two determine to a large extent the changes that will occur in the position of the individual in the operating system. The *temporal pattern* of these changes will be called 'the council member's career'.

For heuristic purposes only let it be assumed that the particular council under consideration has existed in a stable environment for a long time and that within the council member's sector the status and power structures correspond to each other and to the operating system itself. Therefore some committees and some activities are of low status and little power, others occupy middle positions and others are the high status and powerful ones. It is also assumed that individual members wish to progress some way up the hierarchies, though this desire will be modified by a number of personal factors.

The main stages in all council members' careers are: *entry, continuation* and *departure.* From the point of entry to the point of departure the processes will be influenced repeatedly by such factors as the person's individual circumstances, the general state of the system, and the *incumbency* and *seniority* factors.

The point of *entry* to the system is generally regarded as the occasion on which a person is first elected to the council, though a case can be made for regarding first candidature at the start, or in the case of those who have been co-opted, first membership of a committee. If election is chosen then entry may be either at a by-election or an ordinary election (or, in the case of a few aldermen and presiding officers in the traditional system, first co-option). In the short run these may have different effects because in the case of the by-election the system may be adjusted to take into account the difference between the departed and the arriving member, whilst in the latter there is in a sense a restructuring of the whole.

Departure from the council is much more varied. Between elections an individual may cease to be a member through death, disqualification (under several headings) and resignation (for one or more of several reasons); at an election he may not seek to retain office or he may be defeated; also his tenure may be terminated by a 'clean sweep' election or reorganization which abolishes his authority. In the latter cases, if he continues, the observer has the choice of treating the whole as an interrupted career or as two separate careers.

Continuation is simply the result of not experiencing one of the occasions of *departure*. A member continues until his tenure is terminated by one of the above factors. The interest of continuation in the study of local councils lies in the processes that occur whilst a person is a member.

Unless a newcomer to the council has had a prominent high status position in local society he or she will start a council career in a lowly role. The 'freshman' will be allocated to minor committees for the most part and will not be expected to play a prominent part in council debates or to introduce large amounts of new business to committee agendas. As time passes this will change at a rate which will obviously depend partly on the abilities (widely defined) of the member, but will also be influenced by two other factors – *incumbency* and *seniority*.

The *incumbency* factor is one which gives a preference to those who already hold an office and wish to retain it. It is a factor in elections but here it means the tendency for members to remain on a committee until they wish to leave it. The *seniority* factor is one which gives preference to the more senior candidate in terms of council service when two members wish to fill a 'vacancy'. The combination of these two factors defines the *inertia* of the system – the extent to which newcomers to a council can expect to progress within the power and status system of the council.

This point is best examined from the point of view of the individual member. If he wishes he can calculate his life chances within the council by references to these two factors. First, seniority is a relative concept, so that he must look at the drop-out rates of the cohorts more senior than his and at that of his peers. Second, he must look at the turnover rates in committee and other memberships, so that he can estimate the chances of 'vacancies' occurring in different places in the system. His life chances are expressed as a set of probabilities that he will achieve a certain position by a certain time in the future, assuming that he remains a member of the council or returns if defeated.

Thus in the stable, traditional system that has been assumed, a new council member will start in minor committees and, if he remains on one of them, will become chairman; in the meantime he may achieve a more important committee place, and eventually become chairman of that; if he lasts long enough he will be elected to the aldermanic bench, may become party leader and eventually mayor.

The processes described above are never observed in their pure form, because several factors are likely to operate in a given situation to distort or disguise the picture. Two of these relate to the changing environment and two to the personal characteristics of members.

The system of regular and predictable promotion is often destroyed or modified by changing party fortunes in the environment. The extreme case occurs when a new political movement such as a ratepayers' party or a minor national party such as the Liberals or Nationalists experience a sudden upsurge in popular support and make striking gains in the elections. In these cases, as the whole rationale of the movement is a denunciation of the established ways of doing things, the new members are not likely to be satisfied with a system which relegates them to minor roles until they have served for over three years. Much less dramatic adaptation has to take place in systems where the major parties experience an ebb and flow of support which is reflected in the changing party composition of the council. In such cases *seniority* and *incumbency* must bow to *partisan balance*, and the regularity of the system is disturbed.

In addition councils (and political parties) are always on the lookout for new talent, for people who can fulfil what they regard as the key roles in the system. There is usually sufficient flexibility in the system to permit the rapid promotion of a highly suitable person if opinion in the council or party is generally favourable to this. The rules may be reinterpreted, bent or ignored if it suits the leading members of the system. This is aided by the fact that many members settle for lesser roles and lesser participation in the operational and power structures of the council, sometimes because their views on important and unimportant differ from those generally held in the local authority. They are thus happy to serve on what others regard as insignificant committees and carry out minor roles.

The above discussion of council members' roles and careers illustrates the reliance of modern approaches to local government on the development of political science in the last twenty-five years. For councils are miniature legislatures, just as departments are formal organizations. There is nothing in the study of local councils that does not derive from the study of legislative behaviour or some other well defined branch of the study of government. This point, which is fundamental to the conceptual framework recommended in this book can be illustrated again by a consideration of the careers of officers.

The careers of officers

The roles of employees were discussed when the *dramatis personae* of local government were described at the beginning of the analysis of local authorities as miniature political systems. There is no need to repeat or elaborate on this, but it can be taken as the starting point for a discussion of employees' careers, with special emphasis on those in administrative and professional positions, usually called 'officers'. *Career* in this context has its usual meaning.

The effects of departments having the structure of a professional organization are seen throughout the system of career patterns in local government employment. The main consequence is to restrict the chances of getting to the very top to professionally qualified personnel.

For the purpose of understanding organizational behaviour there are two major aspects of a professional qualification. First, it necessitates the acquisition of a specialized body of knowledge, both factual and contextual, which is abstract in fundamentals yet useful in practice. Second, it necessitates the adoption of a code of ethics which requires higher standards of conduct towards others than those of everyday life. The other characteristics attributed conventionally to professions, such as lengthy training, difficult examinations, controlled entry and self-discipline through an authorized body of peers, really depend for their existence on the reality of the code of ethics and the science underlying professional practice.

Local government has always been an institution for *doing*, rather than proposing or requiring; thus it has always needed technically qualified personnel to take action or directly supervise those so doing. The originally significant employees in local authorities were from the classical professions of law, medicine, accountancy and civil engineering, and they needed their professional qualification in order to carry out their duties as then conceived. There can be little doubt that all of these are strictly professions, though with varying degrees of rigour in the disciplines and the code of ethics.

Recruitment to a profession requires reasonable qualifications in general education as a starting point and the ability to carry through lengthy training. It is not therefore surprising that those who are, or expect to be, so qualified expect substantial career opportunities and a decent starting salary. Professional trainees and newly qualified persons are therefore a cadet entry, beginning well up the organizational hierarchy and pre-selected for rapid promotion.

First employment will be to perform a strictly professional task – lawyers will prosecute in court or arrange a mortgage, accountants will audit accounts, engineers will design bridges and architects buildings. But as time goes on the professional will be brought increasingly into touch with council members and the public, and will find increasing elements of organization, supervision, planning and co-ordinating in his daily work. His role becomes more managerial and political in the strict sense of both these words every year.

As work becomes less strictly professional in nature the official is likely to feel personal tension. There may be conflict between the values of work inculcated in his training and the demands of the new role; everyone who has done research on individual authorities in the traditional system is likely to have come across the professional chief officer who still likes to employ the minor skills of his early training – the medical officer of health who takes temperatures and the engineer who visits sites. As a consequence the managerial activities may be badly undertaken; there is no organic connection between professional competence, which was the basis of the promotion of many officers, and managerial ability. In the traditional system many authorities may have exhibited the Peter Principle[10] to an alarming degree: officers stop being promoted only when they achieve a high level of incompetence.

A professional officer who wishes to rise in the hierarchy more rapidly than average has to move between authorities, each time achieving a more responsible position or the same position in a larger authority. The mobility of professionals in contrast to the immobility of generalists and council members is a source of new ideas and values within the system.

In recent years serious consideration has been given to the career patterns of professional officers. Though some have urged that others be given more opportunity to take chief officer positions in departments it is clear that for many years these will be the sphere of the qualified person. Attention has therefore turned to the provision of managerial training in the early and middle years of employment. The Local Government Training Board founded in 1967 made this one of its first priorities, and the Institute of Local Government Studies at Birmingham has found a sustained demand from middle-range professionals. A successful career in local government is increasingly likely to require explicit management training away from the authority itself.

There is some variety in relation to the last step upwards in a career. Some local authorities make a practice of appointing the deputy chief officer to the headship of the department when it falls vacant, having selected and trained him for the succession over a period of time. The crucial step therefore is appointment as deputy. Others make the appointment an open choice, often tending to have a bias against deputies succeeding their chiefs. The rule is usually fairly clear in any authority and an officer may plan his career accordingly.

NON-PROFESSIONAL STAFF

The career patterns of non-professional staff tend to take a different form. In most cases recruitment is on the basis of the possession of some general educational qualification, such as O-level or A-level certificates. The changing educational system has forced many authorities to try to recruit graduates as generalists, as the traditional sources of school leavers have weakened. Not all authorities have come to terms with the problems of providing a career structure for generalists who are graduates, and this may have had some effect on the success of such attempts to exploit new sources of recruitment.

In most cases the generalist will expect to stay within the same authority, moving relatively slowly through a succession of posts with increasing amounts of responsibility and contact with the professional officers within the department. The crucial steps are those that bring a generalist in contact with the most senior professionals, particularly the chief officers, and with the elected element. Thus in many authorities service as a committee clerk will be a significant step in the career pattern; it brings contact with the elected member and with the senior professionals and involves work that is substantially managerial and politically sensitive.

The pressure of life chances in professional organizations has led some generalists to seek the relevant qualification later in life; occasionally a middle-range administrator will be granted secondment to acquire a diploma or certificate which enables him or her to transfer to the professional side of the department's work and thus to restructure employment expectations.

More quantitatively important has been the attempt to create a profession of administration in local government, through the institution of examination systems which provide the generalist with relevant diplomas or other formal qualifications. If these attempts are successful then the generalist will have the chance of a career as a professional administrator, something that would certainly have considerable consequences for local government.

The discussion so far has applied largely to headquarters staff within the main departments of a local authority. Some of the points are relevant to the careers of teachers and policemen who normally work within institutions attached to a department; in some authorities, also, service in an area office might be regarded as part of one ordinary career pattern. Unfortunately there is neither space nor sufficient information available for a proper account of each of these, or of manual employment in local government.

Likewise there is no information at all on the role of temporary and part-time staff in local government. Though some of these will be following a career in which local government service is a phase, most of them cannot be analysed in such terms. This is unfortunate in an analysis which stresses system-environment interactions, because it may well be suspected that such staff play a significant role in the adjustment of the employee organization to short-term and long-term factors within the proximate environment.

Conclusion

This completes another important stage in the argument of this book. In order to interpret local authorities as political systems in their own right it is necessary to have a clear idea of how each one is built up out of diverse elements. The basic elements are individuals, some of whom are elected and some appointed. In their 'raw' state the personnel of the local authority can be described in terms of their general position and characteristics as members of the larger society in which the miniature political system exists. Each type of individual, however, has its characteristic form of aggregate or collective organization; each creates specific institutions *within* the authority for its purposes and activities. These institutions are woven together into the behavioural fabric of the authority by a set of structural relationships and working processes.

Finally, the processes, relationships and institutions interact with the individuals in their 'raw' state to produce characteristic patterns of activity which together create the roles of council members and employees within the operational, power and status systems of the political system. Understanding local government is in large part a matter of being able to interpret the behaviour of different types of person within the local authority and in its proximate environment.

The next stage is to apply the understanding so far gained to some of the subjects that are considered in conventional discussions or descriptions of local government. It is impossible to deal with every one of these, because the logic of the analytical framework necessitates that a topic be treated at length or not at all. System-environment interactions are almost always so complex that to describe them briefly is to misunderstand them.

Part Four
Applications

Introduction

The fourth part of this book has been called 'applications' to distinguish the approach adopted here from the one used by conventional textbooks on local government. In the latter the topics considered in these four chapters, in as much as they are given substantial treatment, are taken with the discussion of the pattern of internal organization in an indiscriminate manner. That is, they are regarded as subjects on the same level as the committee system, the local government service and partisanship.

In contrast it is argued here that these are subjects that can only be properly understood *after* the pattern of systemic behaviour within the context of a specific environment has been grasped. In the first two examples – complex systems of local government and central-local relations – the individual authority, having been abstracted from the country at large, is put back into it, in one case by relating it to other local authorities to whom it has an organic connection, and in the other, to the rest of the system of government which sees it as one of its constituents. In the second two examples – management in local government and the fear of local democracy – aspects of systemic behaviour are considered as such, rather than as objects of external moralizing and external control.

The subjects chosen were selected on several grounds from a long list of possibilities. The first consideration was that there should be one from each of the major spheres of local government, or rather one corresponding to each of the four distinguishing characteristics of primary local government. Second, the subject should be one about which a considerable amount of basic information already existed, even if it is not always interpreted properly. Third, the application of the modern analytical framework should lead to different conclusions from those that are normally drawn in the conventional approach. In practice this means that conventional wisdom on the subject can be shown to be in error.

The test of the approach really does lie in this fourth part. If the application of the concepts to a diverse set of important subjects does not lead to a better understanding of the behaviour of local authorities then the time devoted to mastering a necessarily abstract and complicated argument, vocabulary and point of view is wasted.

Complex systems of local government have been totally ignored in general writings on the subject of local government, yet they always comprised over two-thirds of system and now monopolize it. Understanding complex systems is the most important aspect of the interpretation of the new local government systems' structure of areas and authorities.

Central-local relations have always been largely misunderstood because those who have written about them have invariably done so from the point of view of the centre, as expressed in formal documents such as statutes, regulations and circulars. Once a student begins to examine how an individual local authority has reacted to a particular circular or a specific grant, or how it has interpreted a ministerial request, he finds a very different picture. Indeed, there is the opposite danger – of removing the centre altogether from the analysis and regarding it as a confused, divided and ignorant spectator of the realities of politics and administration at the local level.

The subject of management in local government is particularly apposite for a different sort of reason. Members of local authorities and leading officers have always theorized about the best form of internal organization of the individual council, and in recent years this has become more explicit and more frantic. Thus the framework is being applied to something which is part of the *culture* of the individual political system, and which involves the danger that verbal behaviour will be substituted for an understanding of what is happening.

Logically local democracy should have been considered as the first of the applications, for the local government system gets its original impulses from the institutions of local democracy, and the 'theory' of local democracy depends on the existence of local elections.

But the subjects grouped together under the heading 'fear of local democracy' are more difficult, partly because they are more complicated, but largely because they belong to a neglected sphere of traditional social and political theory. It is appropriate that the more technical applications should be considered first, before an attempt is made to fit the use of the framework into the mainstream of English political thought.

Finally, it should be remarked that even the extended treatment given to each of these subjects here comes nowhere near to exhausting the complexities that local government behaviour exhibits. It is hoped, however, that the applications sketch out in sufficient detail the main features of these aspects of local government, so that a new understanding is obtained of them.

Chapter Nine

Complex Systems of Local Government

There is probably no aspect of local government which is less well understood in general than the structure of complex systems of local government, with the consequent failure to comprehend even the existence of the intricacies of behaviour that it creates.

All local government units must be treated as *complex* in at least two ways. As has been seen, they are systems interacting with their environments in a multitude of ways, and no understanding can even commence unless these relationships are seen from the start as extremely complicated. The previous chapters should also have illustrated the second kind of complexity – that which arises from the elaborately differentiated internal organization of the individual local authority, with the consequent maze of paths or channels that items of business may follow.

Multi-tier local government is complex in a third way; because it necessarily involves the existence of co-ordinate and independent local authorities,[1] it creates complicated patterns of relationships between the upper and the lower levels of local government *within* the boundaries of the whole system. Notice that such systems – for instance, an administrative county, the Greater London area and a metropolitan county – are not themselves local authorities, but geographically circumscribed sets of authorities, with organic connections between them. The appropriate expression is therefore *type* of local government.

This complexity affects behaviour in local government in two main ways. First, it creates behaviour which belongs to the complex system itself, because it exists at two levels or between two authorities. In this chapter such behaviour will be referred to as *systemic* because it contributes to the working of the overall system, and can only be understood as part of the structure of complex local government.[2] Second, the whole system itself is part of the environment of each individual local authority within it – not only the county council, but each district and parish authority. A metropolitan district council can only be understood as part of a metropolitan system.

These fundamental points – factually even more important in the new system – have been missed by virtually every Royal Commission and committee of enquiry into local government, by most individual pieces of research into local government outside the county boroughs, and by every writer of an introductory textbook on local government. This point can be illustrated by considering the proposals made by the majority of the Redcliffe-Maud Commission, and largely adopted by the Labour Government in 1970, for the creation of 'unitary' authorities to govern most of England.[3]

Very few people have commented on the confusion caused by the Commission calling their proposed new authorities 'unitary'. This adjective led most of the commentators and the members of the Commission itself to believe that what they were proposing was a simple system of local government on the lines of the traditional county borough. Nothing could have been farther from the truth. What they in fact proposed was a three-tier system, with provincial councils at the top, the 'unitary authority' in the middle and local councils at the bottom. It is true that originally this was to be a 'middle heavy' system in technical terms, but this cannot obscure the fact that the other councils existed and would have had some role in the overall system. It is well known that administrative forms develop in ways that were not envisaged or prescribed by those who create them – witness the change in the balance of the administrative county in the twentieth century, and the changing role of parish government in the post-war period – and the Redcliffe-Maud structure would have contained strong forces at work to modify the original conception.

The complexity of the proposed system can be appreciated if the position of the individual citizen within it is examined. The individual would have been subject to nine different types of decision-making processes or administrative procedures. He would obviously have been governed by three councils – the provincial, the unitary and the local – and these would have had different impacts on him.

But the system also contained the possibility of three different kinds of delegation or agency arrangement between councils. The provincial council could delegate functions to either the unitary council or the local council (or both) and the unitary council could delegate to the local council (this ignores the three types of upward delegation; these have been very rare in the history of complex systems). All three types of council could if they wished set up their own decentralized administrative machinery – field officers or lay committees responsible for an area within the authority. It is to be expected that extensive authorities of all types would have done this to some extent.

It may be objected that not all of these administrative forms would have existed in every province, and even if they had they would not all have been sufficiently weighty to affect the citizen significantly. Even if this is true it was likely that in most areas most of them would exist – or the system would not have worked in the ways the Commission wanted – and the individual would have been confronted with a system of local government more complex than any he had ever faced before. What is equally important, he would have been quite unaware of the pattern of relationships that would necessarily have developed between the different authorities within the province. Redcliffe-Maud and his Commission wanted to make local government more intelligible to the ordinary citizen; they would only have succeeded in creating the most complex system ever experienced.

The complexities of systemic behaviour generally can be illustrated by a simplified account of one aspect of town and country planning in the old administrative county. In the late 1950s many people became aware that town centres were often functionally and physically obsolescent, and that much money could be made from their redevelopment. This process was a straightforward matter for county borough councils faced with pressure from urban property interests, but in the non-county borough and the urban district it generally required action both by county council and district council.

What happened in many counties was that redevelopment was a joint venture. The county council possessed the legal powers of planning and the technically qualified officers to carry out the research and the implementation of new schemes, but the district council could contribute ancillary legal powers, for instance, in housing, markets, public buildings, even allotments, and local knowledge and interest. A collaboration between the two was therefore one obvious response to the problems of decision making in this field. But the typical situation in many counties was that when the county council proposed to use its legal powers in one part of its territory only it immediately looked to the representatives of that area – the county councillors and the district council. This was the effect of *localism.* The latter was a political and social force of considerable importance in many counties, and involved giving a greater weight to factors relating to the locality than to those relating to the overall system.

The administrative machinery by which the joint venture was carried out was likely to be a joint committee or subcommittee with representatives of both councils on it, often in equal numbers. The way this was likely to work illustrates exactly the importance of systemic considerations. First, the town district council would nominate some of its leading members as representatives on the committee; when the county council chose its members, it would choose those from the area for the most part, some of whom might also be district councillors through dual membership. If the county council chose members from outside the area to represent the county interest then, as the committee would meet for the most part in the town district, these would have a lower attendance rate and would be 'playing away from home'. In the meeting itself, therefore, the values and perceptions of the locality would be reinforced at the expense of those of the county council, despite the formal division of powers. What the actual outcome of decision making was depended on other factors, of course, such as the relative power of officers compared with council members, and the extent to which the full county council reserved a veto role to itself.

It should be clear from the above generalized description that behaviour cannot be understood in a complex system without reference to its systemic aspects. In the sort of case set out above what was seen was the operation of one of the most important systemic forces within complex local government – the force of *localism*.

The description and analysis of complex systems

In order to present a comparative framework in which to describe and analyse the working of complex systems of local government it is first necessary to stipulate what certain words will mean, as there is no widely accepted and appropriate terminology for these purposes.

Each complex system will be referred to as a *county; county government* refers to the overall system. The upper-tier authority will be called the *county council* and all lower-tier authorities *districts;* if there is also a third tier this will be called *parish government.*

The description of any form of county government must begin with the local authorities within it – these are the basic elements of the system. The first point is identify the number of levels of authority within it – two, three, four . . . There will be only one area-wide primary authority – the county council – but there may be one or more secondary authorities with the county as their territory. The first stage in the description of lower-tier authorities is to divide them into distinct legal types, if there are more than one, particularly distinguishing between those that are themselves simple systems and those that are complex – in effect miniature counties, as was the rural district. The legal distinctions may be supplemented with ones based on empirical characteristics if this is thought necessary. One factor that is of general significance is the number of individual authorities within each type of district. The picture of lower-level systems may be completed by the enumeration of the numbers and forms of parish government and secondary authorities with a jurisdiction over only part of the county.

From the information relating to districts it is possible to derive measures of three sorts of geographical balance of the county. *Balance* is measured by the distribution of population (and area if this is important) between legal types of district authority (if more than one), between types of geographical area, and between individual authorities, giving emphasis on the proportion in the largest single district. The distribution of the 'weight' of the system geographically is an important structural factor in all complex systems.

The second stage in the description of county government is the presentation of the division of services between authorities. This can most conveniently be done in terms of separate lists under a number of headings. First, there are the services which in that particular county are allocated to a secondary authority, either throughout the county or in some parts only. Second, some services will be the exclusive duty or right of the county council, and third, some will stand in the same relation to district councils. Fourth, some services will have divided control, in that some aspects have been allocated to the upper and some to the lower tier. Fifth, there are some services whose control is variable, either because they are concurrent powers or because the law does not make a consistent allocation to one or other level. Sixth, some services are subject to compulsory delegation provisions, or 'claiming' as it is more appropriately called. Though these are primarily the responsibility of one level only, in certain closely defined circumstances they may be claimed as of right by an authority in the other level.

From the distribution of responsibilities between levels can be obtained another measure of the *balance* of the system. A system may be either top-heavy, bottom-heavy or balanced, depending on the distribution of services, with account being taken of their relative importance. Instead of a subjective judgement of importance, the analyst may use either the number of staff or one of three financial indices as a measure of the 'weight' of the system.

The easiest and most satisfactory are the financial measures. The basic one is the distribution of expenditure between levels, though in calculating this certain assumptions have to be made. For some purposes it is better to look at income rather than expenditure, in which case the distributions of both grants and tax calls between levels are important. There is the possibility that the weight of the system will be different from the taxation and the expenditure points of view.

The third stage is to set out the legal forms and procedures of the financial processes within the county. Ultimately expenditure decisions, both capital and current, will be in hands of the local council itself, for it fixes its own estimates and rate or precept without direct interference from anyone, including the central government. But various events which involve other authorities may take place before the rate-making meeting. This is particularly noticeable in current finance where matters are delegated and in capital finance when they belong to the category of locally determined schemes.

The administration of local taxation is also a matter of considerable importance. The most significant aspect of this will be assessment of the tax base, especially if this is a district function. But tax collection may also involve interaction between levels; if one is a precepting authority, then the other must act as agent in tax collection for it. The precepting relationship always confers some power on its possessor because the rate collecting authority must always act last, and it may be or feel constrained by what the other has fixed as a tax rate.

Generally the grant system is much less complicated because each authority deals directly with the central government over central grants, but occasionally grants are made within the system, and some systems involve compulsory equalization procedures, over and above those implied by the fact that the county council rate fund is a consolidated fund. In as much as there are elements in the county council level finance operations of differential rating of areas within it, this ceases to be entirely true.

The first three stages are all only matters of discovering the elementary facts of a complex system. To understand its functioning and the behaviour of groups and individuals within it, it is necessary to investigate the structural relationships between distinct authorities. This requires an analysis of much more detailed processes than those indicated above. At least six major headings are required to undertake this.

The first heading concerns elected members. One of the important structural features of county government is the extent and role of dual and triple memberships. The same individual may be a member of both a county council and a district council at the same time, thus uniting what the law puts asunder. Parallel to overlapping memberships of councils are countywide social and political organizations, such as parties and pressure groups, whose internal operating systems will not necessarily reflect the division of the local government system. Again these may be integrating factors, cutting across the division into levels of authority. Council members may also interact in countywide associations, such as a branch of the National Association of Parish Councils (now Local Councils).

Parallel to council member activities are those of officers. An officer may be employed by two or more district authorities at the same time, or by the upper-tier and two or more lower-tier authorities – forms of pluralism. Professional officers also have their countywide associations, for instance of chief financial officers, though the division of services tends to restrict the scope of this to professions employed by the district only, or 'horizontal' officers. There are also an indeterminate number of day-to-day working relationships on an informal basis between officers in different authorities; little is known about the importance of these, though it may be assumed to be at least considerable.

The third aspect consists of relationships between the county council and the district councils as collectivities. Some have already been mentioned, such as the relationships generated by financial processes. Delegation from upper to lower tier can be important in some circumstances. In the traditional system the county council was free to delegate a large number of services if it wished, and had to do so in a small number if a legally qualified council claimed them. In the first case control of the process was entirely in the hands of the upper tier and in the latter in the hands the lower tier. The new system of agency arrangements gave final say to neither level but permitted the central government to determine the matter in cases of dispute, during the transitional year 1973-74.

In addition local authorities may purchase goods and services from each other. For instance a district council may make use of a county supplies department, or buy time on the county computer; it may employ the officers of the county in charge of specialized administrative techniques to carry out a study in its administration. Sometimes, as was seen in town centre redevelopment, the two levels may undertake a joint operation. A good example of this occurs where a county council using its social services powers collaborates with a district using its housing powers to provide grouped dwellings managed by a warden for the elderly.

Finally, there may be an element of *tutelage* by the county council over the district councils in its area. That is, the county council may have some administrative powers, akin to those exercised by the central government, over decision making by the district. It may have default powers or power to approve certain types of decision, as did the traditional county council. Tutelage is relatively unimportant in British systems of local government.

Many of the same points arise with district-district relationships. They may engage in joint operations, forming joint boards or joint committees for this purpose, or very rarely, they may actually form a joint administration. As above they may purchase goods and services from each other. Collectively also they may form county associations of lower-tier authorities.

The fifth aspect is the administrative structure of the county council itself. If the county is an extensive one it is likely that much of its day-to-day administration will be carried out through some form of decentralization. This will possibly mean the creation of area committees or subcommittees, and the creation of area offices – the county's own field administration. The way boundaries of areas are drawn, the location of area offices, the appointment, tenure and powers of personnel are all important aspects of county council administration.

The sixth aspect consists of the factors that contribute to the continuance of the system, and maintain it with at least a minimum degree of coherence. Aggregate political systems, such as counties, are in a state of tension between the forces tending towards disintegration and the forces tending towards greater integration. Though this is not invariably true, often the self-interest of the parts is a force tending to divide the system. The creation of a council is the creation of new interests and demands, and these tend to look for an advantage against the rest of the system. For instance, there are large non-metropolitan districts of a highly urbanized nature, such as Portsmouth and Southampton, which in the next ten years will be looking to form a new metropolitan county and destroy the county just established in that area. The main factor making for integration is the interest of the centre. In complex systems one can detect the interests of the centre which are distinct from the joint interests of the districts, or the interest of any single district or group thereof. The chief officers and elder statesmen of the county council tend to be the defenders of this interest, against the backwoodsmen of the council, the leaders of the districts, and many district chief officers.

In the British context the balance of the complex system is usually tilted in favour of the county council because the central government is the guarantor of the whole system. This role is played through legislation which has tended to stress the role of the county council and through judicial review, or its British equivalent. In complex systems there are many ways of settling disputes between county council and districts, including letting them drag on for years. But a factor of growing importance has been the role of the centre as arbiter when disputes occur. Too little is known at present about this appellate function; it is bound to be of greater importance in future, partly because more and more specific provision has been made for it, and partly because in general district authorities are much larger and more self-confident than they were in the traditional county.

A description of a complex system should include some kind of overall judgement about the way it works. This may be referred to as its political and administrative *style*.

The estimate of the style of government of a particular county must inevitably involve a large element of subjective judgement. This is because the *style* of behaviour is an emergent property of thousands of interactions and requires a knowledge of what is happening in two different kinds of location at the same time. With that proviso it may be said that complex systems can exhibit one of the three following styles: interactions and behaviour may be characterized by *conflict, co-operation* or *interdependence*. The first two are self-explanatory; they refer to what is a characteristic of all interactions, and the allocation to a type depends on the predominance of the indicated attribute. *Interdependence* occurs when the two are mixed up in very complicated ways.

Several factors influence the emergence of styles of county government. One of the most obvious is that of partisanship. Different councils may be controlled by different parties, or operate different types of party system on them. For instance, a county may contain a number of districts that are one party systems controlled by a different party from that which has dominated the county council for many years. In non-partisan areas different types of people may be dominant at the two levels – the county being dominated by the traditional leaders of county society whilst small businessmen control urban councils.

Both measures of the *balance* of a county are important. If a county is dominated by one lower-tier authority then it is highly likely to develop in different ways from a county with fifty districts, none of whom has more than ten per cent of population. A distribution of services which gives both levels substantial functions is perhaps more likely to develop a co-operative or interdependent style.

The strengths of the forces generated by the system are also important. *Localism* obviously tends towards the creation of a situation of conflict, as different local demands can be inconsistent, but if it is built into the system at county level then it may eventually produce a classical example of interdependence, by diffusing a 'something for everybody' attitude throughout the system.

It is suggested that in the long run the institutional features of county government, such as the area administration of the county council and the growth of co-operative activities, are effects of the general style of government, though in the short run they may affect day-to-day attitudes. Factors such as dual membership are harder to interpret because they may result from the style or they may be major factors contributing to it.

Behaviour in complex systems

When the main features of county government have been described it becomes necessary to return to the analysis of systemic behaviour that was set out in Part Three of this book. For county government adds extra dimensions to each aspect of the system.

The first effect is on the diagram which portrays the cycle of meetings within each council as a communication network (p. 140). For those who can draw in several dimensions the meeting cycles of all authorities within the county must be drawn side-by-side, and the links between them shown in the usual manner. Information can now flow from one system to another; indeed, both are now redefined as subsystems of the more inclusive county system. This has implications for the speed and reliability of decision making, and for access to the system. The new system has many more access points than do its two components (if one thinks only of a one district structure), but the redundancy of message transmission is much reduced as there are fewer and less reliable messengers. There is much greater chance of misrouting in all its forms.

The committee system is likely to be affected in a number of ways, but only at the county council level. Committees with an area responsibility, area subcommittees, composition of committees based partly on area balance as a factor – these are the sort of phenomena that will be encountered in complex systems. An extreme example of this occurs when district councillors are co-opted on to county council committees.

The county council's departmental structure and officers are likely to be affected in one respect only (recruitment, training etc. are the same as in the simple system) – field administration will be a major feature of the organizational structure of the department and of the career and working life of many officials. As county government tends to involve large populations and extensive areas, field administration is almost unavoidable.

At the minimum the combination of size of territory and technical demands of services administered requires a system of operating areas in which officers and other employees who provide the service and make contact with individual citizens will work. The county council will therefore have to divide its area into parts and delimit the boundaries of each. It will then choose a location for the area office in each part – not only a town or village but also an actual building. Decisions about status and salary will help to determine what role the head of the area office will have within the departmental hierarchy. This will also affect the degree of discretion given to the area.

Several factors affect the way the above matters are resolved. It may be suggested that in counties where localism is strong, area boundaries will correspond to district boundaries, area officers will be located near district headquarters and area chief officers will be expected to play a more positive role. A rigorous managerial approach will also lead to there being a coherent overall system with areas for different services coinciding.

The council will also face the question whether to attach to each area office an area committee – either a subcommittee of the county council committee or a joint committee with the district councils. In counties where localism is strong it is likely that this will be favoured, or else a further step will be taken – that of delegating to the district council itself.[4] Schemes of delegation themselves are capable of differing tremendously. Administration with either delegation or area committees is clearly very different from simple administration through peripatetic officers from headquarters.

At a more general level the existence of the county affects the daily life of council members and officers in two ways. First, it pervades decision making so that when matters come up for decision which affect only one part of the county a deference will be paid – the equivalent of senatorial courtesy in Congress – to the views of the representatives of that area. If for instance an education committee proposes to close a village school the officers will have to make sure that they can counter localist arguments about numbers of children, ease of access to other schools etc. – or the scheme may not be accepted by the full council. Second, it affects the political culture of the council, so that the local area occupies a central place in the value system of members. These two combine in council meetings where factors such as the 'greater moral virtue' of districts enter into public speeches and also appear to affect decision making.

One consequence of county government that has not generally been recognized is the demands it makes on the time of key members in the county system itself. Service on a district council (unless it be one in a largely rural area) is relatively easy because the council offices will be accessible and the local authority has only a limited range of services; county councils also have less than the full range of local government services, but many members will have to travel more than twenty miles to county headquarters, in circumstances that make a car almost a necessity. The key members, however, are those that bridge the gaps between upper and lower tiers, either by operating at both levels or by filling systemic roles within one. One of the most important features of recruitment of members in county government is the process by which county leaders evolve.

Understanding county government is made more difficult by the fact that events taking place at two different levels influence each other; a local disaster is a problem in the environment of both county and district – and perhaps parish also.

This can be illustrated by examining the concept of a council member's career in the county and the effects of electoral behaviour on this and the work of the county council itself.

When the first genuine complex systems of local government

were being created in the last twenty years of the nineteenth century, it was rightly believed that distinct levels of society could be discovered in small town and rural Britain. The key factor in these areas was the ability to travel, which itself was a function of the availability of means of transport and the individual's income. Thus throughout the county there was a level of society, landowners in rural areas and capitalists in urban, who were able to make the day's journey necessary to serve on a county council. In town districts service was in principle open to everyone who was formally qualified, and special provisions were introduced to ensure that ordinary people could serve on parish councils, leaving the rural district as an intermediate body, the preserve of the small property owner. The county council was described as 'government by horse and trap'.[5]

Those who were elected to the first county councils have been described as *social leaders* because they owed their political position to their socio-economic status. As the latter has tended to disappear in the twentieth century, the 'theory' of county government was undermined and it was necessary to find another sort of individual to fill the roles the system prescribed. These were found in *public persons* – those who obtained a social status from their widespread political and administrative activities.[6]

Once the differentiated society which was the foundation of traditional county government had passed away, the obvious source of upper-tier political leaders was the lower tier. Service on a district council is almost always easier for the individual and elections are more predictable because of socially more meaningful constituencies. A person may therefore begin to establish a reputation for political competence and to acquire a taste for local government. Thus when a 'vacancy' occurs because the serving county councillor dies, becomes an alderman, does not seek re-election or resigns through ill health, a district leader can consider whether to try for 'promotion' to the higher level. If he succeeds and shows an ability in county affairs then he creates a role for himself which links upper and lower tiers and gives him a personal political position in his locality.

The complexities of a career in county government are therefore obvious. The key stage for any individual is the transition from one level to another; for various reasons this is likely to be upwards rather than downwards. The 'fragility' of the system can easily be seen. If socialization processes fail to 'lock' the newcomer in a favourable attitude to the county council, if political conditions change rapidly or if the burden of work proves too great, then the turnover of representatives may be so rapid that it is impossible for individuals to create a political reputation which transcends the locality where they originally entered the system. On the other hand if county council service captures the imagination of members, and political positions are easily created, the system may ossify in a state which reflects the social structure of ten, fifteen, twenty years before. The high proportion of retired members on county councils, compared with other local authorities, may have reflected the commitment they created in their members and the fact that newcomers enter at a relatively late age because their career has started at the lower level.

The careers of council members in county government are thus complicated by the existence of two sets of elections and the transitions between them. Electoral behaviour was seen earlier as one of the proximate influences on the decision-making system of the local authority, and through its effects on council members' behaviour it is one of the important factors in understanding county government.

The study of electoral behaviour in complex systems could proceed by looking at the factors which bring about variations in each aspect – turnout, competitiveness, selectivity etc. – at each level separately, but this would miss the interrelationships between the two which are part of county government. This can be illustrated by a study of the effects of *competitiveness* on the county council. The following is an outline of the process that should be followed in order to understand this aspect of local government.

First, the system by which county electoral divisions have been created should be inspected to see how far the wards have boundaries coincident with district boundaries. Then the relative weight the system assigns to each type of area can be estimated by calculating measures of under- and over-representation.

Second, electoral behaviour in each division should be examined to see how far factors making for stability-instability in the 'delegation' to the county council from each type of area operate. These involve three processes: the rate at which retiring members seek re-election and do not retire in mid-term (the *incumbency* factor); their chances of being unopposed (*competitiveness* and *incumbency* combined); and if opposed, their chances of being re-elected (*incumbency* again). All three processes are affected by such factors as the presence or absence of parties on district councils, the nature of such party conflict, the geographical structure of constituencies, particularly the number of 'centres' they contain, and the liability to experience meteoric political movements.

Thirdly, the effects of elections on the composition of the council should be examined in the light of the 'promotion' system within the council itself. The achievement of influential positions, such as important committee memberships and chairmanships, will depend on a number of factors of which seniority is likely to be one.

Thus a particular county council might be understood in the following terms. Rural areas are greatly over-represented by the electoral system of the county; their 'weight' is increased by the greater political stability of the area (absence of political parties and short-term political movements at district level); more incumbents seek re-election, fewer are opposed and fewer defeated if opposed. Representatives of rural areas are thus more likely to become aldermen, committee chairmen, elder statesmen and part of the council's 'establishment'.[7]

The above discussion has dealt with only a sample of the political and administrative processes of county government, but, it is hoped, one that is sufficient to show the reader how to undertake the study of complex systems of all types, whether they be a small rural district of the traditional system or the government of Greater London today. As an example of how to proceed to unknown systems, an attempt will now be made to evaluate county government in the new local government system.

Creating county government

At the time of writing the new local government system has been in existence for such a short time that none of the complex systems that constitute it can be regarded as having reached relative stability of structure. It is possible to make a tentative evaluation, however, of the formal features of the new pattern, on the basis of an understanding of county government generally, and to reflect on the process of creating multi-tier local government. In what follows no reference is made to other problems of local government but only to those characteristics of the new system which derive from the *county* as a form of local government, and within these, to those factors which are likely to influence its long-term development. Forms of government can change out of all recognition over a period of years and end as institutions quite unlike anything their founders desired or feared.[8]

THE 'BALANCE' OF THE COUNTIES

There is good reason to believe that multi-tier systems are more likely to find a stable and, to the participants, satisfactory state if they are balanced in the senses distinguished above. Geographical balance is achieved by having a sufficient number of lower-tier authorities and by having a distribution of population which does not *de facto* lead to the county being dominated by one district.

The new pattern of local government is substantially different from the old in this respect. Many of the old administrative counties had more than twenty districts within their boundaries: Cheshire had 42, Essex 43 and Devon 47 lower-tier authorities, whilst Kent had 56, the West Riding 89 and Lancashire 109. No new county has more than 14 districts; the great majority (32 out of 45) have 8 or less, and one (the Isle of Wight) has only 2. A small number of districts does not necessarily mean that counties are 'lop-sided', but increases the chances of either one district dominance or an alliance between two or three of similar circumstances against the rest. No English county is as striking as South Glamorgan which is little more than greater Cardiff (72.9 per cent of total population), but Bristol has 46.1 per cent of Avon and Birmingham 39.1 per cent of the West Midlands.

There is no space here to deal with each new county separately, but it may be remarked that judgements are complicated by two facts: the relative sizes of the largest and its nearest rivals, and the extent to which one pre-1972 area has come through unchanged as a high proportion of the new authority. The new metropolitan counties are based very clearly on long established urban areas, and this poses a problem of identity for their inhabitants.[9]

Though at the time of writing there is insufficient evidence available to make a quantitative judgement about the balance between levels in the new counties, it is clear that in general the metropolitan counties are bottom-heavy in that most major responsibilities have been allocated to the district councils, and that the reverse is the case in non-metropolitan counties. In Exeter, for example, the county council is asking of the ratepayers of the City three times as much as their own district council is, whilst in Greater London in 1973-74, 29 of the 33 lower-tier councils levied rates eight times as great as that of the GLC. The question therefore is whether the top tier in metropolitan and the bottom tier in non-metropolitan counties have sufficient responsibilities to enable them to participate happily in the county itself.

THE DIVISION OF SERVICES

There is reason to think that the framers of the 1972 Act were concerned lest one tier in the new system had insufficient work to justify its existence. They therefore divided up local government services in ways that have caused much criticism in the local government world.[10]

In multi-tier systems there is much to be said for making the division of services as clear-cut as possible. Though all public activities are potentially related to all others, in practice some are more closely linked than others. If the division is unclear and involves the joint action of two or more authorities on many occasions, then this is a source of tension and conflict within the system. An unclear division will create jurisdictional disputes both ways as authorities try to claim or disclaim responsibility for particular cases or problems.

In fact a distinction must be drawn between enforced co-operation, where the local authorities have no choice, and that co-operation which arises from problem-solving search behaviour by different authorities who find that in particular instances joint action will provide the answer. The latter is part of the adaptation of the system to the circumstances of individual areas and specific problems, and is of vital importance to the working of complex systems; the former is a source of friction which may invade other aspects of decision making.

The new system involves in general a much less clear division of powers than did the old one. For instance, refuse collection and disposal are divided between upper and lower tier, as are aspects of town and country planning. The highways-transportation-transport group of services is also divided, and recreational services generally, including museums and art galleries, are concurrent functions.

The situation is complicated by the general provisions for agency arrangements. As many districts were previously all-purpose county boroughs they naturally feel that they are quite competent to administer those services which are now the responsibility of the county council. Agency arrangements for services or parts of services involve frequent interaction between authorities, and thus from the point of view of the citizen at least confuse the allocation of responsibility.

THE SETTLEMENT OF DISPUTES

However well powers are divided and boundaries of areas drawn, however well the county council adapts its internal organization to the facts of localism, conflict is inevitable on occasions and this will sometimes lead to open formal dispute.

At present disputes within multi-tier systems may be resolved in a variety of ways. The most common is for one authority to determine the matter unilaterally in its own favour – in many cases not to the satisfaction of the other parties. This form of 'solution' has become less satisfactory since the recent trend of requiring consultation between levels has gathered strength. Very rarely, disputes can be dealt with by the ordinary courts; more common is the invocation of ministerial adjudication which is specifically provided for in some circumstances.

An example of a central body charged with the task of dealing with disputes *de facto* in counties is the Local Government Boundary Commission for England. This body is responsible for preparing schemes for changes in virtually every aspect of areas in local government, including those relating to elections, to be implemented by ministerial order, with or without amendment. It is to be expected that in most cases the driving force for change and the origin of specific proposals will be the authorities within each county. If, as may be expected, many of these proposals will be controversial and strongly opposed by other authorities, the Commission will in effect be presiding over a choice between authorities' desires. This is the role that the Local Government Commission for England (1958-65) prescribed for itself on the previous occasion when permanent machinery for local government reorganization existed.

It will become increasingly obvious that there are great advantages in having a body to whom *all* disputes between authorities within complex systems can be referred – a sort of judicial review, except that it would not be undertaken by the ordinary courts but by a specially created appellate board or commission. This would help the process of adaptation within each system, making the operation of complex systems smoother and more regular.

Such a body would also have the great advantage of being an experiment within the British system of government of a rudimentary administrative court. If successful in dealing with the relations between a few administrative bodies it might provide a precedent for others, or even have its own terms of reference extended to cover the relations between administrative agencies generally and eventually relations between the state and the citizen. It might help to convince the opponents of an administrative court that the introduction of greater openness and regularity into the system was not as dangerous as they fear.

ADAPTABILITY

The basic underlying factor in all of the above discussion is *adaptability*. Each county will seek a *modus vivendi* which will satisfy to a minimum extent both the districts and the county council. It is therefore helpful if no restrictions are placed on the discretion of the individual local authority to determine its own internal organization. Statutory committees and departments are always impertinent; in the case of complex systems they are dangerous. Legal provisions should encourage the authorities within each county to search for satisfactory forms of cohabitation – for this is what they necessarily have to do – and to develop local conventions and customs to regularize the patterns of interaction. Anything which reduces the manoeuvrability of individual councils and permits disputes to become running sores lessens the chances of long-term evolution towards a form of government which citizens will accept wholeheartedly.

The reason why *adaptability* is particularly important for complex systems of local government is that they exist in a more complicated environment. The intricacies of system-environment relationships when only one authority is considered as an individual in its own right are multiplied by the existence of relationships between authorities within the county.

Understanding complex systems of local government is thus one of the most difficult aspects of understanding local government, but it is made more important by the fact that for the foreseeable future the county will be the only form of local government in Britain.

Chapter Ten
Central-Local Relations

For over forty years W. A. Robson has been writing of 'the centralizing tendency which is undermining local government', 'the subordination of local autonomy to the dictates of the central power . . . their [local authorities'] transformation into mere receptacles for government policy',[1] and his judgements have been taken over by virtually every textbook, Royal Commission and committee of enquiry, and the local government world itself. The central domination of local government and the reduction of local authorities to will-less agents of the Government is therefore a common theme of the discussion of local government, and indeed part of a conventional wisdom.

Such a view of central-local relations is misleading to a high degree and is based on a misunderstanding of local government behaviour, or rather an ignorance of what happens in local government. It is a classic example of the legalism and institutionalism that have damaged local government studies for so long. Someone writing from London and having experience of only the statements of the centre, including those in statutes, white papers and circulars, is always in danger of confusing its expressed desires with what is likely to occur.

The extent of the misunderstanding can be estimated by considering two sources of evidence. First, there is the cross-sectional evidence from the econometric-type statistical studies of variations in local government services. Second, there is the evidence of longitudinal studies of central government policy in a number of spheres, in which the centre's own words testify to a weakness of influence over local authorities. The two sources of evidence are in fact the geographical and temporal facets of the same processes.

If the central government was as dominant as the conventional view alleges then there would be uniformity of provision in all the major services for which the government takes explicit and personal responsibility. Yet when measures of local authority behaviour have been constructed and interpreted as outputs or performance indicators, it has been found that the differences between local authorities are so great as to be inexplicable in terms of an automatic reflex reaction to central desires.[2]

As the intention of decentralization is to produce differences between areas it cannot be argued that all such variations are signs of the failure of the centre to impose its will, but in practice the striking differences between authorities in both the form and quantity of service provision, over a wide range of activities, are much greater than can be expected from any simple interaction between local factors and the centre's wishes. Nor as a matter of fact are they easily explicable in terms of purely local factors such as size and wealth of population or party composition of the council. One research group giving evidence to the Redcliffe-Maud Commission came to the conclusion that 'the differences between authorities in performance may have nothing to do with size or wealth or even need, but may be much more closely linked with the effectiveness of the chief officer or the views he holds on how the service should run, or with the influence of a powerful committee chairman or group of councillors with a special interest in a particular service'.[3]

The first way of testing how far local authorities are the will-less agents of the centre is one that has been popular with economists and social administrators of a statistical background. The first step is to choose some area of public services for which local authorities are responsible and which the centre is known to regard as of vital importance, such as primary and secondary education, the personal social services, school meals, council house rent policy, housebuilding, and fluoridation.[4] It is then necessary to develop standardized measures of how local authorities as individuals have behaved and are behaving in providing the chosen public service. These measures of behaviour may or may not be financial; all that is required is that each be applicable to all local authorities in comparable terms.

The next step is to use whatever statistical techniques are deemed appropriate to see what sort of variation within the group of authorities chosen for study exists at a given point in time, and whether this can be accounted for in terms of factors in the locality. In every case the extent to which the observable variations between local authorities can be attributed to the interaction between local factors and the will of the centre is very small; even if there are significant results from the statistical techniques the degree to which the variation is accounted for is generally low. As one author says 'the centre has a part to play in setting the boundaries within which local authorities operate, but the divergence within those boundaries must be explained elsewhere'.[5]

The evidence from the longitudinal studies is of a different sort. Basically it consists of tracing through public statements on a particular subject matter over a period of time, to see how far the central government has been satisfied with the reactions to its previous statements, and, where possible, to look at measures of behavioural change following central public policy announcements. If this is done for a large number of subjects *that have been declared by the central government* to be of great importance, it will be found that over periods as long as fifty years the latter has found it necessary to reiterate its demands and requests. Often there is a pathetic sameness about the centre's complaints that local authorities have ignored or perverted its previous requests. There is no space here to rehearse the evidence in individual services but studies of smoke control, comprehensive education, family planning, rent rebate schemes, the housing of old people, and fluoridation, to take a few examples, show this temporal pattern of repeated pressure by the centre for changes in local authority behaviour, without the former receiving full satisfaction.

It would be wrong to suggest that local authorities never react favourably and immediately to central government requests or demands. On the contrary many do, and others interpret the policies to suit themselves. But the 'central domination' thesis requires that *all* do, and this is not the case.

It should be noted that the evidence against the conventional picture of central-local relations has not relied on cases of extreme conflict and resistance by local authorities which have been highly publicized in recent years. The analysis depends on the evidence of the behaviour of all local authorities, the most conformist as well as the most extreme. But at any given point in time there are always one or two local authorities, or a small group of them, that are in serious conflict with the centre. Examples can be found from Poplar in the inter-war years to Clay Cross in the 1970s.[6] These cases, it will be argued, are only the tip of the iceberg; they involve the exploitation of powers and rights to an extreme degree, but these are being used with different outcomes by all local authorities every day. The understanding that the new approach gives is nowhere more strikingly illustrated than in the field of central-local relations; the framework places the behaviour of both the most conformist and the most deviant local authority in a common context.

Consider first the remote field office of a central government department such as the Inland Revenue or the Department of Health and Social Security. This will receive communications, written or verbal, from headquarters and on receipt it will have to process them within the office. As field offices are relatively uncomplicated organizations this will be a simple matter, yet there is evidence that members of organizations do misunderstand messages, particularly the strength of the imperative in them, and it cannot be assumed that what happens will be what the originator of the message expected.[7]

How much more scope is there for different reactions to the same message or piece of information in an organization as complicated as a local authority. As with the field office the request or demand must be internalized before action can ensue. Part Three of this book set out the many dimensions in which local authorities may differ in respect of their internal processes of decision making and information flow. Central-local relations will therefore be analysed as a case of system-environment interaction, with the central government interpreted as part of the proximate environment of the individual local authority whenever it sends a communication to the latter.

The vehicle of the interaction will be the passage of information in the form of a document, letter or verbal message from the centre (regarded as undifferentiated for the moment) to the local authority. Let it be assumed that it is an official circular. This will be received by the clerk to the council and reports of its existence will be heard by some other officers, some council members and some citizens in the mass media. It may well have started on several different paths through the decision-making procedures of the council. All that can be said in general is that at some time it will be considered by the relevant professional chief officers, by their assistants and by the relevant sections within their departments, by the treasurer's and clerk's departments similarly, by the relevant committees and subcommittees, by party committees if any, by interested groups in the locality, and by a council meeting.

There is in fact no standard path that the item must take through the intricacies of the internal organization of local authorities. Not only may the paths be different from one authority to the next, when they both receive the same circular, but the same authority may process consecutive items quite differently. For instance, a circular may go quite unnoticed by interested outsiders, and when the local authority has determined what action it will take this is sprung on a largely unsuspecting public. But equally government policy innovations may be widely discussed in social and economic groups and a knowledge of the centre's request may be the source of local pressure on the reluctant council to take action of a particular sort.

It is not therefore surprising that after, say, six months the central government will find itself faced with a variety of reactions, including inaction. It will find that local authorities make requests for delay or change in the details, that in some areas vocal citizens groups are complaining to it about the attitude of their council, and that in others good progress is reported.

But though the paths that an item may take cannot be described in detail, or even predicted with confidence, it is possible to say something about the factors that will influence the outcome of the whole process within the authority.

First, allowance must be made for the role of chance factors. Because there are so many points of access to the system and distribution of items between them must contain random elements, no description of them can be more than a list. It may be that behind the apparently irregular inputs of information there are strict patterns but these are not, and in practical terms can never be, accessible to the outside observer. He must therefore treat them as probabilistic phenomena.

Second, there are a number of general conditions in the system of government which regulate the relations between governmental bodies but which are often overlooked. Some of these are restrictions on the freedom of action of the centre.

The statutes that allocate rights and duties to local authorities restrict them to defined spheres of activity, but they also restrict the role of the central government. Once a service has been made the responsibility of local authorities, the intervention in it by the centre must be justified by reference to a specific power to act; often this power is further restricted by procedural requirements. These factors will continue to operate whilst the system of government is based on the rule of law. It may be argued quite rightly that the central government retains the ultimate power to change the law itself and thus to modify central-local relations through an increase in its own rights and powers. But this is itself restricted by pressure on parliamentary time, by the relative significance that is ascribed to something that may be of importance only in relation to a small minority of cases, and by the inability of the centre to devise regulatory systems that do not contain further loopholes.

The centre is not in any event a united organization and there is much scope for conflict within it about what should be done in relation to an individual authority. This relates to another factor; local authorities are each responsible for a prescribed area of land and therefore they face problems which arise from the unique combination or conjunction of circumstances. As has been stressed several times before, the problems that occur in different areas do not necessarily fall into the neat categories used by the central government. Problem solving first requires a definition of the problem and this gives those with first-hand experience of its nature an advantage. A traffic problem may be created by the passage of heavy lorries through a historic city centre, but may also be created by the office building policy of the council. In the first case the building of a by-pass is central, in the second redevelopment aspects of planning relegate roads to a secondary position.

One general factor that is hard to quantify but which must be assumed to be of significance is the fact of popular election of members of the authority. In Britain direct election confers on a person's judgements a certain legitimacy that is lacking in those of the local appointed officer. It does not matter that in fact a local councillor may be at variance with many of his constituents, or that the mandate he claims is fictitious; what counts is the confidence that he brings to dealings with other public bodies. This of course is something that varies tremendously; for instance, if a councillor is elected as part of a sweeping victory for his political party throughout the authority, or if he unexpectedly turns a large minority into a big majority, the degree of self-belief will be much greater than if he is deemed re-elected for a small remote parish of a district council. The fact of popular election has been seen by L. J. Sharpe to be the reason why the rate of capital expenditure on local authority services has been much greater than on similar services controlled by other types of body.[8]

The above are all general factors that the reader may expect to experience in some form or other within his own local authority. They do of course vary in impact between authorities but as sources of differences between localities they are not as important as the factors that are discussed below.

One of the most obvious factors is *partisanship*. Clearly one of the sources of conflict between centre and locality is a difference in political control. Equally, similarity of viewpoint tends to reduce open conflict, but it should not be assumed that everything will always be smooth when there is the same party control; parties contain wings and factions within them, and this is a source of disagreement between party members.

Related to this but of wider significance is the social composition of the council. As was seen earlier, council members are not collectively a microcosm of the whole population. The general social attitudes that accompany these variations are equally diverse. In some areas there is a strong tradition of 'economizing' which is drawn upon by ratepayers' movements. But the observer is constantly being surprised by the attitudes found in council members collectively. For instance, comprehensive education was introduced earlier and more rapidly in some traditional Conservative areas than it was in some more left-wing urban centres.

It may be expected that one of the factors that has a general influence on central-local relations is the size of the authority in terms of population served. The larger the population the greater the work load, the more cases in each specific category, the more likely that highly specialized officers will be employed, the higher the salary that chief officers and their immediate assistants will be paid. It is therefore a reasonable assumption that the more competent and well-qualified officers will be found in the larger authorities. In a sense it does not matter whether this is true or not; what counts is whether the officials themselves believe it to be true. There is some impressionistic evidence that this is the case and that when professionals from the big cities and the urban counties, including Greater London, deal with the central government, they do not feel that they are dealing with their professional superiors. The contrary is in fact often the case. Such attitudes affect the treatment given to messages from the central government departments, which come for the most part from civil servants, or are seen to emanate from them.

Finally, there is the pattern of internal organization. It was shown earlier that each local authority's internal structure involved a status and power system, that committees and departments enjoyed different rankings, that different specialisms were given separate organizational identities, in the committee, subcommittee and chief officer sectors of the authority. The treatment that a circular from the centre will receive will depend on how its 'sponsors' within the system can influence the processes of decision making.

But even if an authority is found in which in a particular case the factors making for differentiation or departure from the norms expected by the centre are absent – the same party is in control, social attitudes support the development of the service, chief officers agree with the centre's professional judgements and they are of high status within the authority – there is still another factor which may lead to a different response from that expected by the government.

It has been stressed repeatedly that each local authority is an individual system having its own unique proximate environment. If this is so, then the problems that are faced by each council when implementing national policy (in the case under consideration) are also unique. It is true that they may be broadly classified so that there is sufficient similarity between members of the same class for the same response to be expected. But in many cases this is not true.

For instance, a local education authority which has just rebuilt most of its secondary schools as purpose-designed secondary moderns, and whose council members and officers have been to a local high prestige direct grant school cannot be expected to react to a call for complete comprehensivization of secondary education in the same way as an authority whose schools are largely obsolete and in need of replacement. An authority with large areas of slums and derelict property, bombed sites still not redeveloped, and abandoned factories can respond enthusiastically to a call for new roads to rehumanize the urban environment in the city centre, especially if backed by the offer of extra funds. But what of the authority faced with a different set of choices? Suppose a solution to city centre traffic problems involves knocking down the cathedral or the historic town hall, or driving a four-lane highway through the most expensive residential area, or else finding a more costly and probably ineffective route in another area of town. To the county borough in the centre of a conurbation a call to clear slums in a massive way may have appeared utopian; even if they had the money to build all the new houses needed to deal with the square miles of (by national standards) inadequate housing, they could not find the land.

This is perhaps only to express the results of the research into differences between authorities in a less quantitative way. What is most lacking in the conventional wisdom about central-local relations is a sense of what is going on in local authorities. As local authorities are systems interacting with their environment, the response to a new act, a circular, or a ministerial speech or letter, will be complex. Members and officers of local authorities cannot be naïve when faced with such a message, even if they wished to be so.

There are therefore several sources of difficulty for the local authority when it receives a circular from a central government department. The information and the request may generate conflicting responses within the organization itself, it may cause tension between system and environment, and it may be sufficiently imprecise to the locality (though not to the centre) so that the correct reaction in specific circumstances may not be obvious.

The relationship then moves into a second phase. The central government now takes over again, and the onus is on it to try to determine the next stage. Its reaction is of course constrained by the level of knowledge that it has of what has happened in a locality. As the local authority is the source of much (perhaps most) of the centre's information about events within its boundaries and its own action and inaction, the government will not necessarily be able to evaluate independently the response of the system.

The centre may choose to send a second communication, to which the locality will respond, again in the complex way structured by the system's interaction with its environment and its own internal organization. This may lead to a third, fourth etc. phase of the relationship. But the major characteristic of the centre-system-environment interaction will change simply because it is in its second, third etc. phase. The style of the relationship may well change towards one of greater consensus; central-local relations involve repeated interaction between the same people and this often leads to a greater appreciation of the other's point of view. But this is not always the case and sometimes the style of relationship is one of increasing hostility leading eventually to severe open conflict. To see how these styles of central-local relations can emerge, it is necessary to look at the methods of control and influence available to the central government in its dealings with local authorities; collectively they reflect the different phases and styles of relationship very accurately.

First, it is necessary to categorize the methods systematically. Too often they are presented as a list without any indication of where they fit into the pattern of central-local relations, or what their structural importance is.

Methods of central control and influence

The first distinction that must be drawn is between administrative control and influence on one hand and legislative/judicial control on the other. Local authorities are bound by law to do and refrain from doing a large number of things, and these prohibitions and obligations are enforceable in the courts. Judicial control of local authorities is thus a necessary corollary of legislative control, and has no force without the obligation that the latter implies, particularly the *ultra vires* doctrine.[9]

Little time need be spent on judicial control by the ordinary courts, for it is constrained by the factors that influence litigation generally in Britain – it is slow, expensive, time consuming and uncertain. In quantitative terms it is unimportant compared with the activities of central departments. But it remains in the background and some have argued that it sets the tone of much local government behaviour by making legal considerations more important than they are for local authorities in other countries.

It has already been remarked that legislation binds the central department in the short run as well as the local authority. Many of the major acts regulating local government services, such as the *Education Act, 1944*, confer a general responsibility for the whole of the service on the relevant minister, but the operational significance of such blanket provisions is small compared with the specific powers to make regulations, issue directives and to inspect the work of local education authorities.

However, the central department through its ministerial head is in a better position than a local authority to have the law changed if it does not suit it. New legislation is sometimes a response to the difficulties that the centre has encountered in dealing with local authorities, and introduces new powers for the government, but on many occasions it results from the initiative of the local government world and can be seen as in a real sense 'liberating' individual local authorities, by making it easier for them to do the sort of things they desire.[10]

There are two methods of central control of local authorities which come halfway between the strictly legislative and judicial control exercised by Parliament and the courts and the strictly administrative controls at the disposal of government ministers. The first is the power to make regulations governing the behaviour of local authorities which have the force of law and the second machinery of district audit which is part of the civil service but which has mainly adjudicatory functions.

Most of the major statutes governing local authority services give the minister the power to make regulations controlling the exercise of the powers of local authorities. The use of these powers results in the creation of abstract rules regulating all the relevant authorities and thus resembles ordinary legislation, but is is controlled by the need to obtain parliamentary approval through a prescribed procedure (though this is usually easily obtained), and is restricted to the subjects enumerated in the original act. As with all statutory instrument procedures it is intended to be more flexible, detailed and easily changed than are the results of Parliamentary processes of legislation. It shares these qualities with the main straightforward methods of administrative control and influence. It thus combines features of both legislative and administrative control.

The district audit service consists of civil servants deployed on a regional basis within the Department of the Environment. Though their position has been changed in a number of respects by the *Local Government Act, 1972*, district auditors are still concerned not only with financial rectitude in the traditional accounting sense but with the legality of payments made by the local authority.[11] They thus act as judicial officials and make the restrictions embodied in legislation a reality, by testing every expense incurred against the provisions of the law. The fact that they are civil servants, however, means that they can on occasion serve administrative purposes, and this has sometimes led to controversy about their role if it is felt in the locality that their work is politically motivated. Of particular importance here is the power of the Secretary of State to call for an extraordinary audit at any time of any individual authority's accounts.

The aspects of central-local relations discussed so far – legislation, actions in the courts, district audit and the making of regulations – are all relatively infrequent in occurrence, though they exercise a general influence on the atmosphere of local authority decision making. The next set of central activities operate in a much more routine manner, and even if they themselves are relatively infrequent, give rise to almost daily and repeated interaction between representatives of the locality and the centre. These are the methods of central influence on local government decision making.

In this context the difference between control and influence is vital for they are associated with distinct styles of interaction between the two levels. Methods of control presume a conflict of wills and make provision, in so far as the law can do this, for the victory of the central point of view. Methods of influence, however, are intended to prevent a conflict of wills ever arising by fostering agreement or consensus between locality and centre so that the 'autocratic' methods, which substitute the judgement of the latter for that of the former, are not brought into play.

It has been remarked that much of British government is a

dialogue, and this is nowhere more obvious than in central-local relations, when the experience of the United Kingdom is compared with that of continental and colonial countries. From the side of the central government this dialogue is conducted through circulars, white papers, ministerial speeches, special research reports, design bulletins and the like. They may contain more than advice, suggestions and persuasion, but these will be a large part of most of the documents, even if they are mixed up with threats and orders. In fact the general tone is hortatory rather than mandatory; they appeal to the self-interest of the local authorities. An objective account of a new method of building a certain type of school which is as good as the traditional ones and much cheaper recommends itself without further comment. The scope for conflict over school construction is thus lessened.

The intrinsically persuasive nature of much of the documentation produced by the centre has now been overlooked by those who have focused attention on control rather than influence. The point is underlined when it is remembered that a considerable number of the innovations that the central department adopts and advocates originated in one or two local authorities. Insufficient consideration has been given to the role of central departments as 'post offices', disseminating what is soon recognized as best practice developed by particular authorities. A well written and constructive document may continue to have an influence long after the immediate impact of its publication and transmission has disappeared.

A similar role can be seen for specific grants. A specific grant is one which is made by the government to a local authority towards the cost of a service or part of a service. It may be calculated on the basis of a fixed amount for every unit of the service provided, or it may be a fixed percentage of total relevant expenditure. In either case the rules for qualifying for the grant will have been announced before the financial year. The effect of a system in which some services or parts of a service have specific grants and others do not, and some have large percentages and others smaller ones, is to change the marginal cost of every service relative to all the others in the direction the creators of the grant system desire. The economic logic of the above argument is more complicated than presented here, but it is probable that if a specific grant system is unchanged for a long period it will produce considerable shifts in the expenditure patterns of individual local authorities. And in governmental systems once an expenditure pattern is well established it tends to maintain itself through 'incrementalism' –

the process of making decisions in terms of increments to or deductions from existing activities.

Again the effect of a specific grant system is to produce an agreement between the two levels about what the locality should do. This is underlined by the few occasions on which an individual authority has rejected the service itself, and has therefore been unaffected by the offer of large grants. The changes in marginal cost can have no effect in such circumstances.

The third method of influence is through central inspection. Not all central departments have permanent inspectorates; some that do are really carrying out substantive functions in relation to society at large, as are the factory inspectors. But in education, child care, police and fire services, they inspect the local authority – or one of its institutions or depots. They are regarded as the 'eyes and ears' of the central department, and their formal reports, which may draw attention to defects (and successes) that they have encountered, are less important than the personal contact and verbal interaction with members and officers of local councils. It has been suggested that inspectors both educate and learn at the same time and, because of their great prestige, can carry knowledge of best practice directly from one authority to another. Inasmuch as they also promote consensus they are acting to prevent overt conflict arising, and are thus a method of influence.

If the essence of administrative influence is that it operates prior to a decision being reached by a local authority, and thus tends to prevent disagreement between the two levels, the essence of control is that it operates afterwards, and substitutes the judgement of the minister for that of the local authority. But as with the transition from legislative/judicial control to administrative action there is machinery that is halfway between influence and control. This is the statutory scheme which the local authority must make and the central minister approve, and which is supposed to govern the future provision of the relevant service.

There are two levels of decision making involved in schemes of this sort. The council has to make decisions about the scheme itself, but these do not become directly operative until further decisions have been made about its application in particular circumstances. Likewise the central department has to make two types of decision; those relating to the scheme itself and those relating to actions within its framework. In making the scheme the minister may be able to substitute his judgement for that of the locality, and this is an element of control; but once the scheme has been accepted it is expected to reduce conflict by providing a framework for future decision making. As with all the other means of influence this may not always succeed, but generally it will provide common ground between centre and locality, and concentrate much of the potential conflict into a short period of time.

It is very rare for a central minister to be able to take over a local authority function or part of one by a straightforward 'seizure', but in one or two cases this is possible. Important planning applications may be 'called in' by the minister for central decisions, and the Secretary of State has a very general but rarely used power to overrule the lawful decisions of local education authorities. The most common method of overruling a local authority is through the approval function. In certain circumstances local authority decisions need the approval of a central minister before they become operative. This may happen in either of two ways; it may be required in every case, as with the confirmation of by-laws and loan sanction, or it may be exercised only on appeal by an aggrieved party, as with appeals against planning decisions. In these cases the minister may support the local authority by rejecting the appeal or he may reverse the original decision by finding for the complainant.

The approval of decisions is a day-to-day matter, occurring frequently and often the occasion for discussion and negotiation. The other two methods of control are very rare and are ones that symbolize severe conflict between centre and locality, indicating that a stage in central-local relations has arrived where the dialogue has ceased. The first of these is the directive, which is an order to a named authority (or authorities) either to do or to refrain from doing some act. Although there is no evidence on this point it may be suspected that the issue of a directive will be a matter of embarrassment, if not shame, for the professional officers concerned, even if the council members are pleased with their stand against central dictation. Directives are relatively rare but of course it is not known how often they are threatened, or how far the knowledge of their existence constrains local authorities to do things that they would not otherwise have done.

Even more rare is the use of default powers. Certain acts provide that if the minister is dissatisfied with the performance of a local authority in a particular service he may temporarily remove that service from its control and either arrange for its administration by another local authority (this is likely to happen mainly in county government) or create a special post or body to carry it out.

In the case of the default by a district council in public health he could transfer the power to the county council, whilst under the *Housing Finance Act, 1972* he could appoint a commissioner to take over the housing functions of the errant council. This is what happened in Clay Cross and in certain urban councils in south Wales.

The use of default powers is so rare that it is impossible to generalize about their use in practice. It is obvious that when they are used conflict between minister and council is so widespread and severe that the normal pattern of relations has disappeared, but how far default administration is effective in providing the service is not established. Again hints can be found that the role of commissioner in these circumstances is not a pleasant one and he may suffer obstruction from the council members in the attempt to carry out his duties.

The circumstances in which directives, default powers and even imprisonment through action in the courts are used are so unusual in the British context that there are likely to be factors in the environment which provide a local justification for what would otherwise be regarded as outrageous behaviour by council members. In such cases the sense in which the minister can win is a very limited one. The members of Poplar Borough Council were imprisoned through action by the Conservative Minister of Health but eventually he was glad to settle with them and forget about the past.

It would be wrong to end the discussion of methods of central control on a note of conflict for this is the unusual side of central-local relations in Britain. The central government has an interest in the details of local government administration for at least four reasons and in respect of some of these it ought to satisfy itself with the way the system works. One of its most fundamental interests is in honest and efficient government and as local authorities spend large amounts of public money and are a large part of the operational state (that which has direct contact with citizens) they cannot be ignored. The central government is also concerned with equality between its citizens, and one aspect of this is territorial justice – the extent to which different areas are treated fairly. In this they are supported by general citizens' attitudes which appear to have become, as a result of increasing diurnal and residential mobility and the mass media, more impatient with differences between areas. Finally, there are national elements in or aspects of most public services; the centre cannot treat what goes on in each locality in respect of most services as purely local affairs.[12]

Although a dispassionate judgement by those involved in either the centre or the localities would be that the centre achieves some of its aims, or all of its aims in part, there are numerous occasions when the centre is ignorant about what is happening or powerless to get what it wants. There is more danger of local government becoming an unacceptable form of local administration of public services through the inefficiency and weakness of the centre than there is of local democracy being destroyed by too effective central control.

Local influence on the centre

The description of central-local relations so far given is incomplete because it leaves out the moves that the individual local authority may make against the centre. Part of the influence that the individual may exert on a central department is exercised collectively, through the general goodwill that local government has in Parliament and more importantly through the local authority associations acting as pressure groups. The most important of the latter are the Association of Metropolitan Authorities (AMA) and the Association of County Councils (ACC).

But because the perspective of this book is the individual authority it is necessary to adopt a different point of view from that adopted when giving an account of the system of central-local relations as a whole. For the local authority associations do not necessarily represent the views and interests of any individual authority at a given point in time. They are often part of the remote environment and concerned more with general rules and principles than with the details of the individual case. What counts for the local political system is the influence that it personally can exercise.

The amount of help a local council can expect from its Member of Parliament will depend partly on relative partisan affiliations, but often there are matters which are bi- or multi-partisan at the local level, and involve opposition to the centre as such, irrespective of the partisan nature of the government of the day. Similar points may be made about the work of the party organizations. Unfortunately so little is known about the articulation of interests through politicians inside or outside the parties in the central-local context that any judgement would be guesswork. It may be assumed that it does happen but how often cannot even be estimated.

One form of influence about which a little more is known is the direct appeal to the minister or department through the petition or deputation. It is believed that the open public 'marches' on London which council members occasionally organize are not so effective as the small private delegation of senior officers and perhaps the committee chairmen who go to argue the case for the local authority verbally to the civil servants and politicians concerned in the centre. There are sometimes hints in council minutes of a successful or unsuccessful approach of this sort.

But most of the power of the locality against the centre comes simply from the fact that it is the moving force in most of the interactions, at least at the operational level. Most of the centre's information about what goes on in a council's area derives from the council itself, and the centre does not generally have the machinery either to check the information or supersede the local authority as administrative agent.

The financial processes of local government

Each local authority now operates within a complex central-local financial system first created by the *Local Government Act, 1966*. The overall financial system will be called the *rate support grant system* because the calculation of the latter is its central feature. The system involves two parallel processes, one taking place in the central government and one taking place in each local authority. The determination of the rate support grant itself is the transition point from the first stage in which decisions about expenditure are made for the coming year to the second stage when the funds prescribed by the process are distributed to local authorities.

Each individual local authority is however such a small proportion of the total that what it does cannot affect the whole process significantly. The main features of the rate support grant as it affects the individual council are fixed outside its jurisdiction; indeed most of the features of the local financial system are so fixed, and the local authority can only react to them and perhaps exploit their potentialities. They appear as given in its environment and impinge on its internal processes in a variety of ways. To understand the financial behaviour of a local council it is necessary to be able to distinguish between those factors which it does not control and those which it can manipulate or exploit in the pursuit of its own values and beliefs.

There are separate though related processes for raising money for capital finance as opposed to current finance. As the former eventually end up as items in the current budget, attention will be concentrated on the finance of current expenditure. Local authorities obtain their income for current expenditure from three sources: fees, charges and profits from trading undertakings; grants from the central government; and the rates. These three items vary in their contribution to the total revenue of the individual authority; for instance, some authorities are in a very much better position to exploit trading powers than others, whilst yet others have such a low tax base per head that they are largely financed by the central government. Some examples are given in Tables 4a-b (pp. 291-2).

Each of these three sources of revenue has its main features fixed outside the local authority decision-making system. The scope for profits from trading undertakings and from charges on consumers of services is restricted by the socio-geographical circumstances of the area. Seaside towns and resorts are in a much better position to make money out of car parking, ferries, deckchairs, concert halls and the like, because the charges will be paid by outsiders rather than citizens. An authority may choose to give the 'profits' of any commercial service to its consumers in the form of lower prices rather than to the ratepayers as a payment in relief of rates.

In fact to talk of profits at all in this context makes no sense unless the features of the accounting system are specified. For a local authority will not necessarily treat the costs or the prices charged in the way that a private firm does. To speak of economic rents of council houses or of the economic fares on local authority buses implies a particular method of calculating both costs and receipts. What this system is will determine whether any 'profits' or 'losses' appear or not.

Local authorities receive two types of grant from the central government – *specific* and *general*, that is, allocated or unallocated to a particular service or part of a service. The specific grant is declared beforehand as a percentage of approved expenditure or as a fixed amount per unit of service provided. The local authority's expenditure decisions determine how much, subject to the necessary special audit, it will receive, and therefore how much it will have to find from its other resources. Housing subsidies are excellent examples of specific grants, for their total depends on the size and composition of the council's housing programme.

The amount of the general grant that a local authority receives is determined by complicated formulae. If it is a rating authority it will receive a share of the domestic and resources elements of the rate support grant, depending on the size of the domestic hereditaments' share of its rateable value and on whether its rateable value per head is below average or not. The main spending authorities within complex systems also receive a share of the needs element of the grant, which is intended to act as a general subsidy towards the cost of the expensive local authority services such as education and personal social services. What the individual authority will receive is determined by complicated formulae which are intended to reflect its needs in relation to listed services (those that are relevant to the calculation of the rate support grant in the first place), compared to other authorities.

In similar manner most of the characteristics of the rating system are fixed by general law, except the wealth of the area which is determined by its economic base and the socio-economic composition of the population.

The rates were a tax on the beneficial occupation of real property and were intended to be a charge on the occupier, not the owner, of an amount determined by the value of the property. Thus *real property* was the equivalent of *income* or *sales* for income and sales taxes respectively. The fiction still remains, but it has been modified in so many ways that it is not a good guide to the system of local taxation. The amount that the individual ratepayer actually pays is affected by so many factors that it can only be understood through a description of the details.

Originally the amount of tax base was to be the rent that the property (literally a hereditament in rating law) would command from a tenant leasing it on a year-to-year basis and doing the sort of things such tenants usually do. But for many classes of property there is little direct evidence of what this notional rent is. In the category of domestic hereditaments, owner-occupied houses, council houses and dwellings controlled under rent acts can not be authoritatively assessed in this way. Many types of commercial and industrial property have no annual value in the sense required by the law; property occupied by the Crown, for instance that used by the armed forces, cannot be envisaged as leased on the open market.

The result has been the development of conventional definitions, sometimes supplemented or replaced by specific enactments, of what the gross value of different types of hereditament should be and from this certain statutory deductions are made, to give the net annual value which is the amount on which the ratepayer will pay the local tax.

The original conception of the rates as a tax on beneficial occupation of real property has been further eroded by statutory modifications. Not only is the basis of valuation largely fictitious, but the liability to pay has been reduced in a number of ways. First, real property in the form of agricultural land and buildings, other than farmhouses, is exempt from the payment of rates, and is no longer even valued. Second, those with small incomes may claim a rate rebate of an amount determined by the Government through a statutory order. Third, charitable and recreational bodies may be excused, at the discretion of the rating authority, from paying a part of their rates. Fourth, domestic ratepayers have the amount that they would pay reduced by the equivalent of a fixed amount (a set rate in the £), which is also fixed by the Government and has been an increasing sum each year. Domestic derating is covered by the domestic element in the rate support grant mentioned above. Finally, a council may resolve to charge a proportion of the rates due on empty property on the owner, if it wishes.

It can be seen that in the above there is little scope for the local authority to change the major aspects of the system. The rateable value of each hereditament is fixed, subject to appeal against assessment, by the valuation officers of the Inland Revenue. This determines the total rateable value which the local authority is able to tax; the reductions in yield of a given rate in the £ are determined by law. The council has some discretion with charities and recreational bodies, with the rating of empty property and with the amount it publicizes the rate rebate scheme over and above the national campaign.

It does, however, have complete control over the rate in the £ it chooses to levy (or precept if it is not a rating authority). The council meeting at which the rate is finally determined is often regarded by outsiders as the most important meeting of the municipal year, but this is a misunderstanding. The chances of it being a significant decision-making occasion are not greater than those of any other meeting. Like these it comes at the end of a long process, most of whose features are determined long before it starts.

On the expenditure side, the local authority has little control over loan charges, continuing wage and salary bills, maintenance and depreciation on existing property.[13] Interest rates are determined by factors well outside the control of the authority; the size of the debt has been fixed by decisions about capital finance in years past; increases in wage and salary bills are now determined by national negotiating machinery; and there is a limit to the extent to which depreciation and maintenance costs may be ignored. Nor does it have much control over the product of a penny rate, which is a concept used solely as a calculating device in local government finance. It is the estimated amount that a rate of one penny in the £ would yield in that local authority. Some authorities are naturally rich and others poor, as a result of the economic and social status of the area, and the richer areas naturally raise a greater amount per head from the product of a penny rate.

Yet local authorities do make changes in their budgets during the five to six months that they are preparing them. What the rate in the £ will be in February is not a foregone conclusion in the previous September. Though the local authority does not have any large element of real discretion (and in meeting another authority's precept it has none) it has some scope throughout the financial system. What use is made of these tends to reflect an interaction with its environment.

Though it would be hard to establish this rigorously, there is some evidence that local authorities generally are expenditure-oriented as a result of the pattern of their internal organization. Professional officers believe in the value of their activities, often intensely, and they are supported by groups of council members who have, as a result of service on a committee, a considerable knowledge by acquaintance of individual services, and have acquired a commitment to them. There is considerable internal pressure to improve local government services – to which may be added the demands of consumers. But these forces, when aggregated, meet certain special features of the local council's sources of income.

First, the amount of money received from central grants is largely determined by national considerations such as changes in prices, the state of the economy and the centre's view of the need for progress, and any individual local authority may find that the national factors do not operate in the average way in its area. Unless its special problems are those which are covered by one of the few remaining specific grants then the grant system will not adapt to them.

Second, raising charges for services provided may meet objections from local citizens and, if done to a large extent, may meet the problem of demand falling very rapidly – total revenue may actually drop if prices are greatly increased, and the problem of evasion also grows.

Third, the rates have a fixed monetary basis, so that in order to raise more money it is necessary to increase the tax rate. The opposite happens in the case of income and sales taxes; the tax rate remains fixed and the yield increases automatically as the tax bases grow in monetary terms. The same effect could be achieved if the total rateable value (and each hereditament within it) was muliplied by some inflationary factor so that the yield would necessarily keep pace with changes in money costs, though the rate would remain constant. Despite the logical similarity the increase in the yield of the rates does not receive the calm acceptance that the same increase in the yield of income tax does.

There are several reasons why the rates should receive this distinctive treatment. One of the traditional ones was that they had to be paid in two lump sums at six-monthly intervals, and this could be very hard on the improvident. Local authorities are now required to make arrangements for payment by instalment for any of its ratepayers who choose, so that this factor is much less important now than it used to be. Another factor is the inability of the taxpayer to see the relation between his income and his tax payments, when the latter are invisibly extracted from him through some automatic method, such as deduction at source. There is also a general awareness that rates are regressive in that poorer people tend to pay a larger share of their income in the tax than do rich people.

Different sorts of political costs are involved in decisions by the local authority relating to the level of local taxation. Council members often show an awareness of the differential effects of rates on the separate types of hereditament – regressiveness for the poorer domestic ratepayers, the vocal political activity that small businessmen can produce and, the possible effects of high rates on locational decisions by developers and new investors. Some areas have been vulnerable to ratepayers' movements, which often contain a high proportion of 'economizers' and which have an accession of support when rate rises are particularly steep, or when revaluation disturbs the pattern of tax demands. In taking into account any of these political costs a council is interacting with its environment – often in the form of anticipated reactions.

Central control and local finance

The central domination thesis held that one of the major reasons for the control of local government by the central departments was the fact that such a high proportion of local current revenue was provided through central grants. The examination of the financial processes of an individual local authority does not support this belief. *A priori,* the conjunction of central finance and central control and influence is as consistent with the hypothesis that grants are paid because control exists, as the opposite. It is equally plausible to assume that both grants and control derive from the same third factor – the desire of the centre to achieve minimum standards of service provision and to protect the national 'interest' in local government services. For the individual local authority, however, most of the activities of the centre are 'givens' once it embarks on the six-month sequence of financial decision making; it is concerned with its local environment, both in the form of inputs of demands and outputs of service provision and tax calls.

In fact, what is most clear is that the level of control and influence achieved in a local authority by central departments individually and collectively is largely independent of the way local government is financed. Central government has at its disposal a large number of formal powers which can in principle be used to influence local authorities in directions that the centre desires, but whether these are so used depends on such factors as the will of the centre, which partly depends on the amount of information it has, and the will of the locality, which depends on many factors in its environment. The analysis of central-local financial relations cannot be divorced from the analysis of the general flow of influence in the system.

Chapter Eleven

Management in Local Government

The growth of the subject *management in local government* is not an isolated phenomenon, but is matched by similar developments in many other spheres of social life where large-scale formal organizations are important. The management movement, as it will be called, has generated multitudes of books, articles and lectures with such titles as 'management in X' and 'the administration of Y', where X and Y are the names of activities normally carried out in such organizations, or are the names of types of organization. The development of management thinking in public administration occurred later than in private commercial and industrial organizations, and this has given the management movement in local government some of its characteristic features.

In one sense, however, *the management of local authorities* is a very old subject, for problems of internal organization have been discussed at length in professional journals and in textbooks under a series of headings such as 'the committee system', 'the training of town clerks' and 'the role of the treasurer's department'. What this literature was like can be seen from past volumes of *Public Administration*, from textbooks such as J. M. Warren's *Municipal Administration*, and from weekly and monthly journals such as the *Local Government Chronicle*, the *Municipal Review* and more specialist publications for the local government professions. Prior to 1960 these carried articles which were often descriptions of some new development or administrative innovation in the local authority with which they were personally acquainted. For instance, the then deputy town clerk of Blackpool, now the Director-General of the Greater London Council, J. C. Swaffield, wrote an article in summer 1960 entitled 'Green Fingers in the Council Chamber' in which he described how his county borough council had set about rationalizing its committee system.[1]

This type of literature will be called the *traditional* approach to management in local government. It had several very important features.

First, it was largely written by officers rather than council members. This introduced systematic biases into the approach and presented most of the problems from an employee's point of view. The special concerns of elected representatives, such as those arising from the existence of the local social and political environment and from partisanship, were given very little weight in the analysis and diagnosis. In fact the local authority tended to be presented as relatively self-contained, solving its organizational problems by reference to internal factors, in contrast to the approach adopted here which denies that the management problems of an individual authority can be treated in isolation from their local environment.

But not all officers were equally inclined to write about the committee system and the departmental structure. Many of those writing were either clerks or treasurers – the two traditional offices which involved a concern with general organizational matters. It is not surprising that one of the main thrusts of the traditional reform proposals was for strengthening the town clerk's office and the finance committee's role within the overall pattern. The literature was also contributed by *chief* officers; the managerial roles of generalists and the organizational problems of the lower tiers were largely ignored.

Second, it was very much a reactive process – the results of detailed problem-solving activities within each authority. The traditional pattern of internal organization was established very early in modern local government history. Specific problems with the committee system, with the meeting cycle, with speed of decision making etc. led to a series of *ad hoc* solutions – merge several committees, introduce five-weekly meetings, delegate more to officers and so on.

Most of the relevant literature has remained unpublished because it consists of internal memoranda from officers and committees on organizational matters – the working documents of the individual authority, and in effect a sample of the culture of the organization.

Those experiments and 'discoveries' which were published could of course be presented simply as descriptions of what occurred in a particular system,[2] but many of the writers obviously thought that their personal experiences and the rules that they formulated in the course of a working life had a wider relevance, which justified presenting them to the local government world at large as organizational principles of some general utility. This process of generalizing from the particular instance to a wider class of cases involves certain logical difficulties. The reasoning was often anecdotal in that 'proof' was offered in the form of a personal experience. In other cases the reason was one of the generalities of everyday life, which are often held to be self-evident, such as the belief that very small committees are always better than large ones or that the professional knows best for his client.

Thirdly, the literature of the 'traditional' approach existed in an almost complete vacuum, having no contact with the general management literature that has developed in the twentieth century. This isolation cannot entirely be attributed to the local government world alone; part of the reason for the separation of two domains of thought about the same sort of thing lay in the nature of administrative thinking generally. The latter developed mainly in large scale commercial and industrial organizations, particularly those of heavy industry, and for many years the literature, including the concepts used, bore the stamp of its origins. This meant that much of it was about problems that were not the pressing ones in the individual local authority, and those that were did not appear in the books and articles. A second reason was that the general management writers showed considerable arrogance in the presentation of their ideas, and denied the necessity for detailed knowledge of specific types of organization. It was at that time difficult to get a dialogue going, because they were so confident that they had grasped the basis of a universal administrative science which would solve the organizational problems of all bodies, public and private.[3] Such attitudes could not recommend the 'theories' to the local government world, which at that time was probably more self-contained than it is now.

The traditional approach has not proved in the long run to be very satisfactory. Even if the fundamental logical flaws it contains are ignored and allowance made for the fact that most of the writers are not professional authors, it often failed the test of usefulness to other practitioners. For if all the writings are taken together they are found to be full of inconsistencies and gaps, both dictated by the accidents of the experiences of those who have chosen to publish their 'findings'. It is hard therefore to decide whether the clerk or treasurer should be both chief executive and administrative leader. But perhaps more important from the point of view of the man wishing to act on the recommendations is the fact that almost invariably they were presented in vague terms. To say that committees should be small, that they should be few in number, that chief officers should always show concern for the welfare of their subordinates and that council members should only decide those things in which they have a special interest, is not to say anything that can be used for definite action. 'Size of committees' must be specified in terms of number of members, 'showing concern for welfare' must be based on a definition of 'welfare' and so on. Once numbers are introduced or 'good' and 'bad' prescribed, then the recommendations immediately become less plausible, partly for intrinsic reasons – the 'proofs' obviously do not support that degree of precision – and partly for extrinsic ones – they make no reference to the environmental circumstances of the individual council. This is the dilemma of the practical man approach – the more precise, the less plausible are the principles, the less precise the principles the less usable in practice.

The modern approach

The modern approach to management in local government starts with assumptions quite different from those that were the basis of the traditional literature. Both insiders and outsiders have come to feel in recent years that general management literature is relevant at heart to the problems of local government administration and internal organization.

Relevance in this context involves two assumptions. The first is that there *is* a subject (discipline, science, theory, call it what you will) which has a very general applicability in all those organizations that are thought of as formal, complex and large-scale. This subject, it is believed, is a body of knowledge, both factual and contextual, which is valuable to those who are in any way responsible for the proper conduct of the organization and for the reasonableness of the behaviour of those in it. This body of knowledge helps the leaders of the organization (often referred to as 'the management') in their decisions about organizational matters. It is a guide to effective managerial behaviour and to rational managerial choice.

This assumption may be encountered in either of two forms. In its weaker version it embodies only the thesis that the knowledge is useful in a practical sense – that if employed with good judgement it helps managers to improve their decision making. In its stronger form it asserts that there is a genuine science of management or administration which stands to *management* in types of organization as physics and chemistry stand to engineering; thus *management in X* stands to behaviour in individual organizations as engineering stands to particular roads and bridges. The difference between the two forms is of course very important but the proponents of general management thinking are often ambivalent, writing as though the stronger form was intended but acting as though the weaker was.

The second assumption now normally made is that there are special problems associated with each type of organization which make it impossible or undesirable to transfer general ideas to the more specific context in a routine manner. The operation is more than a mere formality; it cannot be done in a mechanical fashion, but requires high level skills of a certain type. Some would go further and say that there are always special problems in the application of general ideas in individual organizations. The use of management ideas within a firm or a local authority is also a matter of skill rather than routine.

The two basic assumptions combine to produce definite implications for the subject of this chapter – management in local government in its modern form.

The first implication is that it is necessary to identify the special features of each type of organization (which is the object of management thinking), and then to identify any special features of an individual organization within a type before the ideas can actually be used. The second aspect of this implication will be left until the ramifications of the first have been explored.

In setting out the distinctive features of a type of organization care should be taken not to end up by arguing that the type is unique or too special to be assimilated in any way to other types. But in the case of local government there are a number of special characteristics which can only be ignored at the risk of producing irrelevant nonsense. The following attributes of local authorities are only a sample of the possible ones but they include those that will always be found to be important.

First, local authorities are *public* bodies. As part of the system of government they are largely exempt from the dictates of commerce – the free buying and selling of goods and services – which dominate the activities of capitalist organizations. They are also subject to all the considerations that public accountability entails in the circumstances of democratic decentralization.[4] Finally, they are under the imperative of equality – the need to treat everyone alike, unless and until due cause for differential treatment has been established.

Second, local authorities are a special type of public body, and this introduces further considerations. They are part of the system of decentralization but they are marked off (in the case of primary local government) from most other forms of local administration by four characteristics. Each local authority has a well-defined and relatively permanent territory, with clear boundaries of great operational significance – it can neither go outside them nor disclaim responsibility within them. It is multi-functional in that it is responsible for a variety of services, rather than just one. The governing body is directly elected rather than appointed. Finally, the authority controls an independent source of revenue through taxation and associated with this are constraints which guarantee it degrees both of autonomy and external restriction.

It is not necessary for the purposes of understanding local government to decide that these and only these are the relevant characteristics of local authorities for the construction of a modern management in local government. What is important is the consequence of the existence of *any* special characteristic for the choice of ideas within the general subject *management*.

It is obvious that any ideas to be worth transferring must deal with the sort of features that are distinctive in the type of organization. For example, in the short run it will be found that general management literature is very weak on 'government through committee' – it has scarcely ever concerned itself empirically with the highest levels of organization in private corporations. Knowledge of the shop floor is considerable but knowledge of the boardroom almost non-existent. As a second example, it will be found that *decentralization* scarcely ever refers to territorial division of responsibility but to functional allocation between branches and divisions within the organization; thus there is no account of the sort of decentralization that is of vital importance to the local government student – both because he is concerned with central-local relations and because extensive authorities operate through their own area administration.

For the transfer of ideas from the more to the less general to be successful they must not only be appropriate, they must be right – that is, justified and defensible in their original formulation. There is no point transferring something that has been discredited as part of *management* generally to a new sphere.

This is not the place to discuss the problems of distinguishing between 'good' and 'bad' in management literature generally, but several *caveats* are worth bearing in mind when discussing the subject in the context of local government. The first of these is that there is no homogeneous 'theory' or even 'approach' in administrative thought. On the contrary the writings that are given that title form an extraordinary diverse collection.

They include approaches that have been discredited in several different ways, and which are now better regarded as traditional social and political theory or interesting phases in the history of ideas. Some are so vague as to be little more than pious moralizing. Others are more concrete but not fully tested. But others require a knowledge of mathematics or economics for anyone to be able to use them. Some of these have records of success in narrowly defined fields.

The writings can in fact be grouped into three or four major traditions or classical schools on the basis of the sort of problems they typically confront, the concepts they use and what they count as *proof* of a general point. An important distinction can also be drawn between general administrative thought, which deals with the organization generally, and specialized administrative techniques, which are used to solve specific and precisely defined problems.

The example of specialized administrative techniques

After the above general considerations have been discussed it is possible to illustrate some of the advantages and defects of the modern approach to management in local government. The best place to start is with what the local government world usually calls 'management services' but which are referred to here as *specialized administrative techniques*.

The latter is a more descriptively accurate title for three reasons. They are specialized because each is highly specific – it applies to only a narrow range of problems which can be precisely stated in terms of conditions to be fulfilled, and if these are not, then the technique is non-applicable. They are administrative because they are at the disposal of those in the higher positions in the organization, who are often referred to as 'administrators' or 'managers', and can be used to further values espoused by them. They are techniques because they require skill – a matter of 'knowing how' – on the part of those who put them into effect. Some of them require rare and expensive abilities and training on the part of the practitioners.

The intention of these techniques is to bring about a more effective performance of one or more of the organization's activities. Though they have not yet in general achieved full articulation as useful theories, and only deal with one or a few values, they contain in varying degrees the elements of more promising long-term approaches to management in local government.

There are literally scores of allegedly separate techniques, some of them referred to by memorable acronyms, but differences in name do not always correspond to differences in substance. They may be grouped into four main categories, mainly on the basis of their intellectual foundations. Significantly, the categories differ in intellectual rigour, and, it may be argued, in terms of profitability of use.

Personnel management is the name of a set of techniques that relate individuals to the organization through their personal characteristics and their activities. They include job classification, recruitment, training, control, promotion and 'exit' – every aspect of the organizational life of the individual. Most are based on psychology or sociology, or some combination of the two. In local government there is obviously scope for their deployment in such fields as the specification of the role of a chief executive, the selection of professional trainees, the training of clerks dealing directly with the public, the creation of disciplinary procedures for peripatetic staff, the choice of deputy chief officers and the enforcement of early retirement for senior officers suffering prolonged ill-health.

Work study is the least theoretical of all categories. It is based on pragmatic problem solving, using whatever methods of measurement and close observation are feasible for a given set of work activities. The practitioner uses whatever material comes to hand in addition to the results of previous experience. Work study in the narrow sense tends to relate to manual labour, whilst organization and methods is the work study of clerical operations. Ergonomics, which is the study of ways of adapting working methods and equipment to the features of the individual doing the job, is more rigorously based, and draws on psychology, physiology etc. as needs dictate. Because local authorities are large employers of manual workers and clerical staff, there is obviously great scope for the use of many of the techniques in local government. Highways, bridges, sewers, parks and housing maintenance all offer the opportunity for work study in the narrow sense; filing, record keeping, organization of typing and office layout are suitable for organization and methods.[5]

Operational research is the most intellectually taxing of the groups, because it is a branch of either applied logic or applied mathematics. The foundation of operational research is the construction of a model – a deductive system which is a representation of the data under consideration. The behaviour of the model is believed to simulate the behaviour of the real world and thus by observing the former the latter can be predicted. It is thus a substitute for empirical experimentation. The simplest forms of operational research are those which are a type of network analysis, because these need only the mastery of a few symbols and elementary arithmetic. In contrast linear programming, queueing theory and cybernetics require mathematical imagination and ability of a high order.

Each of the operational research techniques contains great potential for use in local government. Critical path analysis, which uses a network, is of great significance in the building of roads, for its function is to improve the sequencing of activities that must occur in definite temporal order. Potentially it could be of great importance in the design of committee systems, which are at the heart of local authority internal organization. The traffic problems of an urban area are fundamentally complicated patterns of queueing situations, for the output of one road is the input of others; streets export traffic congestion to each other either directly, or through 'backing-up'. This is clearly a case for the employment of the techniques that are called 'queueing theory'.[6]

Management accountancy is a combination of economic reasoning and accountancy. Some of the techniques are cost-receipts analysis, as in traditional economics, but in the public sphere most are regarded as cost-benefit analysis. Generally they are concerned with the use of scarce resources and the evaluation of alternative forms of their deployment. Local authorities own, or in part control, one of society's scarce resources – land in the centre of large urban areas – and are responsible for many aspects of decisions about its use. They ought therefore to turn to those techniques which make more systematic the decisions about the allocation of resources to alternatives. In one sense cost-benefit analysis is only the generalization and systematization of the evaluation function that all local authorities have as the authoritative controllers of public money, staff and land.

Each member of each group of techniques requires that certain precise conditions be fulfilled before it can even be considered for use – the more rigorous the technique the more precisely the conditions are specified. For instance, critical path analysis studies activities that constitute a necessary temporal sequence and have definite starts and finishes. In road construction land has to be acquired through proper legal processes before work can start, excavation must take place before the foundations can be laid, and so on. It is no accident that the building of new highways has benefited tremendously from this technique, for it exemplifies the prescribed conditions perfectly.

Another example is queueing theory which requires that the operation consists of the treatment of cases at service points with a fixed processing capacity, when the pattern of arrival of cases to be served contains random elements – that is, is irregular in a non-predictable way. These conditions are literally the cause of queues and occur frequently in local authorities. Examples include the issue and collection of library books, the manning of information centres, running open clinics and operating a switchboard. In the case of library issues, it takes on average a certain time to deal with one book, but the number of people wanting to be served will be influenced by factors the chief librarian cannot know, such as the weather, alternative attractions and a previous night's television programme.

One could continue the list indefinitely, showing how there are occasions in local government where a particular technique is relevant because the conditions are fulfilled. This general point is not especially useful to an individual authority; what it wants to know is whether in its circumstances it should adopt a given technique, and if so, how it should deploy it. Fortunately it is possible to give an outline answer to these questions which permit the system to adapt to its own environment.

For the individual council the decision whether or not to adopt a technique depends on a comparison of the costs of administering it with the probable benefits, which may or may not be expressed in monetary terms. The cost side is relatively easy to estimate; it consists of payments for the investigation and the implementation of any proposal, both of which tend to occur for a relatively short time period, leaving only small extra running costs, if any, to continue indefinitely. The benefits side is much more problematical.

It is best to think of the benefits as being a function of the size of the operation or set of activities being investigated – in fact as a percentage. This means that the larger the operation the greater the probability of considerable gains compared with the costs of the investigation and implementation. The size of the activity within the system depends on the size of population served and on the environmental factors which increase or reduce demands on the system for that activity. The second consideration is the length of time during which it can be expected that the gains from adopting the proposals will continue to accrue. Administrative systems tend to 'slip' with the passage of time through the impact of external forces and interaction with other parts of the system itself. Sometimes it is found that new organizational structures last only a few months, as they are moulded to the needs of the individuals within and outside them.

The vital factor here is the degree of rigour involved in the use of the technique. All of them can be placed somewhere on a dimension which measures their 'hardness' or 'softness' in terms of the calculations they involve and the precision of the proposals that they generate. The more precisely the operational system is specified and the more clearly the benefits derive from using it, the longer the system will last. Thus the more the technique is logically strict the greater the confidence that the rewards for successful use will in fact be obtained.

All of the above considerations can be combined into a simple decision-making scheme for use by each individual local authority. In short the leaders of the council need to ask themselves a series of questions, in sequence, and to act on the answers. For every individual technique the first question is whether it is needed by the local authority or not. If it is judged to be unnecessary then the matter ends there. But if it is regarded as valuable, the next question is whether there is sufficient work within the authority to justify the employment of full-time staff. If the answer is no then decisions must be taken as to the form in which it will be used – either through outside consultations, by purchase from another local authority or through the creation of joint arrangements with others.

If the employment of full-time specialist staff is regarded as justified then the problem becomes one of integrating them into the departmental and committee system. In the traditional form of internal organization this meant either adding to an existing committee's terms of reference (in which case, which committee?) or creating a new committee. In the newer forms they are at the disposal of the policy committee or management board (or whatever the executive committee is called) as part of its leadership role. At departmental level the new staff could either be made a separate department or integrated in an existing one (in which case the choice of which department arose). In the newer forms they will be closely associated with the chief executive even if they are not literally part of his department.

Though decisions have to be taken about each technique on its merits within the individual system, an authority can adopt one of two general policies. It can decide to treat every technique it chooses to deploy through its own staff in the same way, thus building up a management services unit or department, as they are typically called, or it can make different decisions about each one, allocating some to one department, some to another and so on. Thus in a traditional organization management accountancy techniques might generally be allocated to the treasurer's department whilst work study was part of the engineer's.

The example of the management board system

The use of specialized administrative techniques by individual local authorities illustrates how ideas can be transferred successfully from one level of generality to another. But because they are so straightforward they do not illustrate the sort of problems that typically beset management in local government when it deals with the overall structure of internal organization. The position in relation to general management thinking about creation and reorganization of systems is much less satisfactory.

The difficulties may be illustrated by looking at one of the recent proposals for a more 'managerial' form of organization, made by the Maud Committee in 1967.[7] For various reasons the scheme was almost completely unacceptable to local authorities, but these are not the concern of this section. Attention is focused on the logic of the Committee's proposals.

As was remarked earlier, by the early 1960s a considerable consensus had grown up about the defects of the classical pattern of internal organization adopted by most authorities. These were departmentalism, committee-itis, pseudo-professionalism and over-democratization: all defects which both derived from and contributed to the lack of an executive or leadership body – 'executive organ of government' and 'managing body' as the Maud Committee described it – to integrate the diverse activities of the local authority towards common goals and to stress community of interest – the corporate approach as it is now called.

Few would wish to challenge this analysis of defects, provided it is not presented in terms too stark and derogatory, but the main difficulty appears once people have to think of a new form of organization which will meet all the constraints within the local government system. The new pattern must not only be described in detail but it must also be sufficiently adaptable to permit it to be adjusted to all the varying circumstances that individual authorities encounter.

This trend towards simplification and centralization could find prototypes for reform in several different places. It could look at national government, at business experience and at local government in other countries.

The cabinet system with all its ramifications is obviously a centralized one, but it is clear that it can only be applied in local government with greatest difficulty and in exceptional circumstances, because some of the vital conditions for viable cabinet government do not exist. It is not suitable, for instance, in non-partisan and semi-partisan systems. It could be argued, also, that where conditions were most suitable it already existed to some extent in the party caucus and the dominant role of committee chairmen; the Maud Committee found these facts objectionable in the local government context.

Though it is widely believed that the board of directors in a private firm is a well-documented and well-understood institution, this is not true – or at least not to a sufficient extent to provide a blueprint for local authority organization. Much more is known about the conditions for increasing productivity in small groups of manual workers than of the working structures of boards of conglomerate companies such as Imperial Chemical Industries.

Reformers therefore have been attracted by the experience of other countries, particularly that of the United States, which is well documented. America is familiar with at least four major types of internal organization for local authorities. If these are thought of as model schemes, rather than as abstractions from observed systems, they can be called 'plans'.[8]

The traditional American form of administrative organization for local councils was the *weak mayor-council* plan, in which the mayor and the council members were directly elected but so also were a multitude of heads of departments. This was the aptly-named 'long ballot electoral system': the elector had to vote for a long list of city offices, both administrative and judicial, as well as council members in the British sense. Even in terms of the most fragmented English administration it was extremely decentralized and impossible to co-ordinate within itself.

Towards the end of the nineteenth century three other plans become popular with the middle-class reformers of municipal administration. The first of these simply abolished the host of elected executive offices, and made all heads of departments subordinate to the mayor, appointed and holding tenure at his pleasure. The relations between mayor and council (both directly elected) were modelled on the separation of powers found in the federal presidential system and in many state constitutions. This was the *strong mayor-council* plan.

The other two plans derive their inspiration from business management rather than from the rest of the political system. The first was the *commission* plan in which the council and the directly-elected mayor were replaced by a small group (perhaps five) of heads of departments, directly elected, but acting collectively as the municipal authority. The originators of the plan thought, probably erroneously, that boards of directors were constituted and operated in this manner.

The fourth plan is the one favoured by many reformers today. It provides for the direct election of a small council which collectively is the authority, and which makes only one appointment, that of the council's manager. He is head of the whole administration and appoints all the departmental heads, prepares the budget and generally runs the executive side of the authority's business. The *council-manager* plan is thus the most centralized and simplified structure of the four. This can easily be seen by a comparison of the organizational charts of the four plans which are presented in Figures 9(a)-9(d).

Before the Maud Committee had reported in 1967 a number of local authorities had been thinking about new forms of internal organization based on American patterns or constructed *a priori* from general principles. Some innovations had occurred and though these in fact departed widely from models of business organization and from the transatlantic plans, they were available as sources of ideas.[9]

What it finally chose as the pattern to be recommended should be referred to as the *management board system*, because the management board itself was only a part of the structure. The system was an attempt to combine various intractable features of British local government with the admired features of other forms of administrative organization. A careful reading of the text giving the reasons for the choice shows that it was *de facto* constructed on the classical principles of administration – one of the major traditions of administrative thought mentioned above.

The plan as presented by the Committee is reproduced in Figure 5(c) (p. 137). It is immediately recognizable as a structure based

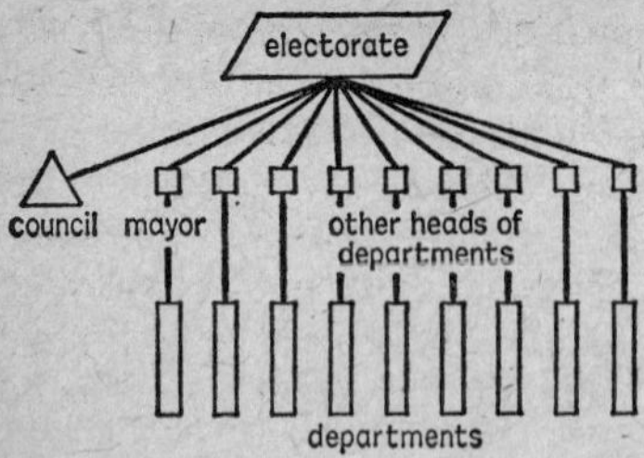

9 (a) **The Weak Mayor-Council System**

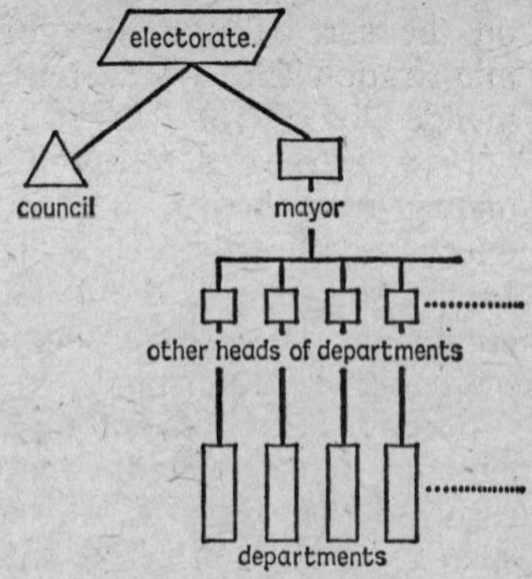

9 (b) **The Strong Mayor-Council System**

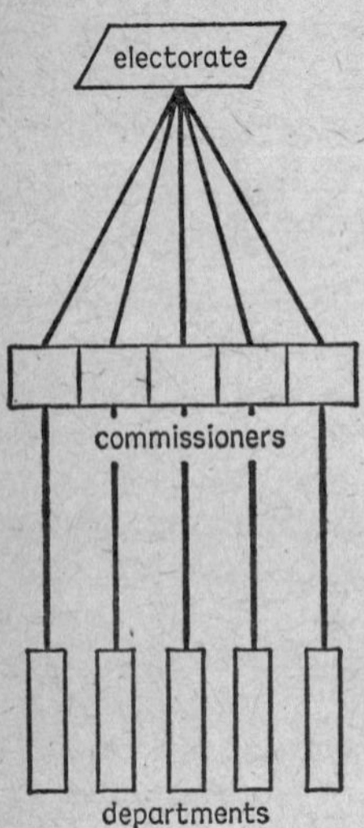

9 (c) **The Commission System**

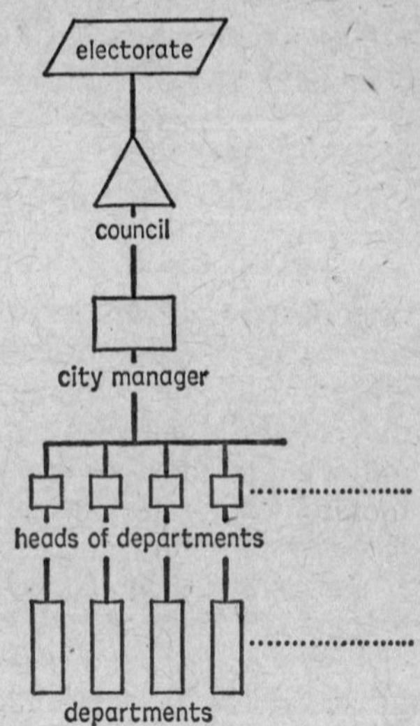

9 (d) **The Council-Manager System**

Figs. 9 (a) – (d) **American 'Plans' for City Administration**

on the sort of principles of organization, management and administration (the words tend to be used interchangeably) recommended by Fayol, Urwick, Mooney and their followers.

First, it creates *unity of command.* The council controls the management board, the management board controls the chief executive officer and he is head of all the council's paid employees. In the language of the classical principles there is a clear line of command running from top to bottom of the organization, and including every person.

Second, it embodies the principle of limited *span of control.* No superior is responsible for more than six subordinates directly (it is assumed that this will be repeated within each department). The span of control principle was one of the most cherished of those of the classical school because it was both exact in meaning and believed to be mathematically provable.

Third, the structure distinguished between *line* and *staff*. The combination of *unity of command* and *span of control* produced this backbone of hierarchical relationships represented by the solid line in the diagram. The contribution of specialist knowledge and interest was provided through the consultative-advisory-informational relationships indicated by the broken lines. This combination of command and advice was known as *line and staff* organization and the management board system obviously exhibited it very clearly.

In order to obey the principles mentioned above the structure drastically reduced the degree of *specialization,* which was another important member of the list of classical principles (in fact it was often listed first). In order to maintain span of control it was necessary to merge departments under the control of a few principal officers, who thus became much less narrowly professional in their duties. The same phenomenon occurred with the merger of committees. The most specialized officers were moved down the official hierarchy and the specialized committees became subcommittees if they were retained.

How should this be evaluated? The first question is whether it matters that the system is based on several of the classical principles of organization in such a straightforward manner. How far is it a justification of a particular model of internal organization to show that it conforms to the recommendations of this school?

Once the question is put in this manner it is easy to answer. For the whole of the classical school of management principles has been discredited. It has been subject to damaging logical analysis by H. A. Simon who has shown that the individual principles are confused and vague, and that as a set they are inconsistent. It has also been discredited by empirical research by organizational sociologists such as Joan Woodward, who have shown that following the classical principles, in so far as this is possible, is not necessarily a formula for success; in some cases it is actually a recipe for failure.[10]

It thus fails the first of the tests for the creation of a modern management in local government – the first aspect of the transferability problem. The second aspect is the extent to which it is possible to be eclectic by borrowing ideas from diverse sources. Though there is nothing logically objectionable to this, in practice it meets two difficulties: how far the diverse elements are compatible and how far it is possible to abstract elements from the original scheme without taking others as well.

Great care needs to be taken when elements from different contexts are mixed together, and the consequences of a failure are well illustrated in the Maud Committee Report. One member disagreed with the majority on the way committees should be integrated in the system and produced a modified version of the management board scheme. Sir Andrew Wheatley said that he would keep committees as executive bodies and give them direct access to the council, whilst retaining a strong management board, chief executive and few principal officers. This is an attempt to combine the characteristics of the traditional system with the new ideas derived from overseas and from business (see Figure 10(a)).

It is a sad commentary on what must have been the intellectual level of the Committee's discussion that the fact that this was self-contradictory was not noticed. For the text says that committees are executive whilst the diagram, through the broken line, says that they are non-executive. The text says that it retains the strong management board, or rather the concept the majority were recommending, but it violates *unity of command* both in relation to committees and to chief officers. But it is simply impossible to mix up different models in this way because they are based on ideas that are not consistent as a set.

As an illustration of the second aspect of this difficulty it may be remarked that the council-manager plan in the United States is only part of a larger scheme for city government. A complete system would include a very small council (five to nine members), at-large elections, compulsory non-partisanship and the involvement of the council in only one executive matter – the appointment of the

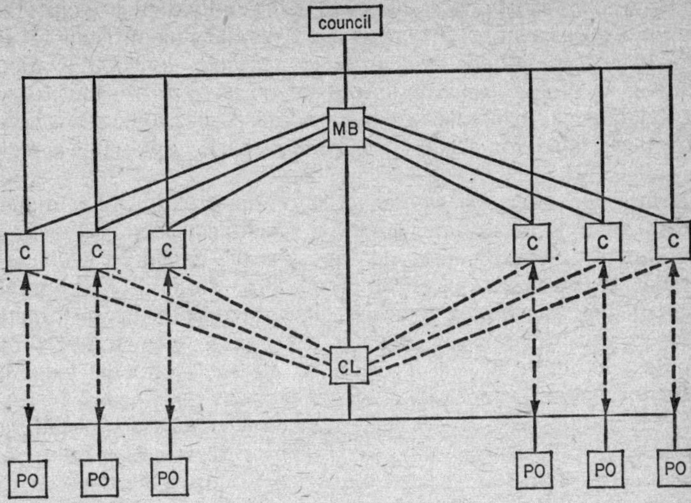

Fig. 10 (a) **Wheatley's Alternative**

reproduced (with permission) from page 156, *Report of the Committee on the Management of Local Government*, HMSO, 1967

council manager. None of these features have been borrowed along with the clear chain of command which the council-manager system necessarily embodies. Nor could they have been copied for they depart so far from the British tradition of local government administration that they would have been completely unacceptable and unworkable. Yet there is American evidence that the viability of this simplified and centralized administrative organization depends on factors in the system-environment interaction. In the United States many local political environments are hostile to the council-manager plan, and in these it has either not been tried, been abandoned or operated quite differently from the way it was intended.[11]

This leads to a third general problem; have the original ideas been understood correctly? In the case of the classical principles of organization it might be argued that this does not matter as they are discredited. But this is not the case with two of the American models – the council-manager plan and the strong major-council plan. Though the fanatics for the former regard their plan as suitable everywhere, there is considerable evidence that what needs to be understood is the relationship between the organizational form and the environment in which it exists. The Maud Committee made no effort to understand foreign experience in terms of a system-environment interaction and indeed they could not, because they relied on superficial impressions gained on a fleeting visit to several countries by one of their members.

What these criticisms amount to is a demand that proposals to change an administrative form (or any other constitutional or political arrangement) should be scrutinized in the same, or greater, detail and with the same care as the existing system was. This means that the proposals should be 'unpacked' by trying to envisage how they would operate in a dynamic model instead of the static one in which they are usually presented first. This involves taking into account the impact of those social and political forces in the existing situation which are not changed by the reform, and considering how present roles, for which there will still be a demand, will be performed.

The example of the corporate approach

The management board proposal was a failure as a model for the reform of the internal organization of local authorities for most local councils implicitly or explicitly rejected it. Even had they accepted it there is good reason to believe that it would have been unworkable in the British context. As a result of the failure to find a generally acceptable prototype a study group was appointed jointly by the Secretary of State for the Environment and the local authority associations in May 1971, to examine 'management principles and structures in local government at both elected member and officer levels'. This led in August 1972 to the document that is commonly known as the 'Bains Committee Report'.

Though the Bains Committee paid tribute to the Maud Committee's work they share nothing in common except the general diagnosis of the ills of departmentalism and related phenomena. The management board concept as described above was based on a systematic selection approach to organization. This type of approach involves first the prescription of a set of roles that constitute the administrative pattern, then the identification of the sorts of people who will fill these roles excellently, followed by changes in recruitment and socialization processes which will lead to the right individuals filling the roles that they can perform extremely well. It is generally assumed that the talents of individuals will ensure that the roles come into existence as originally conceived.

There is no space here to rehearse the arguments against the systematic selection approach to management in local government but a study by the present author concluded 'council members cannot be chosen deliberately to fill a set of previously prescribed roles; the defects of selectivity cannot be remedied by socialization measures and managerial control cannot be instituted in a council and committee system'.[12] The alternative approach is to accept the existing stock of people, and any changes made through the electoral process, and adapt institutional forms to their characteristics. Because of its basic logic this is the *ergonomic* approach.

The Bains Committee adopted the ergonomic approach. It argued that 'at officer level . . . the authority has the responsibility of selection; it has no control over the election of its own membership' (p. 39). Though this is mentioned relatively late in the presentation it is clearly the fundamental starting point for the analysis of a new organizational system. The Committee believed that 'members of local authorities have a wide diversity of aims and interests . . . [it was] impossible to cast them all in the same role . . . the structure of the authority should be such as to provide members with work of thc appropriate type.' (p. 9).

What the Committee wanted was an organizational structure which would foster rather than retard the growth of the *corporate outlook*. This is not specifically defined but means in effect an awareness of responsibility for 'the overall economic, cultural and physical well-being of that community' and of 'the interrelationship of problems in the environment in which it is set'. As these quotations will have illustrated the Bains Committee was much more aware of the diversity within local government and of the fact that each authority exists within its own specific environment. It thus starts from the same point as does this book, and differs only in that it does not pursue the characterization of the *system-environment* relationship much beyond the identification of its existence.

The Committee therefore attempted to replace the traditional professionalism of local government with a corporate outlook, which would also be sufficiently flexible to adapt to all sorts of variation in the environment. In order to do this it completely reversed the approach of the Maud Committee, which strongly favoured simplification and centralization, by producing an outline scheme that was immeasurably more complicated than the management board system and, it may be argued, more complex than the traditional system. In addition, if the proposals for extra council member and officer organization were to work in a predictable manner decision-making power would be spread more widely through the organization.

Though the Bains-type organization is often presented to local authorities as a way of abolishing specialization in favour of the corporate approach, this is obviously incorrect. What it does is reduce traditional types of specialization – on the basis of *services* defined by central government – and supplement or replace them by other types of differentiation. It includes specialization by horizontal function – land, finance and manpower – and by programme area. The question of whether a corporate approach exists or not cannot be guaranteed simply by a different form of specialization.

It may be argued that the real innovation that Bains proposed was the creation of a committee system for officers. Horizontal committees and subcommittees are familiar in the traditional pattern of internal organization, programme committees look like the enlarged vertical committees formed through simple merger, but officer organization would be quite different. In the traditional system the chief officer *was* the department in terms of the local constitution, just as the minister is the ministry in central government, and responsibility rested with the individual. What arrangements each chief officer made for the disposal of his duties were his responsibility.

But if officers are to be organized into a management team of the senior officers, usually the five or six called 'directors', and there are also to be interdepartmental working groups, which are in reality subcommittees of the management team, and interdisciplinary working groups to service the programme committees, the whole will have to be organized into a proper committee system, with fixed times of meeting, regular agendas, the circulation of minutes and reports, and a secretariat to ensure the proper routing of business. In fact eventually standing orders will have to provide accurate terms of reference for each committee and group.

If such a system were to be implemented (and I doubt whether it will be acceptable in practice to chief officers) then it would take power away from the top of the department and disperse it more widely throughout the ranks of middle range and senior employees. If it were to become operational it would be the opposite of the management board because it would decentralize participation in important decisions.

Fig. 10 (b) **An Interpretation of the Bains' Proposals**

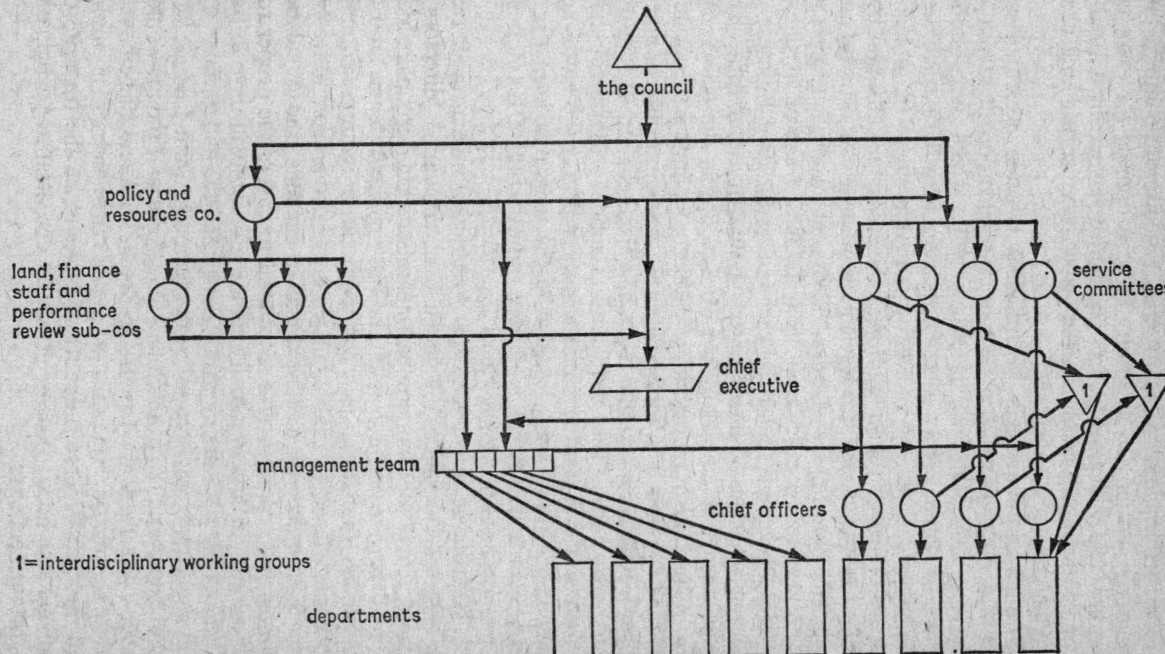

The example of the analysis of committee systems

The Bains Committee Report is an excellent example of the pragmatic practical man approach, in contrast to the more 'principled' approach of the Maud Committee, but these do not exhaust the possible lines of analysis of the internal organization of local authorities. A different approach may be discovered by rejecting a reliance on either the collective wisdom of generations of officers and council members or on the intervention of general management principles between ordinary intellectual criteria and the conclusion of the analysis. This may be thought of as a *reductionist* approach because it reduces all analytical considerations to those of conventional intellectual standards, or as a *do-it-yourself* approach, because the analyst makes up his own rules for understanding and creates rather than borrows the tools of his trade.

In the case-study that follows committee systems are examined with a view to determining how large a council a local authority should have – in fact one of the traditional questions of management in local government. In doing so the example will also illustrate two of the basic points of this book; understanding local government is a matter of increasing rigour in analysis, moving towards quantification, and the internal organization of the individual authority can only be understood in terms of a set of dimensions – *the rule of interpretation.*

The key to understanding committee systems is to describe them in terms of a number of relevant dimensions, to analyse the relationships between them rigorously, and to evaluate them in terms of their organizational consequences, in conjunction if this is necessary. Each dimension is a variable, to be specified in terms of meaning, scale of measurement and range of variability.

The four dimensions of committee systems chosen for this example are:

number of committees (C: discretely, in steps of one, from one to ?)

average number of members per committee (N: continuously, from one to ?)

average number of committee memberships per member (M: continuously, from ? to ?)

total membership of the council (S: discretely, in steps of one, from 3(?) to ?)

If a person were deciding how large the total membership of a council ought to be it might be thought that he could proceed by using the following equation which expresses the logical relations between the four variables:

$$S = \frac{C \times N}{M}$$

Thus if there are 10 committees with 10 members each, and the workload in terms of committee memberships ought to be 2, then the council should have 50 members.

But this is not correct because in default of extra information there is no reason why the equation should not be turned around so that the number of committee memberships (M) (an aspect of workload) was presented as the dependent variable, thus:

$$M = \frac{C \times N}{S}$$

Figure 11 shows that because of the logical relations between variables they are in a situation of arithmetical interdependence and any one of the four can be made the subject of the equation and therefore the dependent variable. If any three of the four are or can be determined externally to the situation itself then the fourth is completely determined. But none is logically prior to the others unless someone by *fiat* or evaluation makes it so.

It must be stressed that the problem that this line of investigation has discovered is not that which occurs when too few obvious variables have been included in the analysis. There are many other dimensions which could have been included without disturbing the central logical relationship. For instance, the notion of council member's workload could be refined by adding the length of meetings and the frequency of meeting to give number of hours of attendance on committee work. The average number of members per committee is changed by the addition of co-opted members.

It is no use whatsoever adding further equations and dimensions of the same sort because these never change the logical relationships of interdependence between members of this set. Nor is it any use reverting to the intuitions of practical men because this does not avoid the problem; it only closes one's eyes to it.

What is needed is a different sort of equation that relates changes

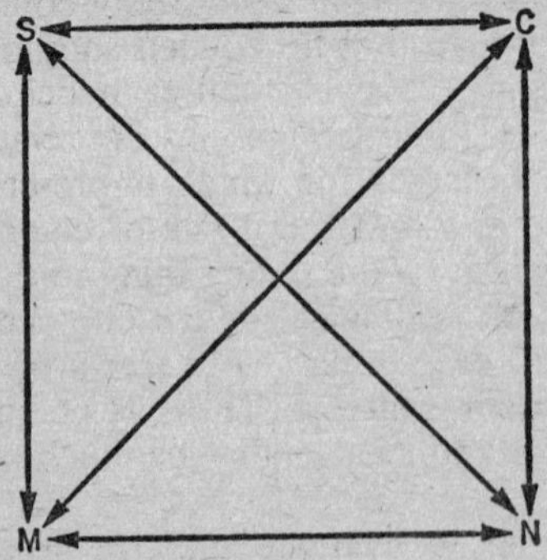

S = size of council

C = number of committees

N = average number of members per committee

M = average number of committee memberships per member

Fig. 11 **The Interdependence of Council Size and Committee Memberships**

in the score on each variable (considered separately) to consequences that are themselves valued by the persons in charge of decision making about the form of internal organization. These consequences are not related logically, as are the variables themselves, but causally to the chosen dimension. Whether the alleged relationship exists is therefore an empirical matter.

For instance, the *workload* of council members affects their willingness to serve and to seek re-election, attendance records, the possibility of interlocking memberships, and perhaps their decision-making efficiency. The *size of committee* affects what sort of group it is, decision making at the meeting, the range of abilities included in the committee, representation of interests and areas, and the satisfaction obtained from membership. The *number of committees* affects the complexity of the communication system and the problems of allocation between committees, the speed of decision making, the amount of detail considered at meetings and the demands on officers' time.

All of these are conventionally evaluated by members, officers and to a lesser extent citizens, and some are 'goods' and others are 'bads'. The problems of dealing with them can be illustrated further by looking at the fourth dimension – the size of council.

The Maud Committee argued that no council should have more than seventy-five members. This is totally inadequate as an approach. First, the Maud Committee ignored the relationship between this and the other variables for which it prescribed values (number of committees (6) and maximum size of committee (15)), which has already been seen to be the wrong thing to do. Secondly, it prescribed a ceiling, which is illogical unless one can be certain that no local authority will ever be larger in terms of business to be dealt with than the existing largest. Third, a ceiling tells one nothing of the right size for councils smaller or much smaller than the largest.

What is required in order to evaluate the size of council is a formula which relates it to its consequences and its context. The first of these relevant factors is *representation*. If the desirable level of intensity of representation (citizens per elected representative) can be established then the formula would be a simple proportional relation, thus:

$$S = \frac{P}{a}$$ (P is size of population, a is intensity of representation)

Likewise it can be established that the amount of business generated is a function of population size, if the composition of the population is held constant. Thus:

$$S = \frac{B}{d}$$ (B is total amount of business and equals the population multiplied by item generation ratio; d is the desirable workload per member.)

But in contrast to these simple proportional relationships the value of the *size of council meeting* as an occasion is curvilinear; costs are high for the very small and the very large meeting. Thus, as the council's size increases from the *intensity of representation* and *amount of business* factors, rapidly increasing costs of large meetings are encountered. Thus in the significant sector of population sizes the two sorts of consideration are inversely related. Though the outcome of the balancing of these two opposed factors cannot be predicted exactly, it may be supposed that the true form of the relationship will be capable of being approximated by a linear equation of the form

$$S = e + fP.$$

In such a case *e* may be regarded as the minimum size of council that is generally acceptable, *f* as the rate of change determined by the combination of intensity of representation, the 'amount of business' factor and the 'size of meeting' factor.

It is interesting to note that in practice the size of councils is related to population in this manner; for instance a study by the present author found the following relationships—

English CBs, 1967	$S = 28.7 + .17P$	$(r = +.89)$
English CCs, 1967	$S = 52.6 + .04P$	$(r = +.77)$

(*r* is the correlation coefficient, measuring the degree of association between the two variables, and *P* is measured in thousands.)

This is perhaps evidence that the previous analysis is on the right lines, but of course a simple description does not mean that the right formula has been discovered. The aim of management thinking is to determine what the equation *should* be.

So far it has been assumed that all councils have a homogeneous environment, but this is obviously not the case. The changing context in which each council operates can easily be accommodated in the model by adding such factors as the number and importance of the services provided, the social composition of the population, population growth and density, all of which affect the volume of business coming before the authority and the representative function.

Those who are familiar with the conventional literature on management in local government, whether it be generated by the practical man approach or by the transfer of general management concepts to local authorities, will recognize that the do-it-yourself approach produces something quite different. The reason why this is so lies in the nature of the presuppositions on which a new understanding of local government must be based. The search for rigour by-passes both the intuitions and impressions of insiders and the conclusions of those who apply general management principles.

A comparison of the examples

Can anything be learned from comparing the fates of the four examples discussed above? Of course such an operation can prove nothing but it may well have considerable heuristic value. The sort of lessons that can be learned are also plausible in the sense that they have a *prima facie* reasonableness which is independent of the local government context.

Some of the considerations that relate to success or failure are intrinsic, that is, they are characteristics of the analysis embodied in the example, whilst others are extrinsic, that is, they relate to the fact that the local political system exists within its own specific environment which strongly influences the pattern of internal organization.

Specialized administrative techniques provide some of the best examples of the successful transfer of ideas from general management thinking to local government for three reasons. First, they involve clear and widely accepted values, such as efficiency, elimination of waste, greater certainty in the face of a fluctuating environment and so on. Second, the reasons that are given in support of them are persuasive because they involve widely accepted premises and factual beliefs, and the conclusions are derived from them by defensible inference processes. Thirdly, the recommendations are framed in precise terms so that what counts as following and not following them is clear. They do not suffer from lack of utility through inconsistency and vagueness. The above judgement is supported by the fact that the techniques vary amongst themselves in respect of all three headings, and the higher they score on these, the more convincing the case for them.

In contrast the Maud Committee's scheme for a management board clashed with widely held values amongst both officers and council members. Indeed it was not always clear how far it would have promoted any previously identified values. The reasons given accepting it were very weak, even if one ignores the abysmally written text, and in many cases belonged to a discredited tradition. Third, though some of the recommendations were exact, for the most part this was a spurious precision, created by simply 'thinking of a number'! In fact many of the recommendations taken together were unworkable as they stood; if one needs excellent judgement to make them into an operational system one might as well have used that judgement by itself.

The Bains Committee was much more successful than the Maud Committee, though not as convincingly so as many of the specialized administrative techniques, because it related to many of the widely held values of both council members and officers. Any lack of acceptability which was experienced in some places seems to be attributable to the fact that it leaned more towards the values of those officers who were likely to be part of the management team than towards those of council members and the more narrowly professional officers. The intellectual difficulty with Bains is that its members did not appreciate fully the significance of what they were proposing and therefore its rationale is not as clearly expressed as it might be. The result is that many of those who have adopted it with enthusiasm as a blueprint have thought they were adopting an improved version of Maud, whereas they were adopting anti-Maud. The question of the imprecision of some of its proposals, however, raises a quite different problem of acceptability which will be discussed below.

The question of the acceptability of the fourth example does not arise in the same way because it was presented simply to show what an alternative approach to management in local government would look like. It should be remarked in passing, however, that it shares several things in common with some of the specialized administrative techniques. It depends on widely accepted values, its reasoning is sufficiently tight to be justified and it ends with precise recommendations of different sorts if it is followed through (that is, further than in this book).

There is a different sort of acceptability involved in the fate of schemes for organizational reform, however, which is the verbal acceptance by participants of the proposals, irrespective of what they do. This arises from the fact that a local authority is a political system set in its own environment and interacting with it, in ways that affect its internal structure in numerous dimensions. The degree and nature of the acceptability of this externally promoted reform depends on the situation of the local authority and often schemes and models become integrated into local political culture, suffering a sea change in the process.

On this interpretation the significance of a new form of organization depends on how it is taken over by those in the local political system and adapted to their pre-existing needs. Vagueness and imprecision become virtues because they give much greater scope for translation into a form which justifies doing what was desired on other grounds. The Wheatley dissent was excellent from this point of view; because it was literally inconsistent it could be used to 'prove' virtually anything. The flexibility that Bains attributed to their proposals also makes the scheme attractive as a source of justifications. This point receives some confirmation from the fact that generally the 'softer' specialized administrative techniques are more popular in local government, despite their lesser payoffs, than the 'hardest' ones, for they also through their lack of complete rigour permit a greater variety of interpretations and manipulation.

In fact the proposal of a committee of enquiry, even if backed by the recommendation of the Government, is simply another input of information into the local authority decision-making system. Like the others it is processed or 'digested' and it emerges in a form that reflects the factors at work within the system.

Chapter Twelve
The Fear of Local Democracy

The fourth 'application' of the general framework of concepts to a specific set of topics is also the conclusion of the book. This is appropriate because it is the fact of direct election of members of the local authority that is the most important characteristic of the British local government system. The other three distinguishing features of primary local government are significant in their own right but some of their interest for the citizen and the student arises because they are part of a structure which is based on institutions of local democracy.

It is also appropriate because local elections, and the political institutions that relate to them, bring into existence some of the questions that have most concerned the citizen, the local activist and the local government officer. Understanding local government must therefore depend on an understanding of local democracy. The latter's institutions and behaviour have already been presented either as a part of the system-environment interaction or as part of systemic behaviour itself. Conventionally, however, such subjects as partisanship, competitiveness and the quality of councillors have been discussed first and foremost as aspects of local political behaviour divorced from the contexts in which they occur with an emphasis on blunt evaluation.

The local community, including the village, the town and the city, has always had a place in traditional social and political theory, though usually a modest one.[1] The government of localities within the overall framework of society and its constitutional arrangements has always raised certain problems. Consideration of these will be limited to the last hundred years when local representative institutions took their place in a system of national democracy. The position assigned to local government in the modern state has been variously referred to as its 'foundations', its 'justification' and as 'theories'.[2] Though most aspects of these have been widely accepted in recent years, attention will not be focused on its values, but on the inconsistencies that usually accompany it in the minds of those who are involved in or write about local democracy.

As its other names suggest, a 'theory' of local government is a list of reasons why local administration of public services through directly elected bodies, responsible to the citizens of an area, is superior to all other forms of decentralization. It thus involves a fear of appointment, through which the centre may dominate the locality, and a fear of local oligarchy, through which traditional elites may continue to govern. These two motives combined in opposition to the control of county government in the nineteenth century by justices of the peace meeting in quarter sessions. Fears of autocracy and oppression by the privileged few are of course one of the sources of democratic theory, but once locally elected institutions have been created other fears take over. Notice that these are not the fears of those who saw local office as a form of personal property or who rejected democracy on other grounds, both attitudes common until the last decades of the nineteenth century. Understanding local government involves an appreciation of the inconsistencies in the minds of those who *believe* in local self-government, as it is now called in developing countries.

The first of these inconsistencies within the theory of local government is between the acceptance in principle of the superiority of local elected institutions and the rejection of democratic behaviour that they make possible. The fear of local democracy is a fear that electors and the elected will behave in ways that are permitted by the system, and whose existence is a central part of the justification of this form of local administration. The fear itself contains two contradictory strands – that local political behaviour will not be democratic enough, and that it will be too democratic. Perhaps the best way to summarize the whole of the following argument is to say that those who evaluate local government are trying to escape from the consequences of local elections – consequences that can be shown to derive from the nature of local government and which are themselves the basis of the 'proof' of its value.

In one sense local democracy is only national democracy translated to the local level with modifications necessitated by the different scale of operations, the different context and its subordinate position. The system is therefore based on free and fair elections, as this expression is conventionally understood. At one time there was a considerable body of opinion which favoured fancy franchises or the restriction of the right to vote to the 'responsible' elements in the local community. The same views led to the desire to limit candidature to those who govern properly if elected. Support for such views has declined continuously since the middle of the nineteenth century, so that today the franchise and the right to submit oneself for election are virtually as wide as they can be. Freedom of electoral choice was guaranteed by the secret ballot and limitations introduced on 'unfair' methods of campaigning, with the result that there is a system of elections similar to that found in national government. The main features of this system were described in an earlier chapter; this book therefore concludes with a consideration of the effects of these within the framework of the 'theory' of local government.

To understand this phase of local government it is necessary to grasp, and to hold on to, one basic fact about free and fair elections in a western context. This basic fact is that elections are not like systematic selection procedures as methods of recruitment. They are externally uncontrollable; if they can be manipulated in the pursuit of values external to the electorate as a collectivity they are rejected as 'undemocratic'. No one can tell the individual that he or she must or cannot stand in a local election, or that a vote must be cast for a particular candidate. This uncontrollability does not mean that local elections are unpredictable; on the contrary sometimes they seem utterly predictable. But in this case to predict is not to control, except in a few uninteresting respects. To try to change electoral outcomes and electoral behaviour, other than through changes in general constitutional rules, would require an interference with democratic processes that would be totally unacceptable in Britain.

Many of those who discuss local government have been unable to reconcile themselves to this fact, and this has had the consequence that many conventional accounts of and arguments about local democracy contain serious inconsistencies. In the following sections an attempt is made to show how these inconsistencies can be eliminated through the concepts embodied in the new approach.

Too little democracy

Whenever and wherever local elections are held it is likely that some aspects of them will raise questions which ultimately relate to traditional problems of democratic government, even if in newspapers and weekly magazines they are presented in a vernacular rather than specialized form. Four aspects of electoral behaviour have in the past been regarded by both local citizens and officials and academic students of government as particularly significant within the context of local democracy. These are, in shorthand, *competitiveness, turnout, partisanship* and *selectivity*. They have already been discussed to some extent because they are related to system-environment interactions and to the *dramatis personae* of local government. The theory of local government involves among other things an attempt to interpret what is believed (often erroneously) to be the true state of affairs in relation to these dimensions of local electoral behaviour.[3] In each case the behaviour of electors and activists is thought to be a threat to local democracy, because it is insufficiently democratic – an odd phraseology, but one which suits the reactions of the critics of local government very well.

COMPETITIVENESS

Competitiveness is the name of a group of features of local elections which all relate in some way to the extent to which the outcome is uncertain. An uncompetitive electoral situation is one in which the result is a foregone conclusion. Uncontested elections are thought to be a sign that all is not well with local democracy; the local elector does not have a chance to exercise the franchise even if he wishes to – and a shortfall of candidates, which occasionally occurs, is thought to be particularly significant as it appears to indicate that local government is of such low prestige locally that it does not even attract the minimum number of people needed to serve.

Competitiveness has different dimensions in partisan and non-partisan situations but in each case it is believed to have effects on the working of the council. The knowledge that an independent councillor is likely to be returned unopposed may well be thought to make him more careless of local opinions and local interests. When elections are dominated by parties an absence of genuine competition is thought to have adverse effects on both the majority, whom it makes complacent and arrogant, and minorities, whom it disheartens and alienates.

Uncontested elections are at the extreme of the *certainty/uncertainty of outcome* dimension of electoral situations, and they occur in both partisan and non-partisan local political systems. Critics of local democracy have therefore focused on the number of unopposed returns that occur in every set of ordinary elections held in Britain. As most rely on the Registrar General's statistics, which present aggregate figures for each authority, they are not able to distinguish the multitude of possible situations within each category. Uncontested elections include those in which there is a shortfall of candidates as well as those in which there is an equality of seats and candidates. Contested elections include those where there are two candidates for one seat, five candidates for one seat, five candidates for four seats and thirty-six candidates for twelve seats. Nor do the gross figures take into account withdrawals after nominations close and invalid nominations. In addition, an uncontested seat may occur when a long serving councillor seeks re-election in a non-partisan system and when a minority party gives up fighting a hopeless ward.

To discuss local elections on the basis of the Registrar General's aggregate statistics (or any other gross figures of this type) is to abstract the local political system from its context. To evaluate the competitiveness of a local political system requires a knowledge of its other features. The problem of uncontested seats can be used to illustrate this point in a very direct manner.

The conventional approach regards the existence of uncontested elections as a sign that local government in an area is of low prestige amongst local citizens. But this ignores a very simple fact about local political systems – they have widely varying *intensity of representation* (which is measured by the number of electors per council member). The number of elected representatives that a given size of electorate has to find varies considerably from place to place. There are some parishes with councils of five, seven or nine members for a population of less than two hundred, whilst Birmingham with an electorate of about 700,000 had only 156 members and Lancashire County Council had only 169 for one and a quarter million electors. Generally the smaller the locality the greater demand on it the electoral system makes; thus a shortfall of candidates in one area means a much greater *intensity of candidature* than a contested election in another.

Not only does the conventional criticism wrongly abstract councils from their environment, it also fails to draw a distinction between willingness to serve on a council and willingness to fight elections. Most candidates and councillors score highly on both these personality dimensions – they want to be councillors and they do not find elections distasteful – but two polar cases have been discovered in local electoral research. The first is the *persistent defeatist*, usually found in highly partisan urban authorities, who is willing to fight hopeless seats time and time again but makes no attempt to get a safer one because he cannot for one reason or another serve on the council. The second is the *deemed re-elected* member who takes advantage of this provision in local electoral law to retain a council seat without risking electoral defeat.

The fact is that both service on a council and fighting local elections involve costs (and benefits of course), both monetary and non-monetary, and these will differ from person to person, and from context to context. No simple inference can be made about the public image of a council in its area from the number of nominations in a local election. If a person does not stand for election this may be because his occupation, social status or personality makes the contesting of elections in public very difficult, even though he may be favourably inclined towards public service.

It is perhaps strange that the other deviation from the ideal of democratic elections that is implicit in the criticisms of local government has not been noted. On occasions a case can be made out that there is a surfeit of candidates, especially in the light of the traditional British first-past-the-post electoral system. In non-partisan areas a large number of candidates, especially in the at-large system, can pose severe problems of choice for electors. The individual elector faced with twenty-one candidates for twelve seats, on a ballot paper nearly two feet long, knowing only the address, sex and occupation of all candidates, has information costs of an enormous size. The easiest solution is to use only a proportion of one's possible votes, but this will be criticized by the democratic purist, and may be a matter of regret if the results show that someone strongly hated just beats a mildly-liked person for the last place. Similar problems of choice arise in multi-party situations. If four or five groups put up candidates for the same seat, or if partisan and independent candidatures are mixed up, the elector is also faced with difficult electoral choices, with the problems of wasted votes and tactical voting, and thus the outcome may be more and more erratic. The pattern of conflict may well vary from ward to ward, so that some parties are seeking control of the council whilst others look only for minority representation.

Thus any departure from the ideal under the British type of voting system, which critics seem to hold, of two candidates for every seat, either all independents or all members of one of only two parties, involves the elector in extra information costs or else deprives him of the proper exercise of the franchise.

Though the existence of uncontested seats by itself tells nothing of the public esteem of local government in a particular area, there is more substance in the assertion of a relationship between the absence of electoral competition in partisan areas and the attitudes and behaviour of council members.[4] Though the evidence is not systematic it does seem as though impregnable one-party systems produce councils that are collectively distinct from multi-party and two-party competitive ones. Competitiveness in party systems has an extra dimension; it refers also to the extent to which the outcome of elections is uncertain in terms of party control of the council. Though in recent years the depths of unpopularity to which national governments have fallen has changed the situation somewhat, in many localities there was a tradition of one-party domination or even monopolization of the council. In these cases the outcome of each election was certain except in a few marginal wards, and these could never upset the balance on the council as a whole. One-party systems are therefore one of the traditional problems of local democracy.

In the context of many theories of democracy, however, it is very difficult to discuss this problem. For it derives directly from the behaviour of the local electorate; the dominance of one party is usually created by the fact that the electorate gives its candidates a large proportion of the vote. To attack local government because it contains one-party systems is like attacking the national electorate for returning a Conservative Government with increased majorities at the general elections of 1955 and 1959 – which led to the premature discovery of 'democratic one-party government' in Britain. It may be regarded as foolish of the electors of industrialized south Wales, south Yorkshire and Durham to vote overwhelmingly for Labour candidates and for the electors of the upper-class London suburbs to do the same for Conservatives, but it can hardly be regarded as undemocratic of the people of a locality to vote for the candidates of their choice.

TURNOUT

Turnout, that is, the percentage of electors voting in contested elections, has also been a matter of controversy over a long period of time. The fact that the proportion voting in local elections in most areas is lower than that in national elections has been taken as a sign of the low standing of local government in the eyes of the electorate.[5] Local democracy can be undermined, it is claimed, by the electors refusing to make use of their democratic right to vote and thus to exercise a choice between different candidates.

One effect that low turnouts have is on the claim of the council members to represent their electors. The legitimacy that attaches to the values and beliefs of representatives from the process of election is felt by some to be reduced by a low turnout – but there is disagreement about counts as 'low' and council members do not seem to be particularly affected by the knowledge that only a small proportion of the electorate voted for them. But in general it is not the *effects* of low turnout that have been of concern to the critics of local government; what has worried them is the belief that non-voting is a sign of apathy in the electorate towards local government.

Conventional discussions of turnout have foundered on one or more of several insidious mistakes – the sort that pious moralizers are always likely to make. First, the figures for turnout are aggregate data, that is, they are the characteristics of the group or collectivity – in this case the ward, the city or some category of local authorities, such as urban districts. But what is true of a set is not necessarily true of each of the individuals that comprise it. *Apathy* is a state of mind of an individual; it is impossible to infer from the fact that 30 per cent of the electorate voted in the Town Ward of Barchester Urban District that John Smith and Richard Robinson are apathetic to local government. Non-voting is as consistent with satisfaction as with apathy, as was pointed out many years ago, and conveniently overlooked by the critics of local democracy.[6]

Second, the figures usually quoted are either national averages or those for individual authorities of whom the commentator has personal knowledge. But is impossible to infer from averages for the whole country what the turnout is in any particular authority. A national percentage of 40 per cent (which would be typical of the post-war period) is consistent with a turnout of 90 per cent in Barchester Urban District and 20 per cent in Barsetshire County Council elections – or *vice versa*. To use non-randomly selected cases is equally pernicious; even if it were the case that local government in 1967 appeared dull and boring to the electors of Maidstone Rural District (14.7 per cent), Ashington Urban District (19.9), Manchester County Borough (30.8) and Leicestershire County Council (32.1), this is completely irrelevant to the electors of Holsworthy Rural District (76.1), Llandovery Non-County Borough (81.4), Castle Donington Rural District (86.6) and Knighton Rural District (89.6). If the conceptual framework of this book is right, one cannot account for high turnouts in some authorities by reference to low turnouts in others, nor for low in one by reference to low in another.

Understanding this aspect of local government is not helped at all by national averages. What counts is variation between authorities, between wards of the same authority and between the same authority in different years. For instance, in Devon alone, town districts ranged in 1967 from 29.9 per cent to 63.6 per cent; in Exeter County Borough in 1966 wards had turnouts varying from 42.1 per cent to 63.8 per cent and one ward in the same city during the post-war period ranged from 36.5 per cent to 65.8 per cent.

There have been numerous attempts to account for the observed variations in the percentage voting in local elections, but most studies have dealt with only limited aspects or a few local authorities, and the findings do not add up to a consistent picture of the forces producing these easily observable differences between local political systems. Few, if any, of the studies have even considered the question whether these variations have any consequences within the miniature system itself.

The interpretation of turnout statistics is complicated by the fact that in general there is a negative relationship between it and seats contested; that is, those areas that have the greatest proportion of seats contested tend to have the lowest turnouts. There was a contrast between Liverpool with high competitiveness and low turnouts and the authorities of west Devon with high turnouts in the few seats that were opposed. But to double the confusion there were places such as Great Torrington Non-County Borough which had high turnouts and all seats contested and Axminster Rural District with low turnouts and few seats contested. The consideration of this factor will be reserved for a later section because it is part of the general problem of appraising local democracy within the context of system-environment relations.

PARTISANSHIP

Worries that democracy will be weakened by uncontested elections and low turnouts are perhaps intelligible in the light of beliefs about democratic duties to serve one's community and to exercise the right to vote, but the fear of partisanship in the local context is much more difficult to understand. Yet it is widely spread through the ranks of academics specializing in local government, and appears in the evidence of practical men to committees of enquiry. It is even present in an attenuated form amongst those who are basically in favour of parties in local government.

The critics of political parties in local government often argue from a stereotype which is more a myth than a caricature of what happens in many partisan authorities.[7] The difficulties begin with the attitude described earlier – 'there is no Conservative or Socialist way of laying a sewer'. This attitude labels partisanship as the 'political element' in local government. With such a definition to describe the provision of local government services as *non-political* is to hold that the attitudes, beliefs and interests of party members are irrelevant to public policy. What is equally erroneous is the assumption that all political conflict is partisan. A moment's reflection will show that this cannot be so, for there are the politics of cricket clubs and senior common rooms, of trade unions and big business, from which partisan organization is absent.

Second, it is believed that party politics was forced on a reluctant local government world by the Labour Party. This is wrong for two reasons: the first is that the present Labour-Conservative conflict only replaced a long standing Liberal-Unionist conflict in many areas; and second, Labour candidates, like those of other parties, are not forced on the local community but always spring out of it and are put into office by its votes. And where the electorate did not want parties on the council they did not vote for their candidates, in which case the Labour Party failed to gain a firm foothold.

Third, there is a widespread belief that party politics leads to the exclusion of many good people from service on local councils, either directly because their party is unsuccessful or indirectly because they are unwilling to declare an open partisan allegiance. But this contention cannot be discussed in isolation from general considerations of 'the quality of councillors' and so will be reserved for the next section.

Fourth, it is sometimes believed that local councillors who are party members act and vote in ways dictated by Transport House and to a lesser extent Conservative Central Office. The bogy of central dictation of local decisions, the more pernicious because it is necessarily secret, is allied to the fear of the caucus – the term of abuse used for meetings of party groups which determine the way members should vote if the authority is organized on disciplined lines.

Those who accepted the earlier analysis of the dimensions of partisanship in local government will recognize the above as more than a misleading simplification. Partisanship is such a complicated phenomenon composed of dozens of major variables that to represent it in terms of a simple model of uniform behaviour is ridiculous. Nor is there any evidence that councillors are the puppets of their respective headquarters.[8] On the contrary there are many occasions when local parties do things that the centre strongly dislikes because it feels that they are bringing the national party into disrepute, especially if local affairs get national publicity.

The fear of party politics in local government brings out much more clearly the oddity of those who believe that the way local elections work involves too little democracy. For the implication of the criticisms of party intervention in local government is that no political system can be democratic if it contains political parties. What the opponent of partisanship is really objecting to is the modern world where organization is as necessary for political activity as it is for sport, business and religion.

The anti-party attitude that has been discussed above should not be confused with *non-partisanship* described in an earlier chapter. The latter was an attitude within the electorate, of varying strengths from place to place, sometimes even being the dominant political force, whilst the former is a frame of mind displayed by outsiders commenting on local government, or by insiders talking about local government generally, as when they give evidence to an official committee. It is probably true that the anti-party attitude has an element of anti-Labour Party bias as well as anti-working class sentiment, though it is also likely to be espoused by officers writing about local government.

The Labour Party has usually regarded local government as more important to it than have Conservatives. George Lansbury is quoted as saying 'We are all clear class-conscious Socialists working together, using the whole machinery of local Government and Parliament for the transformation of Capitalist Society into Socialism. We are under no delusions about the day-to-day work. We are only patching up and making good some of the evils of Capitalism'.[9] The Webbs gave local government a prominent place in their constitution for a socialist commonwealth of Great Britain.[10] But in addition to socialism at the local level through municipalization and the adoption of the right policies for education, health etc., the Labour Party was the vehicle through which ordinary people could enter local councils.

This leads to the fourth problem of local democracy – the fear that local government would fail because it did not attract enough good people as council members. This is the traditional 'quality of councillors' problem.

THE QUALITY OF COUNCILLORS

One of the traditional arguments for democracy, like that of widening entry to the public service, is that it greatly increases the supply of good people for the tasks of political leadership. But its critics argue that local government does not in fact attract the ablest people, and some have added that the situation has been deteriorating in recent decades. For instance the then Permanent Secretary to the Ministry of Housing and Local Government said in 1960 'You hear it widely said, and I believe myself that it is true, despite the first class people there are in every sort and kind of local authority . . . by and large local government is not drawing as good a quality councillor or as many outstanding leaders by way of councillors as it used to do'.[11]

The most sustained attack on council members generally is to be found in E. L. Hasluck's *Local Government in England*,[12] which uses all the conventional judgements in a most violent form. For the author, candidates show a very low standard of capacity – 'not just that there are candidates of illiterate speech and low social standing' but debates in council give the same impression – 'the most childish and ridiculous arguments are brought forward', providing free entertainment for the electorate who attend, and some members are 'so stupid and tongue-tied that they earn the testimonial the sailor gave his parrot "he does not talk much but he thinks a lot" '. Some of those who are elected are 'brainless nobodies' (pp. 48ff). Incidentally it should be remarked that the electors do not escape the same severe censure.

This complaint against local democracy can be analysed under four headings and like the fear of low turnouts, uncontested elections and parties in local government it does not survive the examination in very good shape. The underlying reason for this is that it is blatant pious moralizing and as such can have no place in the attempt to understand local government. Those who have been concerned only to deprecate a state of affairs that they have misunderstood have done a disservice to the study of local government because they have obscured one of the most important and interesting aspects of local political behaviour – the processes of recruitment.

The first element of the fear to be analysed is that of a decline in quality over the years. This is always the sort of problem about which care must be taken, for other times, like other places, may appear to have greener grass – distance lends an enchantment that a microscopic view destroys. Do those who yearn for a bygone political leadership really want men like G. W. Hastings, the first chairman of Worcestershire County Council, for whom council meetings were delayed if he was late because 'we might have to eat our words if we said anything while he was away', but who was subsequently jailed for fraudulent conversion,[13] or Sir William Hodgson, through whose 'pathetic performance' at the Parliamentary Bar over a Manchester Extension Bill, 'the social leader in Cheshire politics was laid to rest'?[14]

It is not surprising that the compositions of councils have changed since the end of the nineteenth century. First, many types of person were excluded by law from being council members. It was only in 1907 that women became generally eligible to serve and those who were not personally ratepayers did not become qualified until 1914 for county and borough councils. Secondly, only in 1948 was the payment of expenses incurred in local government service made a general right, and even then at rates and by methods which appear in retrospect to have been unduly restrictive. Changes therefore were likely because of the enlargement of the pool of possible members and because service was made easier for those other than the well-off.

The above criticisms of those who have talked of a decline in quality of elected representatives is much less important than the following argument. It is easy to speak of a decline generally, or of a low quality without necessarily implying temporal change, but once the critics have been challenged to specify what they mean by 'able', 'high quality' and the like, their views become controversial and to others unacceptable. Nor is there any real agreement amongst the critics themselves.

When pressed, the conventional view cites what it regards as the excessive proportion of housewives and retired people on local councils.[15] This implies that to be male and employed is a sign of quality. Likewise to be young rather than old is a virtue. Professional and upper-middle-class occupations are almost universally favoured by the would-be reformers. At the same time there is a strand in the criticisms which castigates councils for being 'unrepresentative' in that certain occupations or types of occupation are either present or absent in much greater proportion than their shares of the general body of citizens.

The two strands are obviously inconsistent – one cannot argue that the composition of the council should be a mirror image of the composition of the local population *and* that certain 'high quality' groups should be over-represented. But even if this inconsistency is ignored the arguments are still foolish. Why should a married woman with three children who has a doctorate in physics and who is an energetic welfare rights worker be thought to be inferior to a thirty-year chartered accountant who spends his working life helping rich people reduce the incidence of personal taxation? Why should the retired permanent secretary to the ministry of social welfare be worse than an aggressive property speculator?

The latter occupation was chosen as an example to bring to light another inconsistency in the general criticism of the quality of councillors. Often some of the above characteristics are combined to produce demands for more dynamic young businessmen on councils. Yet if the context is changed to one which is part of this subject, but not discussed here for reasons of space – corruption in local government – the problem there is that one way in which young businessmen can show their 'dynamism' is by getting on a council and using the knowledge and influence they acquire to expand their business. Unfortunately trade union officials and housewives have not generally written books and articles on local government so that the 'case' for them and against the categories favoured by the male upper-middle class is never stated.

Underlying the above discussion is the implication that the characteristics chosen as signs of quality are quite inadequate. They are simply those that result from middle-class males showing prejudice in favour of middle-class males, often with an anti-Labour Party social sentiment as an element. But the implication that certain objective social categories are more intelligent, hard working, honest and public-spirited is completely unjustified. Yet it is exactly these sort of attributes that would have to be used if anyone wanted to do an analysis of the 'quality' of councillors that was even *prima facie* plausible. The absence of any such evidence means that the venture must fail before it starts.

This failure to discuss 'quality' in terms of the personal attributes of individuals probably stems from the remnants of the old elitist beliefs that there were certain innate leadership qualities which certain types of upbringing fostered and developed, and which would make the individual the leader in a wide range of situations. This point of view has been totally discredited, and most students of *leadership* now subscribe to some variant of a *situational demands* approach.[16] Yet in discussions of the quality of councillors no reference is ever made to the varying contexts in which councils exist. No evaluation of personnel can begin to make much sense unless it relates the characteristics of the individual to the roles that are to be filled. And as has been shown repeatedly through this book the internal structure of a council depends on the system-environment interaction – which is peculiar to each individual local authority. Thus to say that LlanBarset District Council needs more stockbrokers, accountants and managing directors is ridiculous in default of the analysis of the role structure of the council in relation to its environment.

The above are all minor points, however, in comparison with what is the most important aspect of this element of the fear of local democracy. For all discussion of the quality of councillors must be based on *valuation* – in some cases quite nakedly so, and in others more hypothetically, in terms of consequences. The problem of valuation is always the question of whose values, or who is doing the evaluation? Those who value miners more highly than dentists will differ from those who value probation officers more highly than estate agents, or janitors more highly than university lecturers.

Many of the writings and speeches on the quality of councillors are more perfect examples of pious moralizing than could be constructed as hypothetical instances.

Yet democracy as a form of government is supposed to be a solution to the problem of values, for it states that the values that count in elections are those of the local electorate, and those that count in council work are those of council members. Most of the discussions of the quality of councillors is impertinent, because it tells people what they ought to value, and undemocratic, because it denies that local elections should fulfil the role ascribed by the system of government to them.

Too much democracy

There have been other criticisms of local government which imply that the use the electors make of their rights, which the system of local democracy guarantees to them, will destroy local government. This fear is that local democracy will be damaged, not by local electors who are apathetic or careless of local government, with consequent uncontested elections and low turnouts, but by electors who are too active and too involved.

This fear was first articulated by those who wished to moderate the effects of direct elections of councils by devices which prevented a majority of electors changing the composition of councils too rapidly. The two main devices were the aldermanic system and partial renewal, both of which were said to increase the amount of continuity in council membership in a mechanical fashion. The aldermanic system created a class of council members who served for six years and were indirectly elected; partial renewal made it possible for the electorate to get rid of only a portion of the councillors at any one election.

Such devices only make sense if it is assumed that the electorate are liable to behave erratically, foolishly and whimsically in the short run. The short run is a necessary condition because the safeguards do not work if the behaviour is maintained for three years. A fear of the local electorate is a necessary presupposition, for otherwise the democratic outcomes of each election could be accepted with equanimity.

Two objections may be made to the above reasoning in favour of mechanical devices for ensuring continuity. First, it rejects the democratic assumption that the only people able to evaluate the use of their votes are the voters themselves. If Barsetthorpe parish electors collectively decide to eject the old gang, then elections exist specifically to permit them to do so. To return every one of them is also the prerogative of an electorate.

Second, the devices are only plausible if it can be shown that electors and council members behave differently, that once a person is elected his continued membership of the electorate is no longer a significant influence on his behaviour. For if members of the electorate are irresponsible, temperamental and irrational, if their representatives remain electors they will be too. Neither indirect election nor partial renewal can stop aldermen resigning in mid-term or councillors disqualifying themselves from membership of the council.

In the previous section the fear was that apathy would prevent the ablest people seeking election to local councils. In contrast to this some believed that the fierceness of the democratic struggle would make it impossible for good citizens (that is, those who could make a valuable contribution to council work) even to be candidates. Partisanship would accentuate this because some people were unwilling for various reasons to declare an allegiance openly. The answer has always been co-option. In its original form it meant the aldermanic system, but in later years it has come to mean co-option to committees as a representative or an expert. As has already been shown the latter is in practice not a way of escaping from the forces of the system-environment interaction; on the contrary, the way co-option works demonstrates their existence very clearly.

It is instructive to consider the departed aldermanic system as an example of the fear of too much democracy. As was mentioned earlier, the reasons for its abolition were that the conventional arguments in support of it proved spurious and its obvious defects were brought home to people in different parts of the country on many occasions.

It was first believed that it could be used to offset the fact of popular election by allowing the co-option on to the council itself of high calibre people who for personal reasons were unable to fight elections. Irrespective of the question of what 'high calibre' means, this soon became a fictitious reason. Though the power to elect non-councillors was used on occasions in early years, in most authorities it quickly fell into disuse as aldermanic office took its place in the status system of the council. The one exception to this was in some heavily partisan authorities where the majority avoided by-elections by filling vacancies from outside the council with party members who were often defeated candidates or former members. The rationale of this use was very different from that envisaged in 1888 when the office in its twentieth-century form was created; those co-opted were not people unable for personal reasons to seek popular election – they had often been defeated in doing so.

The second argument was based on the facts that aldermen served for six years rather than three and were elected under a partial renewal system. The institution was believed to provide a degree of protection against the 'winds' of local democracy. The local electorate were thought to be liable to aberrant behaviour which might do permanent damage to a local authority by removing all those with experience of council affairs from its membership. In British government this demand for continuity is something confined to local government (unless one includes some arguments for a second chamber); its oddity is shown by the fact that it is impossible to give a coherent account of its rationale.

In addition to the fact that it was not proof against the sort of perverseness postulated of local people, unless those who were elected are different from those voting – a belief which contradicts the fear expressed in the creation of the system – in certain circumstances the aldermanic system was a source of instability – first in the council's membership and second in its conduct of affairs. In some councils aldermanic seats were less safe than those of most councillors because the council as a whole was evenly balanced, even though most wards were not marginal.[17] A different sort of instability was created in some areas by the bitterness that the system created within and between parties.[18]

In any event, the importance of continuity created by mechanical means will vary with the strength of 'natural' continuity, that is, the continuity provided by the working of the electoral system in the social and political conditions of the locality. In many parts of the country continuity of membership of councils was guaranteed by the electorate who returned the same people, often unopposed, year in and year out. In fact, mechanical continuity without natural continuity can only be a short-term, often very short, phenomenon.

All these points can be summarized in one question – did it make any difference to the citizen, in terms of service provision and good government, whether a council had aldermen or not? For instance, pairs of districts, each consisting of an urban district and a non-county borough matched for powers, social structure and anything else thought relevant, could be selected to see whether the existence of aldermen in the latter made the authority function better in some definite way. In fact this comparison was never tried, because few at heart believed that any of the observed differences in service provision between district authorities could be attributed to the presence or absence of the aldermanic office.

The arguments about the aldermanic system since the late nineteenth century illustrate perfectly the moralizing, legalistic and institutional nature of traditional thinking about local government. Conventional discussion depended entirely on abstracting one political institution from the rest of the constitutional arrangements of local authorities and from the political behaviour, which differed enormously from one system to another, which was associated with them. Not only were the arguments fictitious, they were based on a *misunderstanding* of local government.

Co-option generally has fallen out of favour; at best it is regarded as a useful but very minor device within the committee system. Instead there has been a growth of support for another way of changing the outcome of democratic processes – the introduction of training courses for newly elected council members. Just as the newly recruited member of other organizations is inducted by being given special treatment in his or her first hour, first day, first week and first months in the firm, so, it is argued, the freshman councillor ought to be systematically socialized by courses given by outside 'experts' and by chief officers.

In as much as these courses merely speed up the process of acquiring useful knowledge about the council and local authority which the member will eventually acquire – for instance, the understanding of what a *minute* is, how many pre-1914 schools the education department has to run and so on – they are uncontroversial. But training courses typically include elements of role-training, and role is defined in normative terms, that is, how members *ought* to behave. But neither the views of outsiders – for instance university lecturers on public administration – nor officers have received the legitimation that election gives to newest member's values and perceptions.

Suppose that a councillor has been elected after stating his policy was to fight against the grossly inflated salaries of incompetent chief officers, and to change the administrative policy of the authority which gives too much power to bureaucrats. To send him on a course on which he will be told that this is wrong, that his role is to support these highly trained and dedicated professional men in their expansion of needed public services and to defend them against ill-informed criticisms by members of the general public, is impertinent, an insult to him and his electors doubly compounded by the expenditure of public money to tell them what they do not believe.[19]

The discussion of the fear of too much democracy has deliberately been phrased very strongly in order to draw attention to the anti-democratic basis of valuation that underlies many of the conventional attitudes. Those who are familiar with nineteenth-century opposition to the extension of the franchise and the right to be elected to Parliament will recognize the aristocratic, authoritarian and intolerant elements in both the fears – of too much and too little democracy in the conduct of local affairs.

Local democracy in context

One problem has been found to run like a thread through all of the above discussion of aspects of local democracy. Most of the conventional discussions are based on a refusal to see each facet of the individual political system in its context, that is, in relation to the other facets and to other aspects of local political behaviour. The distinct dimensions of electoral behaviour do not exist independently of each other and of the environment in which they are located. They are not free floating as much of the moralistic literature assumes; if one wishes to appraise the quality of councillors or the aldermanic system this can only be done within each individual political system by itself.

The way two of the dimensions can be related is illustrated very well by *competitiveness* and *turnout*. First, they are related in a mechanical way. If wards vary in their level of turnout then average turnout will depend partly on which wards are contested. This is particularly important when investigating changes from year to year, and also in comparisons of local authorities with all seats contested and those with only a handful.

But more importantly, they are related empirically in that there is a correlation between level of competitiveness and level of turnout but in a negative direction. The greater the proportion of seats contested, the lower the turnout. This poses tremendous problems for those who use both dimensions as measures of apathy towards local government. If turnout is chosen then the small towns and villages of central and north Wales are the least apathetic, for they often have over 70 per cent voting, and not infrequently nearly or over 90 per cent; but if competitiveness is chosen then they are the most apathetic, for only one or two seats are contested at each election. Exactly the reverse is true of the large English cities, including the Greater London area.

A different form of relationship exists between *partisanship* and the composition of councils. Unfortunately, the Maud Committee refused to ask about partisan affiliation in their national study of council members so that extensive countrywide information has not been published. An unpublished study of most of the country's urban councils in 1968 and 1969 by the present author confirms what most people have found at the level of the individual council – that the slates of the different political parties are composed of very different proportions of different types of person. In the large urban areas, therefore, it is impossible to talk about the composition of councils without taking into consideration the nature of partisanship within the particular locality.

It is also very difficult to make sense of competitiveness within the large urban area without taking into account the nature of partisan conflict. The extent to which seats are not contested is related to the competitiveness of the party situation. Two factors affect the extent to which seats are unopposed; the closeness of the overall conflict within the locality and party attitudes to finding candidates for 'hopeless' seats. It is clear that many of the observed differences between different types of authority in respect of proportion of seats contested are accounted for by differing party policies towards candidature in such seats.

The relationship between *partisanship* and *turnout* is more complex. There are structural reasons for believing that in the traditional system parties to some extent made good the lack of official information to electors about the election and simplified the voting decision by reducing its information costs. It may be expected that parties would raise turnout generally but it is very hard to test this rigorously because it is impossible to control the socio-geographical factors that also appear to have an influence on turnout. There is also conflicting evidence on the effect of the marginality of a ward on turnout, some people having found that the closer the contest the higher the turnout, whilst others found different factors affecting such variations in voting.

The above are all examples of the relationships between aspects of local political behaviour, intended to show how the conventional discussion of local democracy has wrongly divorced each of these from the behavioural context in which it occurred. One of the major reasons why these dimensions are related to each other is that they are all influenced by environment in which the council is located. This is the other aspect of the *context* of local democracy.

If only the simplest features of the local environment are taken, for instance, the size, density, social composition and change of population of the locality, it can be shown that competitiveness, turnout and partisanship are systematically related to these. For instance, the small stable town remote from the large centres of population will have non-partisan politics, with a tendency towards uncontested elections, but with high turnouts if an opposed election does occur. The large city will be intensely partisan, have all seats always contested, but will have low turnouts. The fortunes of the major political parties in the locality will be determined by the standing of their national counterparts as indicated by the opinion polls.

Were there space available it would be easy to continue with examples of how the system-environment interaction provides a context in which the dimensions of local democracy must be placed. Some of the best examples come from the study of complex systems of local government, for in these quasi-federal structures each aspect takes on a different colour. The systemic significance of differing patterns of competition, different mixes of partisanship and different social structures of area 'delegations' to the centre is considerable.

Conclusion

The conclusion to this examination of local democracy is also the conclusion to the book. Though this may appear somewhat unusual it has the advantage of ending with a consideration of subjects with which both the student and the citizen are familiar. No one who has taken an interest in local government, either through traditional textbooks or through newspapers and weekly journals, can be unaware of the 'local government in crisis' or 'local democracy in a sorry state' literature. These sweeping denunciations of most aspects of local government often make the failure of local democratic institutions the central point of the criticisms, for it is harder to see how the nature of local democratic processes may be changed than to conceive of, say, the reform of local government finance.

The significant fact about the traditional approach to the problems of local democracy was that it generated a form of blindness in those who wanted to understand local government. The legalistic emphasis of earlier writings prevented authors from even bothering about the striking variations in behaviour that can be discovered within the framework of uniform laws. The statements of those responsible for the creation of a particular institution were taken far too literally; what was alleged about aldermen by the Unionist Government of 1888 was still dominating the discussion in the 1950s. Above all, pious moralizing is a form of blindness deliberately self-inflicted, for it prevents the self-righteous critic from seeking out the facts, which might not support the denunciation.

For instance, one severe attack on county government (meaning the county council) as undemocratic in comparison with the government of cities depended on a judicious selection of figures from unofficial sources. But no statistics are given for one half of the comparison – town elections, particularly those in county boroughs – and only those facts which support the case are quoted.[20] Where few seats are contested this is cited and where turnout is low this is cited. The result is that Cheshire County Council is criticized because 44 seats were uncontested but no mention is made of the fact that turnout in the contested ones was 44 per cent, and if 1922 had been chosen instead of 1925, it would have been 51 per cent. A method whereby a long list of cases is scanned for favourable ones permits the critic to 'prove' almost anything.

Similarly one official study concluded that 'party politics are to be deplored when they produce, as they sometimes do, irrelevant and sterile debate or stifle discussion, and when they dictate the approach towards issues which are manifestly non-political'.[21] This is of course true for the authors in virtue of the meanings of the evaluative expressions – 'deplore', 'irrelevant', 'sterile' and 'stifle' – and they did not think it necessary to investigate the behavioural content of the other phrases. Why is it that party relationships take the forms they do – sometimes co-operative, sometimes hostile or various mixtures of the two styles of human relations?

The blindness that pious moralizing produces prevents the moralizer from feeling the fascination of local government. Above all, local government is a set of local democratic systems, each with its own particular environment, and this produces a tremendous variety of patterns of local democracy. Though the academic student is concerned with all local authorities, the citizen as an individual will experience only one or a few local political systems. Even if the results of pious moralizing were not untenable, after examination they would be irrelevant, for they are ascribed to local government in general. The citizen wants to know how his own system works, not how others do. Once the observer gains a sense of the variety that local government involves, which is the first step in understanding, he will begin to feel the interest that the subject has for the specialist. Even an unsuccessful attempt at understanding can be a source of satisfaction if it creates the sense of the variety of human responses to a changing environment.

Appendix
Local Government Services, Finance and Employment

The purpose of this Appendix is to give a picture of the activities for which local authorities have been and are responsible, through a historical perspective and through their 'reflections' in financial and employment statistics. As corollaries these also provide a glimpse of the sources of local revenue, and their variability between authorities, and of the range of occupations found in local government.

The activities or public services for which local authorities are responsible have changed and been changed over the past 140 years by processes of addition, subtraction and differentiation. In the early part of the period the main emphasis was on the initiatives of individual local authorities struggling to contend with the problems of growing urban environments. Towns gradually developed a whole series of activities to deal with the physical environment – street lighting and cleansing, refuse collection and disposal, sewerage and sewage disposal, treatment of the dead, slum clearance – which are the foundations of the twentieth-century public health functions, and which also led to the growing consumer protection services through the elaboration of food and drugs inspection.

The nineteenth century also saw the growth of the great public utilities and of municipal trading. The latter is the name of a whole host of activities such as the provision of markets, fairs, theatres etc., which were expected to make a profit – 'for the relief of rates'. More important were the public utilities – water supply, gas, electricity and public transport – which grew up either in order to make profits for ratepayers or as a form of municipal socialism, in competition with private provision.

The other great development in local government services was the increasing elaboration of the poor law. This illustrates the process of differentation of public activities through greater specialization and professionalism. The 'old poor law' was the main source of four groups of state activity – the personal social services, the personal health services (other than the general practitioner area), the hospitals and social security. Education, which was introduced in the form of elementary education in the late nineteenth century, also shows the process of differentiation very clearly – basic education has now been complemented by nursery, secondary, further, special and higher education.

The nineteenth century also saw the growth of local authority police forces and fire brigades. Despite the pressures of 'nationalization' these have remained important local authority functions. Highways had always been a local function but in the later decades of the nineteenth century roads became of less social importance because of the growth of the railways; the twentieth century has reversed this state of affairs and highway expenditure has become of significance to local authorities again.

If the process of differentiation is ignored, then the first three decades of the twentieth century were the high tide of local government within the state; since that time local authorities have lost responsibility for services and parts of services over a wide range of activities. Gas and electricity undertakings and hospitals were nationalized immediately after the Second World War, and water supply transferred to *ad hoc* bodies in 1974, as were the personal health services left to local authorities in 1946. In the 1930s and 1940s the involvement of local government in agriculture was lessened (it had never been very great), and it lost responsibility for main roads. Different aspects of social security were transferred one by one to the central government during this period. The result was that many commentators regarded local government as in a serious decline.

Nevertheless local government expenditure has been an increasing proportion of the national income since the end of the Second World War and governments have found themselves unable to restrict this growth to any large extent. This is because most local government activities have become increasing differentiated, so that they are to all intents and purposes groups of related specialisms. The personal social services illustrate this perfectly, as do housing, education and consumer protection. The financial statistics presented in Table 2 show the range of local government activities at the end of the traditional system and also their relative importance in terms of expenditure.

Table 1: **Numbers and Sizes of Primary Authorities, England and Wales, 1961 & 1974**

authority	*size of population served* *smallest*	*average*	*largest*
the traditional system*			
the County of London			
London County Council			
28 metropolitan boroughs	21,596	114,111	347,209
The City of London			
83 county boroughs	30,376	164,960	1,105,651
61 administrative counties			
61 county councils	18,431	479,138	2,230,093
317 non-county boroughs	880	{26,304}	213,700
564 urban districts	490		122,600
474 rural districts	1510	19,450	95,620
about 11,000 parishes			
the new system**			
the Greater London system			
The Greater London Council			
32 Greater London boroughs	139,420	229,663	334,000
The City of London			
6 metropolitan counties			
6 metropolitan county councils	1,198,390	1,995,390	2,785,460
36 metropolitan districts	172,990	325,898	1,087,660
39 non-metropolitan counties			
39 non-metropolitan county councils	109,680	702,744	1,434,960
296 non-metropolitan districts	24,060	92,951	421,800
about 10,300 parishes			
8 Welsh counties			
8 Welsh county councils	99,370	343,660	536,080
37 Welsh districts	18,670	70,494	285,760
about 1000 communities			

*as of April, 1961 **as of April, 1974

(The average population is given for town districts (NCBs and UDs) together – there is no easy way of calculating them separately because of the way the statistics are presented.)

Table 2: **Expenditure of Local Authorities out of Revenue and Special Funds, England & Wales, 1972-3**

	%	%
Education		36·3
Housing		14·4
Housing Revenue Account Services	12·4	
other housing	2·0	
Public Health		8·0
Sewerage and sewage disposal	2·4	
Water supply	2·3	
Refuse collection and disposal	1·8	
Environmental health	·8	
Baths and laundries	·5	
Cemeteries and cremetoria	·2	
Highways and Transport		7·1
Highways, lighting and parking	5·9	
Passenger transport	1·0	
Harbours, docks and piers	·2	
Personal Services		7·0
Local authority social services	4·9	
Local authority personal health services	2·1	
Police and Justice		6·4
The police service	5·8	
Administration of justice	·6	
Recreation and Leisure		2·4
Parks and open spaces	1·3	
Libraries, museums and art galleries	1·1	
The Fire Service		1·3
Town and Country Planning		1·2
others		5·9
expenditure not allocated to specific services		9·9

(source: *Annual Abstract of Statistics*, 1974, table 365)

Expenditure on the above services was financed from three sources: fees, sales, profits etc. on local services; central government grants; rates. In 1971-2 their relative contributions were:

Table 3: **Sources of Income, 1971-2**

	%	%
fees etc.		20·3
Central government grants		44·9
Rate rebate and domestic element	2·4	
Rate support grant – needs and resources	37·3	
Specific grants	5·2	
Rates		34·9

(source: *Local Government Financial Statistics, England and Wales, 1971-2*, HMSO, 1973)

Individual authorities differed enormously in the extent to which they could draw on each source, and even when the figures were aggregated for types of authority there are still clear differences – as the following table shows.

Table 4 (a): **Aspects of Finance, 1973-4**

area	RV per head	Rate call per head	Resources element of RSG as a % of expenditure that would otherwise be borne by rates
	£	£	%
England and Wales	134	52	13·4
England	137	53	9·7
Wales	89	40	31·2
CBs	121	52	11·9
NCBs	122	48	15·3
UDs	112	44	19·9
RDs	101	35	25·9

The variations encountered can be illustrated by comparing two types of area – prosperous London suburbs in Surrey and remote authorities in Montgomeryshire.

Table 4 (b) **Contrasting Authorities**

Epsom and Ewell NCB	144	64	0
Esher UD	167	70	0
Montgomery NCB	53	15	61·1
Machlynlleth RD	51	12	61·7

(source for Tables 4(a) and 4(b): *Rates and Rateable Values in England and Wales, 1973-4*, HMSO, 1973)

Differences between authorities are also illustrated by the next table which shows figures for the districts in one metropolitan area and one non-metropolitan county – Greater Manchester and Bedfordshire. This shows the sources of revenue for the expenditure financed from rates and grants (that is, ignoring the contribution of fees etc.) and the amount spent per head.

Table 5: **Sources of Local Income, 1974-5**

	expenditure per head	% met from stated source				
area	total	1	2	3	4	5
	£	%	%	%	%	%
Bolton	140	50·8	5·0	29·7	13·2	1·3
Bury	125	57·3	6·3	25·4	10·0	·9
Manchester	198	44·8	3·4	31·1	20·3	·5
Oldham	155	49·0	4·1	26·0	17·4	3·4
Rochdale	157	51·5	3·9	25·6	18·3	·8
Salford	159	45·5	4·6	28·5	21·0	·4
Stockport	130	52·2	7·4	30·9	8·9	·7
Trafford	146	57·0	6·7	25·4	10·9	0
Wigan	130	56·9	5·1	29·0	8·6	·3
(no figures are given for Tameside)						
Bedford	138	59·1	6·3	24·8	9·7	0
Luton	181	43·7	3·8	21·1	9·6	21·7
Mid Bedfordshire	133	58·6	6·4	26·1	8·9	0
South Bedfordshire	158	58·9	6·4	23·5	11·3	0

1=rates+resources element of RSG; 2=domestic element of RSG; 3=needs element of RSG; 4=specific grants including housing subsidies; 5=contribution from balances etc. (Source: *Return of Rates 1974–5*, compiled and puplished by CIPFA).

The variety of services for which local authorities are responsible is reflected in the wide range of occupations that are employed in local government. It is not possible to give authoritative figures but the following tables illustrate some of the variety and also the locations in which they are found.

Table 6: **Main Categories of Local Government Employment**

The local government service	934,000
Local authority construction workers	128,000
Teachers and lecturers	674,000
Policemen	109,000

(Note: these figures are derived from various sources and are approximate only.)

Table 7: **Staff Employed in Personal Social Services**

headquarters and area office staff	
management and supervisory	3495
social workers	10,323
administrative	3209
clerical	7913
others	2564
institutional staff	
residential	
wardens, matrons etc. and deputies	17,589
others (assistants, clerical, works, maintenance domestic etc.)	46,663
day-time	
managers and controllers	2014
others (as above)	12,842

peripatetic staff	
home help	
organizers and assistant organizers	1363
home helps	38,341

(source: *Personal Health and Social Service Statistics*, 1973, HMSO)

Table 8: **Numbers and Types of Policemen**

rank	men	women	total
chief constable	41	0	41
assistant chief constable	140	0	140
chief superintendent	441	4	445
superintendent	1038	33	1071
chief inspector	1715	45	1760
inspector	4131	136	4267
sergeant	13,126	574	13,700
constable	61,961	3596	65,557

(source: *County Councils Gazette*, January 1975, pp. 261-2)

The figures do not include the City of London and Metropolitan Police forces, or those on central service and secondment.

Table 9: **Library Staff, 1975–6**

Professional posts	4101
other non-manual posts	8567
manual posts	1851

(source: *County Councils Gazette*, July 1975, p. 115)

Footnotes and References

[References to case-studies cited in the Bibliography are mentioned by author's name and date only.]

Preface

1 The system in mid-nineteenth century is described in V. D. Lipman, *Local Government Areas, 1834-1945*, Blackwell, 1949, chs. 2 & 3, where Goschen's views are quoted at length.
2 For an extended discussion of the processes of administrative reform in general see B. C. Smith and J. Stanyer, *Administering Britain*, Fontana Studies in Public Administration, 1976, ch. 8.
3 Decentralization is described and discussed in Smith and Stanyer, *op. cit*, ch. 4.
4 The brief description of old and new structures of local government is elaborated in Chapter 2, to which the reader is referred if in doubt about the meanings of the technical words in italics.

Chapter 1 The study of Local Government

1 Exact figures for each of these indices of 'importance' are not given here because what they are depends on decisions about what to include and exclude and how to calculate the measures. They also change over time so that published ones are always out of date.
2 The question of what services local government is and has been responsible for is dealt with in the Appendix.
3 Royal Commission on Local Government in England, 1966-69, *Research Studies*, nos. 3, 4, 5, HMSO, 1969. For Professor Robson's views see *The Development of Local Government*, Allen and Unwin, first edition 1931, and its successor, *Local Government in Crisis*, Allen and Unwin, 1966.
4 A good example of a new approach is found in N. T. Boaden, *Urban Policy-Making*, Cambridge University Press, 1971.
5 For detailed examples of pious moralizing in an official report see J. Stanyer, 'The Maud Committee Report', *Social and Economic*

Administration, vol. 1, no. 4, pp. 3-19.

6 See Chapter 10 for a description of default powers and their place in central-local relations.

7 Scientific management was based on the belief that those in charge of large firms had little idea of what occurred on the shop floor, and the Hawthorne Investigations, 1927-32, provided systematic evidence that this was so. This generalization has been confirmed repeatedly by sociological research into organizational behaviour.

8 For *co-option* see Chapter 5 and for the *aldermanic system* see Chapter 12.

9 Muller, 1950.

10 These are technical terms which are defined and used later in the book.

11 For instance, the studies of individual systems published in L. J. Sharpe (ed.), 1967, were undertaken on an agreed common framework.

12 See Chapter 12 for the discussion of this point.

13 See the references in footnote 3 of this chapter.

Chapter 2 Traditional and New Systems of Local Government

1 For instance, C. A. Cross, *Principles of Local Government Law*, Sweet and Maxwell, fifth edition 1974, and W. O. Hart and J. G. Garner, *Hart's Local Government and Administration*, Butterworths, ninth edition 1973.

2 This characterization of local government systems is based on the analysis of decentralization in Smith and Stanyer, *op cit*, 1976, ch. 4.

3 For the new administrative structure of the National Health Service see R. G. S. Brown, *The Management of Welfare*, Fontana Studies in Public Administration, 1975, ch. 6.

4 For a discussion of the principles of area delimitation see V. D. Lipman, *op cit*, Part 3.

5 Both of these problems were well documented in evidence to the Local Government Commission for England, 1958-65, and are summarized in the *Reports and Final Proposals* produced by that body.

6 For an account of parish government see C. Arnold-Baker, *Parish Administration*, Methuen, first edition 1958.

7 For an account of the rural district see J. Stanyer, *County Government in England and Wales*, Library of Political Studies, Routledge and Kegan Paul, 1967, ch. 8.

8 For an account of county government see J. Stanyer, *op cit*, esp. chs. 4-6.

9 For London before reform see W. E. Jackson, *Achievement*, Longmans, 1965.

10 For an example of the creation of a joint board see D. L. Rydz, 'The Formation of the Great Ouse Water Authority', Parts One and Two, *Public Administration,* vol. 49, Summer and Autumn, 1971.
11 Some aspects of the administration of county council services are examined in P. G. Richards, *Delegation in Local Government*, New Town and County Hall Series, Allen and Unwin, 1956.
12 Greater Manchester is examined in L. P. Green, *Provincial Metropolis*, Allen and Unwin, 1959.
13 The problems of local government in Wales are discussed in I. B. Rees, *Government by Community*, Charles Knight, 1971.
14 *Report of the Royal Commission on Local Government in Greater London, 1957-60*, Cmnd. 1164, 1960.
15 For an account of reform under the *Local Government Act, 1958*, see J. Stanyer, 'The Local Government Commissions', in H. V. Wiseman (ed.), *Local Government in England, 1958-69*, Routledge and Kegan Paul, 1970.

Chapter 3 Miniature Political Systems

1 Both the vernacular and functional uses of *system* can be illustrated by studies of 'machine politics' or 'the boss system' in American city government. A functional analysis by R. K. Merton and several accounts in less technical terms by politicians can be found in E. C. Banfield (ed.), *Urban Government*, Free Press, Glencoe, 1961.
2 For readers interested in an exposition of the logic of systems analysis one of the best books is W. R. Ashby, *An Introduction to Cybernetics*, University Paperbacks, Methuen, 1964, but it requires very careful reading.
3 See E. R. Leach, *The Political Systems of Highland Burma*, Bell and Sons, 1954.
4 It has been alleged that British colonial administrators were particularly prone to take literally what some of the indigenous population told them, and thus gravely misunderstood local social and political structure. See Leach, *op cit*, p. 198.
5 See P. Haggett, *Locational Analysis in Human Geography*, Arnold, 1965, esp. ch. 2.
6 A Spanish study of *comarcas* (a traditional unit of government) showed exactly this. See V. D. Lipman, *op cit*, pp. 318-19.
7 P. Haggett, *op cit*, cites studies of the *Bridgewater Mercury*, shopping centres in the San Francisco Bay area, and the Shenandoah national park (p. 41).
8 This problem was well illustrated by the research done for the Redcliffe-Maud Commission and published as Research Study no. 9 →

Community Attitudes Survey, HMSO, 1969.

9 See L. J. Sharpe, 'Theories and Values of Local Government', *Political Studies*, vol. 18, no. 2, 1970.

10 See J. Stanyer in H. V. Wiseman (ed.), *op cit*, for an account of this process.

Chapter 4 The Local Environment

1 For a detailed account of how changes in the national standing of political parties can affect local authorities see J. Stanyer, 'On the Study of Urban Electoral Behaviour', in K. G. Young (ed.), *Essays on the Study of Urban Politics*, Macmillan, 1975.

2 The sources referred to below are as follows: General Register Office, *Census, 1951, Census, 1961, Census, 1966, Census, 1971* (each of these contains a large number of relevant volumes); Ministry of Agriculture, Fisheries and Food, Agricultural Statistics, England and Wales, Agricultural Census's and Production published annually since 1866; Department of the Environment, *Rates and Rateable Values*, published annually.

3 See W. P. Grant, '"Local" Parties in British Local Politics', *Political Studies*, vol. 19, no. 2, 1971.

4 Some of the case-studies listed in the bibliography deal largely with one-party systems; see Butterworth, 1966, Bulpitt, 1967, Brennan *et al*, 1954a, 1954b, and Rees and Smith, 1964, for examples.

5 Wolverhampton during the period studied by G. W. Jones was a good example of a highly competitive system. Party conflict was eventually pursued through legal action over a disputed aldermanic election in 1961.

6 The changes in the political system of Exeter which were brought about by the rise of Liberalism and a ratepayers' movement are described in Chapter 5 of L. J. Sharpe (ed.), 1967.

7 The only general account of pressure groups in local government is found in J. Dearlove, 1973, esp. ch. 8.

8 For an example of the influence of an interest sector see J. Stanyer, 'Farming Politics: Devon and Cheshire Compared', in *Decision Making in Britain, III*, Parts 6-9: *Agriculture*, published by the Open University, 1975.

9 The concept of a local elite and aternative approaches to power in local communities are discussed in two articles by K. Newton: 'City Politics in Britain and the United States', *Political Studies*, vol. 17, no. 2, 1969, and 'A Critique of the Pluralist Model', *Acta Sociologica*, vol. 12, no. 4, 1969.

10 See W. P. Grant, 'Non-partisanship in British Local Politics',

Policy and Politics, vol. 1, no. 3, 1973.
11 The Government said in 1971 that 'it is of great importance for the new health authorities to forge effective links and foster close understanding with their counterparts, the local authorities responsible for personal social services, education, housing and public health' and set up a working party on Collaboration between the NHS and Local Government, which reported in 1973.

Chapter 5 Dramatis Personae: Council Members

1 One Liberal in Exeter served an unexpired term of office after winning a by-election in 1963; was re-elected in 1965 but had to seek further election the following year when the ward boundaries were re-drawn. In this election he came third, and was defeated when he had to seek re-election in 1967, as the successful 1966 candidate with least votes. He thus won three elections in order to serve for just over four years.
2 One third of the new members entering Devon County Council between 1946 and 1972 inclusive joined at a by-election and 38 per cent at ordinary elections where the incumbent did not seek re-election.
3 It had in fact been a source of controversy since reform of municipal corporations gathered momentum in the early 1830s. See B. Keith-Lucas, *The English Local Government Franchise*, Blackwell, 1952, pp. 186 ff.
4 The aldermanic system in Wolverhampton is discussed in G. W. Jones, 1969, pp. 259-67, where many of these points are illustrated: 'the very title of Alderman is prized. To be an Alderman is regarded as a high honour' (p. 259). For bitter partisan relations see chapter 16 – 'Crisis in Wolverhampton, 1961-2'.
5 Sir Godfrey Baring was chairman of the Isle of Wight County Council from 1898 to 1957; J. M. Lee, 1963, p. 227.
6 *Report of the Committee on the Management of Local Government*, vol. 2: *The Local Government Councillor*, HMSO, 1967.
7 There has been sporadic criticism over the years, on the same grounds, of the composition of national bodies, such as Royal Commissions, and regional and local executive boards and committees, such as those in the National Health Service. Generally appointed bodies show a more 'unrepresentative' membership than do local councils. The House of Commons has a membership which departs even more markedly from the population from which it is drawn than do those of local councils.
8 Centre for Urban Studies, *Statement of Evidence* (to the Herbert

Commission), 1959; D. Hill, *Participating in Local Affairs*, Penguin, 1970, ch. 5.

9 The ramifications of the Poulson case may have made the general public over-conscious of 'corruption in local government'. The Prime Minister's Committee found very little evidence to support the newspaper denunciations of local authorities in general, and what evidence there is shows that the involvement of employees, other public servants and outsiders is as great as that of council members. See *Conduct in Local Government*: Volume 1, *Report of the Committee*, Cmnd. 5636, HMSO, 1974.

10 There have been a number of studies of local communities which give varying amounts of attention to local government, but whose main interest is with local society. Most of these are summarized and discussed in R. Frankenberg, *Communities in Britain*, Penguin, 1966, and C. Bell & H. Newby, *Community Studies*, Studies in Sociology, Allen and Unwin, 1971 (the latter also deals with American and other studies).

Chapter 6 Dramatis Personae: Employees

1 Further consideration is given to these *locations* in the next chapter. Here they are used only to characterize local government employees in their 'raw' state.

2 Further consideration is given to the structural importance of the difference between specialists and generalists in the next chapter.

3 The directly elected school boards were abolished in 1902 and their staff and responsibilities transferred to the recently created multi-functional councils.

4 The Institute of Local Government Studies, Birmingham University, has published a number of papers and articles based on its research into the changing patterns of local authority administration. See, for instance, R. Greenwood *et al.*, 'Recent Changes in the Internal Organization of County Boroughs: Part II. Delegation and Departmental Reorganization', *Public Administration*, vol. 47, Autumn, 1969, and numerous articles in the journal *Local Government Studies*. Weekly publications such as *The Local Government Chronicle* have accounts of individual reorganizations, as do the publications of the local authority associations, *County Councils' Gazette*, *Municipal Review* and *District Councils' Review*.

5 Further aspects of the lay administrative officer in local government are discussed in the next chapters.

6 In addition, though there have been studies of local activists of various sorts, few published papers report research that can easily be adapted to the framework used here.

Chapter 7 Internal Organization: Elements of Structure

1 See M. J. C. Vile, *Constitutionalism and the Separation of Powers*, Oxford University Press, 1967, pp. 277 ff.
2 'we doubt whether it is possible to divide the total management process into two separate halves, one for members and the other for officers . . . the two elements in local government management are in fact likely to be present at every stage of the management process.' (*The New Local Authorities: Management and Structure*, HMSO, 1972, p. 10.)
3 Though this point may be forgotten by people in an individual authority for long periods, when a crisis arises they may be forcefully reminded of it. For an example of this see 'Exeter' in L. J. Sharpe (ed.), 1967, where the problems of 1962-66 are briefly mentioned.
4 The pattern set in the *Education Act, 1944*, was followed by a number of other statutes over a period of years. One of the most important and striking was the *Local Authority Social Services Act, 1970.*
5 J. Elliott, 'The Harris Experiment in Newcastle-upon-Tyne', *Public Administration*, vol. 49, Summer, 1971.
6 Figure 6 following is an alternative dynamic model of a committee system.
7 For examples of the financial processes of an individual authority see F. R. Oliver and J. Stanyer, 'Local Government Finance' in H. V. Wiseman (ed.), *op cit*, 1970, pp. 146-52, and F. R. Oliver, 'The Exeter Rate Crisis of 1972', *South Western Review of Public Administration*, volumes 12 & 13, 1973.
8 This is the picture of council meetings in Barking presented by Rees and Smith, 1964 – 'Council meetings are no more than hastily-performed monthly rituals which rubber-stamp the decisions of committees' (p. 81).
9 Some of the factors relating to size of council are further considered in Chapter 11.
10 This subject is dealt with by R. Burke, *The Murky Cloak*, Charles Knight, 1970, which gives numerous examples of press-authority relations from different parts of the country.
11 For one example of a fully partisan authority see H. V. Wiseman, 1963, 1967.
12 For a discussion of these aspects of partisanship see J. G. Bulpitt, 1967.

13 For an example see P. Spencer, 1971.
14 For a discussion of the significance of the difference see A. Etzioni, *Modern Organizations*, Foundations of Modern Sociology, Prentice-Hall, 1964, ch. 8.
15 See for an example Bob Deacon & Crescy Cannan, 'The Area Social Work Team Concept in Islington', *Social and Economic Administration*, vol. 4, no. 3, 1970.
16 Problems of field authority are considered in B. C. Smith, *Field Administration*, Library of Political Studies, Routledge and Kegan Paul, 1967.

Chapter 8 Internal Organization: Relationships and Processes

1 Personnel management consists of a set of specialized administrative techniques and these are briefly considered in Chapter 11.
2 These are described at more length in J. H. Warren, *Municipal Administration*, Pitman, second edition 1954, ch. 9.
3 These are discussed in the *Report of the Committee on the Management of Local Government*, HMSO, 1967, vol. 1, ch. 3.
4 See R. Greenwood *et al.*, 'The Policy Committee in English Local Government', *Public Administration*, vol. 50, Summer, 1972.
5 J. D. Barber, *The Lawmakers*, Yale Studies in Political Science, 11, Yale University Press, 1965.
6 J. M. Lee, 1963.
7 J. G. Bulpitt, 1967, ch. 3.
8 T. Burns & G. M. Stalker, *The Management of Innovation*, Tavistock Publications, 1961, ch. 7, 'Working Organization, Political System, and Status Structure within the Concern'.
9 C. Argyris, *Interpersonal Competence and Organizational Effectiveness*, Tavistock Publications, 1962, p. 1 – 'The individual's strategy for existence is at crucial points antagonistic to the strategy that guides the formal organization. This may lead to a continual conflict between the individual and the organization.'
10 L. J. Peter & R. Hull, *The Peter Principle*, Souvenir Press, 1969.

Chapter 9 Complex Systems of Local Government

1 This phrase is part of the classical definition of federalism. See K. C. Wheare, *Federal Government*, fourth edition, Oxford Paperbacks, 1963, p. 14.
2 A similar point is made by M. J. C. Vile in *The Structure of American Federalism*, Oxford University Press, 1961, about introduc-

tions to the American system of government. 'There is a tendency amongst political scientists to treat the Federal and State political systems . . . as two separate subjects of study, only occasionally acknowledging the interdependency of these two (or, more properly, fifty-one) units.' (p. 1.)

3 *Report of the Royal Commission on Local Government in England, 1966-69*, volume 1, Cmnd. 4040, 1969.

4 See P. G. Richards, *Delegation in Local Government*, New Town and County Hall Series, Allen and Unwin, 1956.

5 J. F. Redlich & F. Hirst, *Local Government in England*, Bk. II, Pt. II, Macmillan, 1903, p. 31.

6 J. M. Lee, 1963.

7 This is in fact an accurate picture of Devon County Council from 1945 to 1972, as drawn in unpublished research by the present author.

8 See J. P. D. Dunbabin, 'Expectations of the New County Councils, and their Realization', *Historical Journal*, vol. 8, no. 3, 1965.

9 Most of the metropolitan districts are either a former county borough, as in the case of Wolverhampton and Liverpool, or one with extended boundaries, such as Sheffield and Coventry. In fact 28 are based on a central county borough, 5 are unions of two county boroughs and only 3 contain none within their boundaries.

10 The allocation of functions within the new system is set out in the joint publication of the Department of the Environment and the Welsh Office, *Local Government in England and Wales: A Guide to the New System*, HMSO, 1974, pp. 6-13.

Chapter 10 Central-Local Relations

1 W. A. Robson, 'The Central Domination of Local Government', *Political Quarterly*, vol. 4, no. 1, 1933, p. 89.

2 For a discussion of this and related evidence see N. T. Boaden, *Urban Policy-Making*, Cambridge University Press, 1971.

3 Royal Commission on Local Government in England, 1966-69, Research Study no. 1, *Local Government in South East England*, HMSO, 1969, p. 5.

4 Many of the earlier relevant studies are referred to in N. T. Boaden, *op cit*.

5 N. T. Boaden, *op cit*, p. 20.

6 See B. Keith-Lucas, 'Poplarism', *Public Law*, Spring, 1962; G. W. Jones, 'Herbert Morrison and Poplarism', *Public Law*, Spring, 1973; A. Mitchell, 'Clay Cross', *Political Quarterly*, vol. 45, no. 2, 1974; R. Minns, 'The Significance of Clay Cross', *Policy and Politics*, vol. 2, no. 4, 1974.

7 For an account of one field organization see M. Hill, 'The Exercise of Discretion in the National Assistance Board', *Public Administration*, vol. 47, Spring, 1969.
8 L. J. Sharpe, *Why Local Democracy?*, Fabian Tract no. 361, The Fabian Society, 1965.
9 The *ultra vires* doctrine is the expression of the legal obligation on public bodies to do only those things that they are specifically empowered to do. In contrast the individual citizen can do all those things he or she is not specifically debarred from doing.
10 The *Housing Finance Act, 1972*, was in part an example of the first type of central action, whilst its repeal was an example of the second.
11 For an account of the district auditor under the traditional system see L. M. Helmore, *The District Auditor*, Macdonald and Evans, 1961. For the 1972 changes see P. G. Richards, *The Reformed Local Government System*, The New Local Government Series, Allen and Unwin, 1975, pp. 161-63.
12 Central departments differ amongst themselves in the attitudes they take towards local authorities. Some are regulatory, some *laissez-faire* and others promotional in the way they generally treat local authorities. See J. A. G. Griffith, *Central Departments and Local Authorities*, Allen and Unwin for the Royal Institute of Public Administration, 1966. This book also contains descriptions of many of the powers available to the centre in its relationships with local authorities, though within a different framework from that adopted here.
13 Under the pressure of the economic crisis of 1974 and 1975 councils were reported as leaving unfilled established posts in their services. It is to be presumed that this pressure also meant that the amount of repair and renewal of existing property was reduced.

Chapter 11 Management in Local Government

1 *Public Administration*, vol. 38, Summer, 1960.
2 See 'The Basildon Experiment', *Public Administration*, vol. 44, Summer, 1966. This is a series of extracts from a report published by the Urban District Council which led to the introduction of a town manager system, amongst other things.
3 Many of the interwar writings of L. F. Urwick give exactly this impression. He engaged in a controversy on the relevance of his ideas to the central government in the journal *Public Administration* in the mid 1930s.
4 These are discussed with special reference to devolution in J. Stan-

yer, 'Divided Responsibilities: Accountability in Decentralized Government', *Public Administration Bulletin*, no. 17, December, 1974.

5 See T. P. Sherman, *O & M in Local Government*, Pergamon Press, 1969, Part 2 – 'Particular Applications'.

6 Some examples are given in R. A. Ward, *Operational Research in Local Government*, Allen and Unwin for the Royal Institute of Public Administration, 1964.

7 *Report of the Committee on the Management of Local Government*, vol. 1, HMSO, 1967.

8 They are described in most textbooks on American local government. See, for instance, the successive editions of A. F. Macdonald, *American City Government and Administration*, Thomas Y. Crowell Company, New York (sixth edition 1956).

9 The Basildon and Harris experiments mentioned above were examples.

10 This judgement may seem sweeping and harsh, but few who have read both H. A. Simon's *Administrative Behaviour*, The Macmillan Company, New York, second edition, 1957, and J. Woodward's *Management and Technology*, DSIR Problems and Progress in Industry, no. 3, HMSO, 1958, will disagree.

11 See J. H. Kessel, 'Governmental Structure and Political Environment', *American Political Science Review*, vol. 56, no. 3, 1962.

12 J. Stanyer, 'Elected Representatives and Management in Local Government: A Case of Applied Sociology and Applied Economics', *Public Administration*, vol. 49, no. 1, 1971.

Chapter 12 The Fear of Local Democracy

1 The place of the locality in social and political theory over the centuries is described in W. H. Wickwar, *The Political Theory of Local Government*, University of South Carolina Press, 1970.

2 H. Whalen, 'Ideology, Democracy and the Foundations of Local Self-Government', *Canadian Journal of Economics and Political Science*, vol. 26, no. 3, 1960; B. C. Smith, 'The Justification of Local Government', in L. D. Feldman & M. D. Goldrick (eds.), *Politics and Government of Urban Canada*, Methuen, 1969; L. J. Sharpe, 'Theories and Values of Local Government', *Political Studies*, vol. 18, no. 2, 1970. (The articles by Whalen and Sharpe are also reprinted in Feldman & Goldrick, *op cit.*)

3 Much of the discussion of local democracy is not very well informed in the factual sense. Sometimes an impression is given from a few selected examples of a general position quite different from that which actually obtains. It is therefore worthwhile describing the main sources of accurate information relating to these fears of local democracy. It should be remembered that three facets of the statistics are required: the average for the whole country and for different classes of authority, the variability within each category, and the figures for each individual authority.

Figures for *seats contested* and *turnout* for all authorities in England and Wales since the end of the Second World War may be obtained from the same document – the Registrar General's *Statistical Review*, published annually, Part Two: 'Civil Tables'. The statistics are presented for each individual local authority as a whole and if more detailed information is needed this can only be obtained from original research within the area.

There is no general record of the social composition of local councils, but the sample survey by the Maud Committee in 1964-65 gives a picture of the overall position at that time. This was published as Volume 2: *The Local Government Councillor*, HMSO, 1967. Some individual councils are described in case-studies of a local political system; the studies of individual councils or groups of councils usually give a considerable amount of information about the sort of people serving at that time. For other councils it is necessary to use local newspapers and council handbooks, but these are very variable in their coverage of members.

Information relating to the partisan composition of most councils can be found in the *Municipal Year Book*, published annually. The section on 'The Political Composition of Councils' has been included every year since 1956, except for 1960. A picture of the state of partisan conflict at a given election can be obtained from *The Economist* in the weeks immediately before and after each set of ordinary elections. A more superficial picture is also usually given in the *Sunday Times*, *Observer* and *The Times* of the appropriate dates.

No information about co-option, the aldermanic system and training courses is generally available.

4 The studies by Butterworth, 1966, and Rees & Smith, 1964, are examples of the effects of one party dominance in an area – Islington and Barking.

5 Though there has been some variation from year to year the national average has been about 40 per cent in the post-war period, compared with 75-80 per cent in general elections. Figures for 1945-67 for both turnout and seats contested are given in Table 4 of H. V. Wiseman (ed.), 1970.

6 W. H. Morris-Jones, 'In Defence of Apathy', *Political Studies*, vol. 2, no. 1, 1954.

7 Anti-party attitudes are well described in R. Freeman, *Becoming a Councillor*, Charles Knight, 1970, ch. 4. They are also effectively criticized by the author.

8 See Freeman, *op cit*, p. 45 – '[the head of a party's local government organization] had to tread with some delicacy when suggesting possible courses of action to the party groups . . . never heard of ordinary day-to-day decisions being influenced in any way by national party organizations.'

9 Quoted in B. Keith-Lucas, *art cit*, 1962, p. 57.

10 S. & B. Webb, *A Constitution for the Socialist Commonwealth of Great Britain*, Longmans, Green, 1920.

11 E. Sharp, 'What's Wrong with Local Government?', *Municipal Review*, vol. 31, no. 371, November, 1960.

12 Cambridge University Press, second edition, 1948.

13 J. P. D. Dunbabin, *art cit*, p. 372.

14 J. M. Lee, *op cit*, pp. 111-12.

15 'Petticoat and Pensioner Rule in Council Chambers', *The Times*, 9/7/63. In contrast the Maud Committee found that retired people comprised 20 per cent of council members compared with 7 per cent of the general population, and housewives were 7 per cent compared with 27 per cent. Only about 13 per cent of council members were female, of whom over 40 per cent were employed.

16 See the collection of articles in C. A. Gibb (ed.), *Leadership*, Penguin Modern Psychology Readings, 1969.

17 See G. W. Jones, *op cit*, p. 263.

18 This was true in Exeter from 1962 to 1964, when the Conservatives' retention of control through the aldermanic system infuriated the parties with growing popular support.

19 Elements of this fictional case can be found in the campaigns of many ratepayers' movements and sometimes in Liberalism.

20 W. A. Robson, *The Development of Local Government*, Allen and Unwin, 1931, pp. 87-8.

21 *Report of the Committee on the Management of Local Government*, HMSO, 1967, p. 114.

Bibliography

This bibliography consists of references which are largely case-studies of individual authorities, or groups of authority, in England and Wales. It includes those studies which focus mainly on the local community rather than the local authority, and those which deal with only limited aspects of political behaviour, but which start from the same sorts of assumption as are made in this book; namely that a local political system can only be understood as an individual entity whose behaviour is located firmly within a specific environment. There are a large number of studies of aspects of internal organization, usually contributed by practitioners or consultants, but these are omitted as they are not generally based on these assumptions. The area studied is cited in brackets after each reference.

F. Bealey *et al.*, *Constituency Politics*, Society Today and Tomorrow, Faber and Faber, 1965 (Newcastle-under-Lyme NCB and RD).

H. Benham, *Two Cheers for the Town Hall*, Hutchinson, 1964 (north-east Essex).

A. H. Birch, *Small Town Politics*, Oxford University Press, 1959 (Glossop NCB).

J. Blondel and R. Hall, 'Conflict, Decision-making and the Perceptions of Local Councillors', *Political Studies*, vol. 15, no. 3, 1967 (Colchester NCB and Maldon NCB).

T. Brennan *et al.*, 'Party Politics and Local Government in Western South Wales', *Political Quarterly*, vol. 25, no. 1, 1954a (west Glamorgan AC, Swansea CB, east Carmarthen AC).

T. Brennan *et al.*, *Social Change in West South Wales*, The New Thinker's Library, Watts, 1954 (as above).

J. G. Bulpitt, *Party Politics in English Local Government*, Monographs in Politics, Longmans, 1967 (Manchester CB, Salford CB, Rochdale CB and Middleton NCB).

R. Butterworth, 'Islington Borough Council: Some Aspects of Single-Party Rule', *Politics*, vol. 1, no. 1, 1966 (Islington MB).

R. V. Clements, *Local Notables and the City Council*, Macmillan, 1969 (Bristol CB).
M. Cole, *Servant of the County*, Dobson, 1956 (London County Council).
L. Corina, 'Elected Representatives in a Party System: A Typology', *Policy and Politics*, vol. 3, no. 1, 1974 (Halifax CB).
H. Cox and D. Morgan, *City Politics and the Press*, Cambridge University Press, 1973 (Merseyside).
R. Crichton, *Commuters' Village*, David and Charles, 1964 (Stratford Mortimer, a village in Berkshire).
J. Dearlove, 'Councillors and Interest Groups in Kensington and Chelsea', *British Journal of Political Science*, vol. 1, no, 2, 1971 (Kensington and Chelsea GLB).
J. Dearlove, *The Politics of Policy in Local Government*, Cambridge University Press, 1973 (as above).
I. Emmett, *A North Wales Parish*, Routledge and Kegan Paul, 1964 ('Llan', a parish in Merionethshire).
R. Frankenberg, *Village on the Border*, Cohen and West, 1957 ('Pentrediwaith', a village in north Wales).
J. K. Friend and W. N. Jessop, *Local Government and Strategic Choice*, Tavistock Publications, 1969 (Coventry CB).
W. Hampton, *Democracy and Community*, Oxford University Press, 1970 (Sheffield CB).
H. H. Heclo, 'The Councillor's Job', *Public Administration*, vol. 47, no. 2, 1969 (Manchester CB).
G. W. Jones, *Borough Politics*, Macmillan, 1969 (Wolverhampton CB).
P. Kantor, 'The Governable City: Islands of Power and Political Parties in London', *Polity*, vol. 7, no. 1, 1974 (Brent, Havering and Newham GLBs).
J. M. Lee, *Social Leaders and Public Persons*, Oxford University Press, 1963 (Cheshire CC).
J. M. Lee *et al.*, *The Scope of Local Initiative*, Martin Robertson, 1974 (Cheshire CC).
J. Littlejohn, *Westrigg: The Sociology of a Cheviot Parish*, Routledge and Kegan Paul, 1964 (Westrigg, a Scottish border parish).
H. Maddick and E. P. Pritchard, 'The Conventions of Local Authorities in the West Midlands', Parts 1 & 2, *Public Administration*, vol. 36, no. 2, and vol. 37, no. 2, 1958, 1959 (eight CBs, 10 NCBs, 1 UD and 6 RDs in the west Midlands).
P. J. Madgwick *et al.*, *The Politics of Rural Wales*, Hutchinson, 1973 (Cardiganshire CC).

E. W. Martin, *The Shearers and the Shorn*, Dartington Hall Studies in Rural Sociology, Routledge and Kegan Paul, 1965 (the Okehampton area of Devon).
D. C. Miller, 'Decision-making Cliques in Community Power Structures', *American Journal of Sociology*, vol. 64, 1958 (Bristol CB and an American city).
D. C. Miller, 'Industry and Community Power Structure', *American Sociological Review*, vol. 23, no. 1, 1958 (Bristol CB and an American city).
G. D. Mitchell, 'Depopulation and Rural Social Structure', *Sociological Review*, vol. 42, no. 1, 1950 (parishes in south Devon).
G. D. Mitchell, 'Social Disintegration in a Rural Community', *Human Relations*, vol. 3, no. 3, 1950 (as above).
G. D. Mitchell, 'The Parish Council and the Rural Community', *Public Administration*, vol. 29, no. 4, 1951 (as above).
H. Morrison, *How London is Governed*, People's Universities Press, 1949 (London County Council).
K. Newton, 'Links between Leaders and Citizens in a Local Political System', *Policy and Politics*, vol. 1, no. 4, 1973 (Birmingham CB).
K. Newton, 'Role Orientations and their Sources among Elected Representatives in English Local Politics', *The Journal of Politics*, vol. 36, no. 3, 1975 (Birmingham CB).
A. M. Rees and T. A. Smith, *Town Councillors*, Acton Society Trust, 1964 (Barking NCB).
I. W. Scarf, 'The Government of Haslingden', *Manchester School of Economics and Social Science*, vol. 18, no. 1, 1950 (Haslingden NCB).
L. J. Sharpe, *A Metropolis Votes*, Greater London Paper no. 8, 1962 (London County Council).
L. J. Sharpe, 'The Politics of Local Government in Greater London', *Public Administration*, vol. 38, no. 2, 1960 (local authorities in the Greater London area).
L. J. Sharpe (ed.), *Voting in Cities*, Macmillan, 1967 (Bradford, Bristol, Chester, Exeter, Leeds, Oxford, Southampton, West Hartlepool and Wolverhampton CBs, Durham and Torquay NCBs).
E. D. Simon, *A City Council from Within*, Longmans, Green, 1926 (Manchester CB).
P. Spencer, 'Party Politics and the Processes of Local Democracy in an English Town Council', in A. Richards and A. Kuper (eds.), *Councils in Action*, Cambridge Studies in Social Anthropology, 6,

Cambridge University Press, 1971 ('Aberton', a northern county borough).
M. Stacey, *Tradition and Change*, Oxford University Press, 1960 (Banbury NCB).
M. Stacey *et al.*, *Power, Persistence and Change*, Routledge and Kegan Paul, 1975 (Banbury NCB).
W. M. Williams, *The Sociology of an English Village*, Routledge and Kegan Paul, 1956 ('Gosforth', a parish in Cumberland).
W. M. Williams, *A West Country Village*, Dartington Hall Studies in Rural Sociology, Routledge and Kegan Paul, 1963 ('Ashworthy', a village in west Devon).
H. V. Wiseman, *Local Government at Work*, Library of Political Studies, Routledge and Kegan Paul, 1967 (Leeds CB).
H. V. Wiseman, 'Local Government in Leeds', Parts 1 & 2, *Public Administration*, vol. 41, nos. 1 & 2, 1963 (Leeds C.B.).

Index

Note: for reasons of space this index does not include references to the following – individual local authorities (Devon CC, Glossop NCB, etc.); individual public services (police, education, etc.); individual occupations (accountancy, refuse collection, etc.); individual institutions (clinics, libraries, etc.); individual academic disciplines (economics, physics, etc.). Readers should consult general heading.